PASSE-PARTOUT

1

Daphne Philpot & Judy Somerville

Teacher's Book

Nelson

Introduction

Passe-partout

PASSE-PARTOUT is a four-stage French course for beginners. It is particularly suitable for lower to middle-ability students, but also provides extension material for more able learners. Stages 1 and 2 of the course each consist of the following components:

Students' Book

Teacher's Book

Copymasters and assessment

Flashcards

Cassette pack (7 cassettes, including one self study, duplicating master cassette)

Structure of Passe-partout

Stages 1–3 of the course are each divided into six Modules, representing approximately half a term's work per Module. The Modules are sub-divided into three *Objectifs*, providing manageable, short term goals for students. These goals are represented visually at the beginning of each Module in the Students' Book and the Teacher's Notes provide guidance on how to present the goals to students, so that they have a clear understanding of what they can expect to achieve. At the end of each Module, the key language which has been covered is listed in the *Sommaire* pages and the content of the three *Objectifs* is brought together in a project-style activity, *Porte ouverte!* which provides wide-ranging opportunities for creativity.

Methodology

The themes covered in each Module of PASSE-PARTOUT are designed to reflect students' own interests or experiences and the language content of each Module of PASSE-PARTOUT has been carefully selected and controlled, so as not to overwhelm students. The structures introduced have been chosen on the basis of relevance to the student and transferability of language from one context to another. Each batch of new language is introduced on a step-by-step basis, with support for students provided at all stages in the learning process. The steps are:

- goal setting
- presentation of new language
- checking for comprehension
- imitation of a model
- practice and consolidation
- recognising grammatical patterns
- independent and creative use of language.

Support comes in the form of: 1) *Mots Clefs* Copymasters, which contain all the key vocabulary for an *Objectif* or part of an *Objectif*, the majority of which are also provided on the self-study cassette, for pronunciation practice; 2) a clear written or spoken example or full model for each activity which students undertake; 3) clear, simple rubrics in French, supported by a glossary of Instructions at the back of the Students' Book; 4) the *Sommaire* pages at the end of each Module; and 5) a comprehensive, two-way, bilingual *Glossaire* in which students can look up words which they do not know or cannot remember. Additional suggestions for support are made on an activity-by activity basis, in the Teacher's Notes.

Differentiation

PASSE-PARTOUT provides a wealth of suggestions and material to promote differentiation by support, by task, by text and by outcome. The Teacher's Notes signal opportunities for differentiation, either for consolidation or extension, for example, by adding or removing support, or by limiting or extending the scope of a task. In addition, the *Extra!* Copymasters (or *Extra!* tasks on core Copymasters) provide regular extension activities for able students. And the *Porte ouverte!* and other open-ended activities encourage students to perform at a level suited to their individual capabilities.

Grammar

Grammar is presented in ways accessible to a wide range of learners. Initially, structures are presented in context and learned as lexical items. The Teacher's Notes then suggest ways of discussing or clarifying grammar points, by using very simple target language, pointing, miming, gesturing, drawing boxes, colouring, etc. In addition, all flashcards of nouns have colour-coded borders (blue for masculine, red for feminine, purple for plural). This convention is continued in the *Attention!* feature in the Students' Book, which summarises grammar points in a simple, often visual, form; for example, adjective and past participle endings follow the colour coding of the flashcards. Grammar practice activities are provided on the Copymasters and there is a brief summary, in the *Pages grammaires*, at the back of the Students' Book, of key verbs and tenses which have been covered. Finally, students can compile their own notes on Copymasters 74–86 which support the grammar points covered in each Module.

Assessment

Activities throughout each Module, including the *Porte ouverte!* feature at the end of the Module, provide opportunities for both formative and summative assessment.

In addition, there are three cumulative 'tests' after Module 2, Module 4, and Module 6. Teachers in England, Wales and Northern Ireland may wish to know that these have been modelled on the optional Key Stage 3 tests, published by SCAA and provide differentiated test items in listening, speaking, reading and writing. Each skill area test consists of three activities, in ascending order of difficulty, and is designed to be quickly and easily administered. The test material for the students and the Teacher's Notes for this assessment material are provided on Copymasters 88–127. Cassettes 2, 4 and 6 contain the material for the listening tests.

Learning skills and strategies

Each Module of PASSE-PARTOUT has a full-page feature, to support the acquisition of key language-learning strategies, such as memorising a list of vocabulary or phrases, using a bilingual glossary or dictionary, reading for gist or detail, listening for gist and detail and using reference materials. The skills covered in each stage of the course are listed in the contents page of the Students' Book. These gradually build into a portfolio of skills and strategies, to support increased learner autonomy.

Pronunciation

Many of the *Mots Clefs* Copymasters are supported by pronunciation practice of key vocabulary and phrases on the self-study cassette. In addition, the *Comment ça se prononce?* page in each Module of the Students' Book focuses on a group of key sounds in the French language, with practice activities on cassette. The activities encourage recognition of the relationship between the spoken and written forms. The use of rhyme, rhythm and song helps students to improve their pronunciation through enjoyable and memorable activities. The sounds chosen are exemplified through words which have been covered in the Module in question.

Student and teacher use of target language

PASSE-PARTOUT encourages teachers and students to make maximum use of the target language in lessons. All rubrics in the students' material are in simple French and suggested target language for introducing more complex activities, including games and the explanation of grammatical points, is given throughout the Teacher's Notes.

In addition, a cartoon feature, *La classe d'enfer*, in every Module, introduces and practises key aspects of classroom language, such as asking for classroom objects, seeking help and clarification, explaining or making excuses and asking permission. These are listed in the contents pages of the Students' Book and gradually build up as a repertoire of language, which enables students and teachers to conduct as much of the lesson as possible in French.

Reading for interest and enjoyment

Both the SOED 5–14 Guidelines and the National Curriculum require students to be given regular opportunities to read for interest and enjoyment. In every Module of PASSE-PARTOUT, two pages of material provide suitable reading material of this kind. The first page, *Entre-temps…*, is a collection of short items from books or magazines, such as articles, cartoons, quizzes and jokes, which link broadly to the content of the Module. The second, *Nous les copains*, is a cartoon story about a group of characters who feature throughout stages 1 and 2 of PASSE-PARTOUT. The language in these stories is mostly familiar and each story is available on cassette, for support. Students are asked to note down key language on the copymaster *Mes découvertes* (Copymaster 23), which encourages them to consider how they discovered the meaning of new vocabulary.

Self-study cassette

The self-study cassette is a duplicating master, which teachers may copy for students. It is designed to be used for independent listening work, in class or at home; in order to provide maximum support for students working without a teacher, instructions on this cassette are given in English. The material for each Module includes pronunciation work, linked to the *Mots Clefs* Copymasters, songs, rhymes and occasional, lighter listening material, such as sports results, quizzes or advertisements. Most items on the self-study cassette will require students to refer to a copymaster or a page of the Students' Book and this is always made clear in the instructions on the cassette itself.

Revision

The emphasis in PASSE-PARTOUT is on the learning of transferable language, which is recycled in new contexts from Module to Module and from one stage of the course to another. This provides a supportive framework for the frequent revision and extension of key vocabulary and structures. The sixth and final Module of each stage of the course is designed mainly to revise and consolidate the language of the previous five Modules. New and revised language is listed at the appropriate points throughout the Teacher's Notes for each Module.

Information Technology

The Teacher's Notes for PASSE-PARTOUT promote the use of IT in Modern Languages. Bearing in mind the diverse hardware in schools, reference is made to generic programmes and their applications. For example, word-processing for drafting and re-drafting, databases for recording the results of a *Sondage* and CD-ROM and the Internet for background information and further reading.

National Curriculum and SOED 5–14

A detailed document, cross-referencing each stage of PASSE-PARTOUT to the SOED 5–14 Guidelines, is available on request from Thomas Nelson (Tel: 01932 252211).

National Curriculum Attainment Targets and Levels are listed at the beginning of each activity in the Teacher's Notes. The Area(s) of Experience covered are also listed in the Teacher's Notes, at the beginning of each Module. In addition, an overview of how the Programmes of Study are covered (and an activity-by-activity list of the Attainment Targets and Levels for each Module) is provided in a separate document, available from Thomas Nelson (Tel: 01932 252211).

Games cupboard

There are many games which can effectively promote language learning. They should support the appropriate learning step within the ongoing learning process. They need to be used therefore with thought and purposefulness as well as with the idea of providing motivation and enjoyment.

Where a game is particularly appropriate to practise a specific area of language, it has also been included in the Teacher's Notes at the relevant point for easy reference.

As a general rule, encourage students to take responsibility for the game, taking over the teacher's role as soon as possible. To ensure maximum participation, encourage students wherever possible to continue the game in small groups. In elimination games it is advisable to give students several lives to ensure sustained interest and involvement.

Games to practise numbers

Loto
Students can write down a selection of numbers and cross them out as you call them. When checking, students could read back the numbers in French. (This game also provides excellent practice for other items of vocabulary.) Students can either play as a whole class or in groups but in either case the winner of the game becomes the next caller.

Chef d'orchestre
Divide the class into two teams: *en avant* and *en arrière*. Call out a number. The *en avant* team has to give the next number, the *en arrière* team gives the previous number. Play one team against another, giving a point for each correct response.

Plouf!
Write numbers to be practised on the board, in the form of stepping stones across a river e.g.

8		12		16		7	
	6		13		15		
20		14		3		19	

Divide the class into teams. Ask a team to cross the 'river' using the stepping stones. Students may choose any route to 'cross the river'. If there is hesitation or a mistake, the other team shout *Plouf!* as the playing team 'falls into the river'.

Trop grand, trop petit
Think of a number and ask the class to guess it. The only clue you give them as they guess the number is that it is *trop grand* or *trop petit*. This game will work best with a limited range of numbers.

Encerclez/Effacez/Touchez
Write numbers randomly on the board. Divide the class into two teams and ask a representative from each one to come to the board. Call out a number. The one that either circles, rubs out or touches the correct number first wins a point for the team. Alternatively give each team member a number (preferably on a piece of paper as a reminder) and call out one of these numbers first to bring the students to the board. This will encourage the active involvement of all students. This game can be played with other items of vocabulary.

Comptez comme ça
Start by saying *Comptez comme ça* and begin to count in a particular way e.g. forwards, backwards, alternate numbers, or in easy multiples of 2/3. Students join in as soon as they can with the right sequence and are out if they say the wrong number. Change the sequence at intervals by saying *Comptez comme ça* and begin again. A group version can be played. Call on a specific group to count. If the group fails to join in after the first three or four numbers, they are out.

Réveille-toi
Students choose a number for the day. This is written on the board either in number or word form. Students stand up whenever they hear that particular number called.

Jeu de dés
Students can throw dice in pairs or groups and call out the numbers. According to the mathematical ability of the groups, the complexity of the numbers can build up by: increasing the number of dice; moving from adding to multiplying; adding up scores over a series of an agreed number of goes.

L'échelle
Students draw two or more six-rung ladders with a number on each rung. Students play in groups. Each member throws a dice and reads out the number. If it is the next number on the ladder, it is crossed off and the player moves up to the next rung of the ladder. The winner reaches the top rung first. This game can also be used with other vocabulary items.

Games using flashcards

C'est vrai
One student has a pile of flashcards. At random he or she picks up a card and says something about it. The others decide if it is *vrai* or *faux*.

Jeu de mimes
Show a flashcard to a volunteer student who mimes it for the others to guess. The volunteer then chooses another card for the winner to mime.

Jeu de Kim
Put on the board a number of related flashcards and then ask the students to try and remember what they were. When they can identify all of them, tell the students to close their eyes. Remove a card and ask them which one is missing.

Jeu de mémoire
Blutak a number of flashcards to the board and write a number next to each one. Remove the flashcards one at a time, giving the appropriate language. Call out the language relating to a missing flashcard and ask students to give the correct number. Replace the flashcard when its number has been given. Later reverse this process by calling out a number and asking students to give the appropriate language.

Cinq questions
Hold a card so that the class cannot see it. Ask an appropriate question e.g. *Quel temps fait-il?* Students have five questions to

guess what the card is. Play this as a teacher against the class game, setting up the challenge and marking up points *classe/prof.*

L'intrus

Show four cards. Ask students to decide which is the odd one out. This game is useful for revision of vocabulary from other areas.

Qu'est-ce que c'est?

Play this game with any flashcards depicting nouns. Shuffle the cards and place a plain piece of paper on the top to hide the image. The caller asks *Qu'est-ce que c'est?* other students ask *C'est un/une ...?* The student who guesses correctly is the next caller and looks at the next card or chooses any card before asking *Qu'est-ce que c'est?* Alternatively to give students a clue, have a circle or peephole in the top sheet. An intact top sheet could also be dragged across the card slowly revealing the picture until the students give the correct answer.

The game can be extended to other language by altering the question e.g. *Qu'est-ce que tu fais? Quelle heure est-il? Quel temps fait-il?*

Vrai ou faux?

This is a version of 'Simon says'. Pick a card from a pile of flashcards and show it to the class making a statement about it in French. If the statement is *vrai*, everyone repeats it but if it is *faux* they keep quiet. Anyone failing to react correctly is out. The winner is the next caller.

La chasse au trésor

A volunteer leaves the room. The rest of the class choose where to hide a flashcard. The volunteer comes back into the room. The class says the language appropriate to the card e.g. *Je fais du patin* and tells the volunteer to look for the card *Cherche la bonne carte.* They repeat *Je fais du patin* softly if the volunteer is at a distance from the card and increase the volume as the seeker comes nearer.

Trouve le trésor

The class identify a number of flashcards as they are laid face down around the classroom. Choose one of the cards. A volunteer then has to find the right one as the others say the language appropriate to that card. The overall winner is the one who finds the card with the least number of repetitions. From time to time reposition the cards to maintain the challenge.

Jeu de morpion

Mark up a noughts and crosses shape on the board that is large enough to take a flashcard in the spaces that would normally have a nought or cross. Divide the class into two teams: one the noughts and one the crosses team. In turns the teams choose and identify their flashcard. On successful identification, remove the card and enter a nought or cross as appropriate. The winning team is the first to have a completed line as in the original game.

Other games

Oui et Non

A volunteer comes to the front of the class. Ask him/her questions. The student must reply without using *oui* or *non*. Keep a score of how many questions the student has answered. Questions like *Tu joues au foot?* can be answered by *Je joue au foot./Je ne joue pas au foot.* A good way of catching students out is to ask a question that requires a factual answer and then repeat their answer for confirmation e.g.

Teacher: *Quelle est la date de ton anniversaire?*
Student: *Le 14 juillet.*
Teacher: *Le 14 juillet?*
Student: *Oui.*

Combat naval

Adapt the game of battleships to practise various items of language. In its simplest form, give students the language to be practised e.g. parts of a verb, numbers, days of the week, or put a set of flashcards on display as a reminder. Each student writes down any three alternatives. Each in turn guesses what their partner has written and if the guess is correct, the partner must cross it out. The first one to eliminate all three of their partner's items is the winner.

Je pense à quelque chose qui commence par la lettre ...

This game provides alphabet practice of the chosen range of language.

La chaise qui brûle

Students take it in turns to answer for 30 seconds any questions fired at them. Initially write the questions on the board. Students can play this as a class then in groups.

La bonne chaise

Divide the class into two teams. Take four chairs: two chairs for each team. Label each pair of chairs: one *vrai* and the other *faux*. Make appropriate language statements in French. In response, team representatives must sit on the appropriate chair.

Contre la montre

Agree a time limit and challenge the class to give a number of items within the time limit. To encourage careful listening, penalise the scoring for any repeated items. Decrease the time limit or raise the number of items to increase the challenge. The language may be topic based but for revision purposes give a letter of the alphabet and all items must begin with that letter.

Silhouettes

This game is most effective on the OHP. First put a piece of paper/card on the OHP. Then place OHT versions of the flashcards (*Mots Clefs* visuals lend themselves to this). Reveal the items as students guess them. The silhouette shapes can fit the theme e.g. map of France for the weather, house for members of the family, Noah's ark for pets, sports bag for sports.

Introduction

Changez de chaises

This is an active game and is a version of musical chairs. Give out a piece of paper with a word/phrase (there should be three/four of each item) to all of the students. Arrange the chairs in a circle but have one chair less than required. One student stands in the centre without a chair. Say one of the items e.g. *Un chat. Changez de chaises*. The four students who have this item must change chairs and the student in the centre tries to occupy a chair during the changeover. To increase the listening and the number of students involved in the changeover, give more than one item at a time.

On fait le tour

Students stand in an inner and outer circle facing one another. Give a question to those in the outer circle that must be answered by the facing student in the inner circle e.g. *Quelle est la date de ton anniversaire? Le 14 juillet*. The students in the outer circle move in a clockwise direction to ask the same question to the next student. The inner circle stands still. Students then change places from the inner to the outer circle and now ask the questions instead of giving the answers.

List of flashcards

1	le français	34	Je joue au tennis.	68	Nous faisons de la voile.
2	le dessin	35	Je joue au tennis de table.	69	Nous faisons des excursions.
3	la musique	36	Je joue au basket.	70	un hot-dog
4	la géographie	37	Je joue au foot.	71	un hamburger
5	la technologie	38	Je joue au rugby.	72	un sandwich au fromage
6	l'anglais	39	Je joue au hockey.	73	un sandwich au jambon
7	l'informatique	40	Je joue avec l'ordinateur.	74	un croque-monsieur
8	l'histoire	41	Je joue aux cartes.	75	une crêpe
9	l'éducation physique	42	Je fais du vélo.	76	une gaufre
10	les maths	43	Je fais du patin à roulettes.	77	une portion de frites
11	les sciences	44	Je fais de la natation.	78	une portion de pizza
12	l'allemand	45	Je fais des promenades.	79	un coca
13	l'espagnol	46	Je regarde la télé.	80	un café
14	l'éducation religieuse	47	Je regarde les vidéos.	81	un café-crème
15	l'éducation civique	48	J'écoute de la musique.	82	un jus d'orange
16	J'aime	49	Je lis.	83	un jus de pomme
17	visual to accompany J'aime	50	Je vais au cinéma.	84	un orangina
18	J'adore	51	Je vais à la pêche.	85	un thé au lait
19	visual to accompany J'adore	52	Je vais chez les copains.	86	un thé citron
20	Je préfère	53	Je vais en ville.	87	un chocolat
21	visual to accompany Je préfère	54	un chien	88	une limonade
22	Je n'aime pas	55	un chat	89	Il pleut.
23	visual to accompany Je n'aime pas	56	un lapin	90	Il neige.
24	Je déteste	57	un cheval	91	Il fait beau.
25	visual to accompany Je déteste	58	un cochon d'Inde	92	Il fait mauvais.
26	Tu aimes ...?	59	un hamster	93	Il fait chaud.
27	visual to accompany Tu aimes ...?	60	un oiseau	94	Il fait froid.
28	J'arrive	61	un poisson	95	Il fait du soleil.
29	Je mange	62	une gerbille	96	Il fait du vent.
30	Je quitte le collège.	63	une souris	97	Il fait du brouillard.
31	Je parle avec mes copains.	64	rouge, bleu, jaune, vert	98	à la montagne
32	Je reste au lit.	65	noir, blanc, gris, brun	99	au bord de la mer
33	Je joue au volley.	66	Nous ...	100	à la campagne
		67	Nous faisons du canoë-kayak.	101	en ville

National Curriculum Programme of Study Part 1 Overview

* = occurs frequently throughout Module

Module 1 Bienvenue!

1a pairs, groups	*	2f pronunciation and intonation	* SB p.8 Ça va?
1b language for real purposes	SB p.9 Ça s'écrit comment?	2h personal feelings and opinions	SB p.8 Ça va?
1c range of language activities	*	2k copy	* CM 5 Moi et toi
1d imaginative and creative	* SB p.22 Porte ouverte!	2o vary language	SB p.15 Comment dit-on ... ?
1e everyday classroom events	SB p.14 Sortez vos affaires!	3a learn by heart	SB p.13 Le vocabulaire? ...
1g personal enjoyment	SB p.19 Entre-temps ...	3c independent learning	* Self-study cassette
1h different types of spoken language	*	3e use context / clues	SB p.11 Au jardin public
1i handwritten and printed texts / read aloud	SB p.10 Villes rythmiques	3f patterns, rules, exceptions	SB p.13 Attention!
1j produce variety of writing	*	3g experiment with language	CM 5 Moi et toi
2a listen for gist / detail	*	3h formal and informal language	SB p.6 Salut!, SB p.15
2b follow instructions / directions	*	4a authentic materials	SB p.19 Entre-temps ...
2d ask / answer questions, give instructions	*	4b native speakers	*
2e ask for / give information, explanations	*	4e cultural attitudes, social conventions	SB p.15 Comment dit-on ...?

Module 2 Au collège

1a pairs, groups	*	2h agreement / disagreement, opinions	SB p.26 Mes opinions
1b language for real purposes	CM 9, ex 3 Fais des panneaux	2j skim and scan texts	SB p.39 Collège des vampires, ex d
1c range of language activities	*	2k copy	CM 9 Les matières
1d imaginative and creative	*SB pp.38-39 Collège des vampires!	2l make notes	SB p.32 Les heures sonores
1e everyday classroom events	SB p.28 Vite, vite!	2n redraft	SB p.42 Porte ouverte!
1f discuss own ideas, interests etc.	CM 13 Sondage!	3a learn by heart	CM 11, ex 1 Matières rythmiques
1g personal enjoyment	SB p.40 Entre-temps ...	3b acquire strategies for memorising	SB p.29 Attention! (TN)
1h different types of spoken language	*	3c independent learning	CM 20 L'heure précise
1i handwritten and printed texts / read aloud	SB p.27 Pas de panique!	3d dictionaries / reference	SB p.35 Le glossaire, c'est clair!
1j produce variety of writing	*	3e use context / clues	SB p.34 La vie scolaire
1k range of communication resources	SB p.30 Une lettre de Sophie	3f patterns, rules, exceptions	SB p.37 Le premier cours ... ?
2a listen for gist / detail	*	3g experiment with language	SB p.42 Porte ouverte!
2b follow instructions / directions	*	4a authentic materials	SB p.40 Entre-temps ...
2d ask / answer questions, give instructions	*	4b native speakers	*
2e ask for / give information, explanations	CM 13 Sondage!	4c consider and compare cultures	CM 22 Toi et moi!
2f pronunciation and intonation	SB p.31 Comment ça se prononce?		

Module 3 Vive les passe-temps!

1a pairs and groups	*	2f pronunciation	* CM 24 Les passe-temps
1b language for real purposes	*	2g initiate and develop conversations	SB p.53 Ce n'est pas vrai!
1c range of language activities	*	2h personal feelings and opinions	*
1d imaginative and creative	* SB p.50 Grimaud	2j skim and scan texts	SB p.61 Radio Jeunes
1e everyday classroom events	SB p.51 J'ai un problème	2k copy words, phrases and sentences	*
1g personal enjoyment	SB p.56 Entre-temps ...	2l make notes from what they hear or read	SB p.61 Radio Jeunes
1h different types of spoken language	* SB p.58 La tombola!	2n redraft their writing	SB p.62 Porte ouverte!
1i handwritten and printed texts / read aloud	SB p.45 Et les copains?	2o vary language	*
1j produce variety of writing	SB p.55 Lettre d'un corres.	3a tongue twisters	SB p.57 Phrases fantastiques!
2a listen for gist / detail	SB p.60 J'écoute - pas de panique!	3b acquire strategies for memorising	CM 24 Les passe-temps
		3c independent learning	* Self-study cassette
2b follow instructions / directions	*	3e use context and clues	SB p.54 C'est impossible!
2c ask about meaning, seek clarification, repetition	CM 27 Au secours!	3f understand and apply patterns	CM 31 Positif ou négatif?
2d ask / answer questions, give instructions	SB p.52 Questions, toujours des questions!	3g experiment with language	*
		4a authentic materials	SB p.56 Entre-temps ...
		4b native speakers	*
2e ask for / give information	*	4e social conventions	*

Introduction

Module 4 En famille

1a pairs, groups	*	2k copy	*
1b language for real purposes	CM 40 Cherche corres.	2l make notes	SB p.73 Grand concours d'animaux!
1c range of language activities	*		
1d imaginative and creative	* SB p.82 Porte ouverte!	2m summarise and report	SB p.81 Salut, Dominique!
1e everyday classroom events	SB p.75 Aïe!	2n redrafting	SB p.73 A toi!
1g personal enjoyment	SB p.74 Entre-temps …	3a learn by heart	SB p.70 Tu as un animal à la maison?
1h different types of spoken language	*	3b strategies for memorising	SB p.71 Moi, j'ai des animaux!
1i handwritten and printed texts / read aloud	SB p.80 Rue St. Lazare	3c independent learning	* Self-study cassette
1k variety of communication resources	SB p.73 A toi!	3d dictionaries and reference materials	SB p.72 Le glossaire anglais - français
1j produce variety of writing	*		
2a listen for gist / detail	*	3e use context / clues	SB p.74 Entre-temps …
2b follow instructions / directions	*	3f patterns, rules, exceptions	*
2d ask / answer questions, give instructions	*	3g experiment with language	*
2e ask for / give information, explanations	*	4a authentic materials	SB p.74 Entre-temps …
2f pronunciation and intonation	* CM 41 Ma famille et moi	4b native speakers	*
2h personal feelings and opinions	SB p.76 A toi!		
2j skimming and scanning	SB p.81 Interview avec Mathieu!	4e cultural attitudes, social conventions	CM 45 Pas de panique!

Module 5 Visite scolaire

1a pairs, groups	*	2j skimming and scanning	SB p.100 Le désert, c'est super!
1b language for real purposes	CM 60 Ça fait combien?	2k copy	*
1c range of language activities	*	2l make notes	SB p.90 Visite d'une journaliste
1d imaginative and creative	* SB p.102 Porte ouverte!	2n redrafting	SB p.102 Porte ouverte!
1e everyday classroom events	SB p.91 J'en ai marre!	2o vary language	SB p.88 Temps libre
1g personal enjoyment	SB p.99 Entre-temps …	3a learn by heart	SB p.95 Aide-mémoire
1h different types of spoken language	*	3b strategies for memorising	B p.95 Aide-mémoire
1i handwritten and printed texts / read aloud	SB p.90 Visite d'une journaliste	3c independent learning	* Self-study cassette
1k variety of communication resources	SB p.90 Visite d'une journaliste	3d dictionaries and reference materials	SB p.99 Entre-temps …
1j produce variety of writing	*	3e use context / clues	SB p.94 Tu veux une glace?
2a listen for gist / detail	*	3f patterns, rules, exceptions	*
2b follow instructions / directions	*	3g experiment with language	*
2d ask / answer questions, give instructions	*	3h formal and informal language	SB p.88 Temps libre
2e ask for / give information, explanations	*	4a authentic materials	SB p.99 Entre-temps …
2f pronunciation and intonation	* SB p.89 Comment ça se prononce?	4b native speakers	*
		4c consider and compare cultures	SB p.92 C'est combien?
2h personal feelings	SB p.91 J'en ai marre!	4e cultural attitudes, social conventions	SB p.97 L'addition, s'il vous plaît!

Module 6 Tour de France

1a pairs, groups	*	2k copy	*
1b language for real purposes	CM 62 Jeu de météo	2l make notes	SB p.121 Porte ouverte!
1c range of language activities	*	2n redrafting	SB p.121 Porte ouverte!
1d imaginative and creative	* SB p.121 Porte ouverte!	2o vary language	SB pp.116-117 Le Rallye de Mauville
1e everyday classroom events	SB p.109 Asseyez-vous, svp!		
1g personal enjoyment	SB p.118 Entre-temps …	3a learn by heart	SB p.106 Comment ça se prononce?
1h different types of spoken language	*	3b strategies for memorising	SB p.104 Quel temps fait-il, aujourd'hui?
1i handwritten and printed texts / read aloud	SB p.110 Les coureurs arrivent!		
1j produce variety of writing	*	3c independent learning	* Self-study cassette
1k variety of communication resources	SB p.121 Porte ouverte!	3d dictionaries and reference materials	SB p.118 Entre-temps …
2a listen for gist / detail	*	3e use context / clues	SB p.113 Qu'est-ce qui se passe?
2b follow instructions / directions	*	3f patterns, rules, exceptions	*
2d ask / answer questions, give instructions	*	3g experiment with language	
2e ask for / give information, explanations	*	3h formal and informal language	SB p.120 Recherche!
2f pronunciation and intonation	* SB p.106 Comment ça se prononce?	4a authentic materials	SB p.118 Entre-temps …
		4b native speakers	*
2h personal feelings	SB p.108 C'est pas vrai!	4c consider cultures	SB p.110 Les coureurs arrivent!
2j skimming and scanning	SB p.118 Entre-temps …		

1 BIENVENUE!

In this module, students learn how to:

Greet people
Bonjour / Au revoir (monsieur/madame)

Say what their name is and ask others their name
Je m'appelle … / Tu t'appelles comment?

Understand classroom instructions
Asseyez-vous / Rangez vos affaires

Use numbers 0 – 60

Ask others how they are and say how they are feeling
Ça va? / Ça va / Non, ça ne va pas

Ask how something is spelled and use the French alphabet
Ça s'écrit comment? (etc.)

Say where they live and ask others where they live
J'habite à … / Tu habites où?

Say their age and ask others how old they are
J'ai … ans / Tu as quel âge?

Say when their birthday is and ask others when their birthday is
Mon anniversaire est le … / Quelle est la date de ton anniversaire?

Use phrases for playing games
C'est à toi! / J'ai gagné

Ask others whether they have classroom objects
Tu as/Avez-vous un stylo/une gomme s'il te plaît?/ s'il vous plaît?

Materials needed
Students' Book pages 4 – 23
Copymasters 1 – 8
Class cassette A
Self-study cassette

Introductory activities
New language introduced
Bonjour! / Au revoir!
Je m'appelle …
(Receptive only)*Levez-vous / Asseyez-vous / Ecoutez / Regardez / Levez la main / Répétez / Entrez / Sortez vos affaires / Rangez vos affaires / Rangez les chaises*
Numbers 0 – 10

Presentation of:
Bonjour!
Je m'appelle …

Greetings and introductions

AT 1 – 1, AT 2 – 1

- Invite students into the classroom, saying, *Bonjour! Entrez. Asseyez-vous* … and supporting the French with appropriate mimes and gestures.
- Introduce yourself, saying, *Bonjour! Je m'appelle* … and giving your name. Then use *Bonjour!* only and move around the classroom, greeting students and shaking their hands. As soon as possible, encourage individuals to say *Bonjour!* back to you. Instruct the whole class to listen to and repeat *Bonjour!*

T: Ecoutez: Bonjour! Répétez: Bonjour! (Indicate that students should listen by putting your hand to your ear and pointing to yourself while you say the greeting. Then indicate that the class should repeat by pointing to them as you give the second part of the instruction.)

- Tell students that they should now practise this in pairs, shaking their partner's hand.

T: Avec un(e) une partenaire: 'Bonjour!' 'Bonjour!' etcetera. (Stress the word *partenaire* and demonstrate how to carry out this activity, making it clear through gesture and mime that all students are to work in pairs.)

- Focus on the phrase *Je m'appelle* … . Practise repetition of the phrase without any name attached. Then give the whole phrase with your name and prompt students to give their names.

T: *Je m'appelle Monsieur/Madame … (give your name). Un(e) volontaire! (Gesture to the class and hold up your hand as if volunteering.) Je m'appelle … ? (Prompt and wait for a volunteer, giving extra support if necessary by helping to say the beginning of the phrase as the student starts speaking.)*

- Encourage more volunteers to join in giving their names. When they are confident, encourage the class to reuse *Bonjour!* and instruct them, using demonstration, to introduce themselves to their partner.

Presentation of classroom instructions

AT 1 – 1

- As a break from greetings and introductions, practise comprehension of some of the instructions given so far and teach others. Tell the students to watch, listen and copy you: *Regardez, écoutez et copiez!* Since these are your instructions to the class, there is no need for them to repeat the French phrase. Instead, support the language with an accompanying mime or gesture and encourage students simply to listen and copy the actions as you say each of the following instructions:

  Levez-vous.

  Asseyez-vous.

  Ecoutez.

  Regardez.

  Levez la main.

  Répétez. (Give an actual word to repeat afterwards, e.g. Bonjour!)

  Entrez.

  Sortez vos affaires.

  Rangez vos affaires.

  Rangez les chaises.

- Keep practising the instructions and gradually remove the support of your mimes, so that students have to remember the actions without your help. When they are confident, play games of *Jacques a dit* to practise listening skills and comprehension of these instructions.

Presentation of numbers 0 – 10

AT 1 – 1, AT 2 – 1

- Introduce the numbers 0 – 10, writing the figures on the board and saying them aloud as you do so.

- Tell students to repeat the numbers after you and say them again in sequence, pointing to each number as you say it.

- Write blocks of figures on the board and encourage repetition/chanting of these groups of numbers in sequence, for example:

  0

  1 2 3

  4 5 6

  7 8 9

  10

- Build up the size of the number groups, but always in sequence. Gradually remove the repetition element until students can chant all the numbers in sequence.

- Leave the figures in sequence on the board and point to a random incorrect figure, e.g. 7.

T: *Zéro. Oui ou non? (Demonstrate meaning by nodding and shaking your head.)*

- Repeat with another obviously incorrect number and ask a volunteer to come to the front and point out the number for you.

T: *Alors, montrez-moi le numéro zéro. Un(e) volontaire, s'il vous plaît. Viens ici. … Très bien!*

- Repeat several times with different numbers.
- Demonstrate and play comprehension activities and games, for example:
  - Say random numbers and tell the class to write down the figures on pieces of rough paper.
  - Divide the class into two teams and ask a volunteer from each team to come to the front of the class. Call out one of the numbers at random. The first student to point to the correct number wins a point for his or her team. Prompting by the rest of the team should be penalised!
  - *Effacez!* and *Encerclez!* are variations of the above game in which, rather than pointing, students race to rub out or to circle the number. For a more challenging game, write the numbers on the board in random order.
- Move on to activities involving oral production of the numbers, for example:
  - Throw a soft ball from one student to another at random around the classroom. The student who catches the ball must say the next number in the sequence.

- *Je pense à un numéro*. Write down your chosen number on a piece of paper and conceal it. Students guess which number you are thinking of. Confirm the correct number afterwards by showing your piece of paper. The student who guesses correctly can choose the next number. Hand over the activity to students to play in pairs. Encourage them to keep a tally of their partner's number of guesses and to see if they can beat their partner by using fewer guesses.
- *Jeu de morpion.* Play a version of Noughts and crosses. Fill the usual grid with figures. Teams or pairs of students take it in turns to say the number in the square of their choice to win the square.

Presentation of: *Au revoir*

AT 1 – 1, AT 2 – 1/2

- Introduce the phrase *Au revoir* well before the end of the first lesson, so that there is plenty of time to practise it before using it as a natural part of the end of the lesson. Revise *Bonjour! Je m'appelle ...* as you greet one of the students again, shake his or her hand and encourage him or her to reply. This time, wave and add *Au revoir!* as you walk away. Focus on *Au revoir!* and instruct the whole class to repeat the phrase and wave goodbye. When the class can pronounce the farewell with some degree of accuracy, tell students to practise *Bonjour! Au revoir!* in pairs.
- Remind students of *Je m'appelle ...* and choose a student with whom to act out the full dialogue *Bonjour! Je m'appelle ... / Bonjour! Je m'appelle ... / Au revoir! / Au revoir!* Shake hands at the beginning of the dialogue and wave goodbye at the end. Students practise this in pairs and move around the class introducing themselves.
- Use *Au revoir!* when dismissing the class at the end of the lesson and encourage students to use the phrase as their password or *passe-partout du jour/de la semaine* in order to be able to leave the classroom at the end of the lesson!

The class is now ready to move on to the **PASSE-PARTOUT** course materials.

New language introduced

Tu t'appelles comment?
Oui/Non, monsieur/madame
Ouvrez/Fermez les livres
Tournez à la page ...
The French alphabet

- Revise greetings and introductions, saying *Bonjour! Entrez. Asseyez-vous.*
- Quickly revise comprehension of other instructions taught previously and chant numbers 0 – 10 to 'warm up' the class.

Presentation of: *Tu t'appelles comment?*

- Remind students of *Je m'appelle ...* and practise this around the class. Introduce *Tu t'appelles comment?* receptively, to prompt students to give their names.

Presentation of: *Oui / Non, monsieur/madame*

- If appropriate, introduce the phrase *Je fais l'appel* and call the register, encouraging students to answer *Oui, monsieur/madame*, or, if someone is absent, *Non, monsieur/madame*. Encourage students to use *Bonjour, monsieur/madame* when they greet you in future.

La France   (CM 1)

AT 1 – 1, AT 2 – 1, AT 3 – 1

- Use an OHT version of Copymaster 1 or a large wall map to introduce France and some of the country's larger towns and cities. Begin by showing the whole of France and briefly pointing out its location in relation to the UK.

T: *Voici la France ... et voici l'Angleterre.*

- Draw a quick sketch on the board or point out roughly where your school is in relation to France.

T: *Et voici ... !*

- Work around the map of France familiarising students with the cities as you point them out and say them. Point out the French pronunciation of Paris and the fact that it is the capital.

T: *Et la capitale de la France est ... Tours?, Calais?, Paris?, Cherbourg? ... Oui! Très bien! Paris est la capitale. Attention! Regardez et écoutez: Paris. Répétez: Paris.*

- Encourage students to repeat this and other city names and to have fun imitating the French sounds.

- At this point, you may wish briefly to spend some time in English, discussing some of the other countries in the world where French is spoken and why this is so. It may also be appropriate to encourage students to think of some reasons why they personally might find French useful.

Presentation of the alphabet

On chante l'alphabet

AT 1 – 1, AT 2 – 1

- Introduce the alphabet.

T: Et maintenant l'alphabet ... Alors, regardez et écoutez.

- Write the letters on the board in the following groups as you say them, encouraging the students to repeat three or four letters at a time, before building up to each whole line of letters:
  A B C D E F G
  H I J K L M N O P
  Q R S T U V W
  X Y Z
- When students are confident in repeating each line, sing or use the class cassette to introduce the marine chant version of the alphabet. Students should listen the first time they hear the letters and then join in with the repetition in the second run-through of the chant on cassette.

T: Et maintenant on chante l'alphabet. (Demonstrate the meaning of on chante by singing a few bars of music.) Alors, regardez les lettres, écoutez et répétez.

- Point to the rows of letters and mime listening to them and repeating them.

A, B, C, D, E, F, G
A, B, C, D, E, F, G
H, I, J, K, L, M, N
H, I, J, K, L, M, N
O, P, Q, R, S, T, U,
O, P, Q, R, S, T, U,
V, W, X, Y, Z
V, W, X, Y, Z

A, B, C, D, E, F, G
H, I, J, K, L, M, N
O, P, Q, R, S, T, U,
V, W, X, Y, Z

- When the chant has been mastered, split the class in half and support one half in leading the chant and the other half in replying to it, until eventually the students can do this without support. For variety, encourage students to sing with increasing/decreasing volume.
- Further work on the alphabet is introduced later in this module (see Teacher's Notes, p. 9).

Presentation of:
Ouvrez/Fermez les livres / Tournez à la page ...

La France   (SB p.4)

AT 1 – 1, AT 2 – 1, AT 3 – 1

- Hold up some copies of the Students' Book, saying *Voici vos livres*. Hand them out, encouraging students to reply *Merci, monsieur/madame* as they receive their copy. Explain the title and practise saying it with the class before allowing time to look through the book. Then tell students to turn to page 4.

T: Ouvrez les livres et tournez à la page quatre. (Mime and remind students of numbers, e.g. Zéro, un, deux, trois, quatre.) Tournez à la page quatre. (Hold up a book which is open at the correct page.)

- Refamiliarise students with the map, pointing out that it shows the cities which they looked at earlier, and reminding them of the pronunciation.

T: Ah, voici la France, et voici Calais, Boulogne, Rouen, Paris, Bordeaux (etc.).

- Use the map to practise comprehension of letters. Link it to the alphabet, spelling out one of the cities as you write it on the board, e.g. *B – O – R – D – E – A – U – X. Bordeaux.* Encourage students to repeat the spelling and then spell out some more cities on the map, but without the support of simultaneous writing on the board. Tell the class to listen to the spelling, look at the map and to give you the name of the correct location.
- Now that students are using the textbook, revise the classroom instructions introduced previously (see Teacher's Notes, p. 2) and extend them to include:

Ouvrez les livres.
Fermez les livres.
Tournez à la page ... + revision of numbers 1 – 10.

- Introduce a variety of games and activities to give students opportunities to practise this language.

La France   (SB p.4)
En France   (SB p.5)

AT 3 – 1

- The map on page 4 and the collage on page 5 can be used to stimulate students' interest in and awareness of France. It may be helpful to provide some direction and a degree of support, by briefly asking questions such as:
  - What is the name of the famous landmark in Paris which you can see on the map and in the collage?
  - Look at the stamp. In our country we have pounds and pence. What is the currency in France?
  - What famous French foods can you see on the map and in the collage?
  - Name some other well-known French foods.
  - What famous French sporting event can you see in the collage?
  - What are the colours of the French flag? Which way are the stripes and in which order?

- If appropriate, students could be encouraged to make a *coin français* in their classroom. For homework they could try to find or draw items for this class collage, e.g. French stamps; postcards; decorated names of French cities shown on the map; pictures of French sports events and celebrities, cars, food, drink, towns etc. from magazines, newspapers, travel brochures; any 'real' food and drink labels or packets, etc.
- At a later date this could be broadened to include information and pictures related to other French-speaking countries.

Student goals   (SB p.6)

- Use the bottom half of this page to familiarise students with the module's main teaching points and goals. Read out the title *'Bienvenue!'* and direct students to the different elements of the picture, as you read out the French contained within each.
- In this initial module it may be more appropriate to move out of the target language and to explain the title of the unit and discuss in English the visual representation of its three sections.
- Encourage students to deduce the meaning of the sub-titles of the sections and the language contained within the pictures. This could be done orally with students finding and piecing together the 'clues' contained within the pictures of the goals.
- Afterwards, this can form the basis of some brief introductory work on simple reading skills. Ask students to explain how the 'clues' helped them to guess the themes. This should give rise to comments about pictures, and words which are the same or similar in both languages. Draw together their comments and point out that these techniques can often be used to help understand the meaning of new French language.
- Point out the open door in the visual representation of the goals. Explain that when the students have worked through the three sections of the module, the new language they have learned will be a *passe-partout* or skeleton key, allowing them to 'open the door' to a special final activity.

Objectif 1 Salut!

New language introduced
Salut!
Ça va? / Ça va / (Non,) ça na va pas
Et toi?
Ça s'écrit comment?
Merci
J'habite à ...
Tu habites où?
Numbers 11 – 20

Salut!   (SB p.6)
La France   (CM 1)

AT 1 – 1/2, AT 2 – 1/2, AT 3 – 1/2

- Remind students of the first of the goals on page 6, e.g. point to the picture of the first goal and say, *Bon. Objectif un – 'Salut!'*

- Use the class cassette and page 6 to introduce the main characters, location and background context of the course.

T: Voici une cassette ... (Hold it up.) Dans un moment vous allez écouter la cassette. (Mime.) Bon. Tournez à la page six. (Mime.) Regardez: 'Salut!' (Point to the title.) Voici deux photos. Alors une photo, deux photos ... . (Direct students to the photos.) Regardez ... (point to the photo of Marc.) C'est une photo de Monsieur/Madame 'X'? (use your own name). Non. Alors, ça c'est Monsieur/Madame 'X'? (Point to the photo of Claire and again use your own name). Bon. Ecoutez la cassette et regardez les photos et les images à la page six. (Mime.)

Marc:	Salut! Je m'appelle Marc.
Claire:	Bonjour! Je m'appelle Claire.
Marc et Claire:	Au revoir!
Marc et Claire:	Bonjour!
Yannick:	Salut! Je m'appelle Yannick.

- Use an OHT version of the map on Copymaster 1 or redirect students to the map on page 4. Point out the towns of Bordeaux, Toulouse and Albi.

T: Regardez la carte. (Mime.) Voici Bordeaux et voici Toulouse. (Point to the two towns on the main map.) Et voici Toulouse et Albi. (Point to the inset map.) Alors, Bordeaux, Toulouse, Albi. (Write the names of the three towns on the board and represent the approximate size and location of each in relation to one another by means of a cross next to each.) La famille de Marc et Claire déménage. Au revoir, Bordeaux! Bonjour, Albi! (Support this final statement with drawings on the board 'map' and with mimes.)

- Tell the students to turn back to page 6 and to listen to the cassette again.

T: Bon. Encore une fois. (Mime.) Tournez à la page six. Ecoutez la cassette et regardez la page. (Mime.)

- Finally, check understanding of the context by asking who can explain what's happening on this page in English. Ask students what they think *Salut!* means and explain the difference in register between this and the greeting *Bonjour!*

Je me présente (CM 2)

- Revise numbers 1 – 10 and play number games to practise aural comprehension and oral production of these numbers. (See Games section in Teacher's Notes introduction, p. iv.)

1 Ecoute. C'est quel numéro?

AT 1 – 1, AT 3 – 1/2

- Move on to more detailed practice in linking spoken and written sounds, using the first section of the copymaster, and the class cassette. Students listen to the cassette, read the five statements on the copymaster and number them in the order in which they hear them.

Boy:	Salut!
Claire:	Je m'appelle Claire.
Girl:	Bonjour!
Marc:	Je m'appelle Marc.
Boy:	Au revoir.

Solution

Salut! 1
Bonjour! 3
Je m'appelle Marc. 4
Je m'appelle Claire. 2
Au revoir. 5

- When students have matched the phrases with those on the cassette, tell them to look again at the statements and to think about the sounds they have heard. Encourage them to discuss briefly anything which they have noticed about the spelling compared with the sound of French. Emphasise the importance of learning both.

- Before directing students to the other activities on the copymaster, remind them of the difference in the register of *Bonjour!* and *Salut!* Draw attention briefly to the existence and function of the apostrophe in the phrase *Je m'appelle ...* .

2 Complète.

AT 4 – 1/2

- Students can then demonstrate their attention to detail by concentrating on copying accurately, as they complete the gaps in the speech bubbles.

3 Moi! Complète.

AT 4 – 1/2

- In the final activity, students complete a bubble of their own, using any one of the phrases from exercise 1 of the copymaster and adding their own photo or drawing.

Differentiation – Extension

AT 4 – 1/2

- Some students could create further bubbles of their own, copying and illustrating the other phrases from section 1 of the copymaster. These could be personalised and/or humorous.

AT 4 – 1/2

- A variety of other tasks can be undertaken during lesson or homework time to give additional practice of writing these phrases. For example, students could:
  - Make a *Bonjour!, Salut!* or *Au revoir!* poster for display in the classroom or around the school.
  - Design a large badge or a name sign for their desk labelled *Bonjour! / Salut! Je m'appelle …* , to help you learn their names.
  - Begin an introductory page about themselves on the first page of their exercise book or file, showing a drawing or photo and a greeting and information about themselves in French. Other information can be added as students progress through the module and encounter more language. They could also/alternatively begin an ongoing *dossier personnel* on disk.
- Encourage all students to learn how to give a greeting, say their name and say goodbye by heart.

Je m'appelle … (SB p.7)

AT 1 – 2, AT 2 – 2, AT 3 – 2

- Explain the context of page 7 of the Students' Book by pointing out the cartoon of Yannick at the bottom of page 6 and the group photo of him and his friends in Albi at the top of page 7.

*T:	Tournez à la page six. Regardez Yannick. (Point.) Bon. Regardez la photo à la page sept. (Point.) C'est une photo de Yannick et ses copains à Albi. Un, deux, trois, quatre, cinq, six. (Point.) Il y a six copains. Et regardez: un, deux, trois, quatre copains. (Point to the four individual photos at the top of the page.) 'Copains', c'est quoi en anglais? … Bon. Alors, regardez la page et écoutez la cassette. (Mime.)*

- Use the class cassette to introduce the group of friends living in Albi, whom Marc and Claire are now going to meet. Students hear different voices as they listen to the class cassette whilst following the text.

Yannick:	Bonjour! Je m'appelle Yannick.
Sophie:	Salut! Je m'appelle Sophie.
Olivier:	Salut! Je m'appelle Olivier.
Sandrine:	Bonjour! Je m'appelle Sandrine.

- Practise pronunciation of the four new names and revise pronunciation of *Marc* and *Claire*. Students can then work in small groups, taking on the roles of the friends and Marc or Claire and introducing themselves to one another.

Tu t'appelles comment? (SB p.7)
a Ecoute et lis.

AT 1 – 2, AT 3 – 2

- Remind the class of the question *Tu t'appelles comment?* by pretending to be forgetful and asking a few individuals their names. Then use the class cassette in conjunction with page 7 to present the written form of the question and introduce the rest of the group of friends in Albi.
- Students listen to their first short dialogues, whilst following the texts in their books.

1

| Marc: | Salut! Je m'appelle Marc. Tu t'appelles comment? |
| Frédéric: | Je m'appelle Frédéric. |

2

Louise: Bonjour! Je m'appelle Louise. Tu t'appelles comment?

Claire: Je m'appelle Claire.

- Practise pronunciation of the question *Tu t'appelles comment?* and the names *Frédéric* and *Louise,* using teacher – class repetition. Draw attention briefly to the existence and function of *é* which occurs twice in the name Frédéric.
- Students practise reading the dialogues aloud in pairs. They can then vary the conversations by substituting their own names or by taking on the roles of the other friends at the top of page 7.
- Quickly revise the numbers 1 – 6 orally, e.g. prompt students to chant the numbers in sequence and then write random figures on the board and encourage students to call them out in French, etc.

b A deux.

AT 2 – 2

- Direct students to the pairwork activity and model the example dialogue, showing how it relates to the numbered group photo above. If necessary, quickly practise pronunciation of the six names again, before asking students to work in pairs.

AT 3 – 2, AT 4 – 2/3

- Students write their own version of the conversation '*Tu t'appelles comment?*', using magazine cut-outs and writing accompanying speech bubbles.

Actions!   (CM 3)

- Revise the classroom instruction language introduced earlier, saying the phrases, using actions and encouraging students to join in the actions. (See Teacher's Notes p. 2 – *Levez-vous, Asseyez-vous, Ecoutez,* etc. and p. 4 – *Ouvrez les livres, Fermez les livres,* etc.)

1 Ecoute et lis.

AT 1 – 1, AT 3 – 1

- Use the class cassette to consolidate the instructions, whilst students follow the labelled pictures on Copymaster 3.

1 Entrez
2 Asseyez-vous
3 Levez-vous
4 Sortez vos affaires
5 Rangez vos affaires
6 Rangez les chaises
7 Levez la main
8 Regardez
9 Ecoutez
10 Répétez
11 Ouvrez le livre
12 Fermez le livre

2 Ecoute. C'est quel numéro?

AT 1 – 1, AT 3 – 1

- As a final check of understanding, students listen to the random instructions on the cassette and refer to the pictures on the copymaster, noting the numbers of the instructions. They can then keep the copymaster as a reference page.

Asseyez-vous	Ecoutez
Rangez vos affaires	Levez-vous
Répétez	Entrez
Levez la main	

Solution

2, 9, 5, 3, 10, 1, 7

- You may also wish to enlarge the copymaster and use it as a classroom poster for ongoing student reference.

Presentation of:
Ça va? Ça va. (Non,) Ça ne va pas. Et toi?

Ça va?   (SB p.8)

a Ecoute et lis.

AT 1 – 1/2/3, AT 3 – 2/3

- Use the cartoon at the top of page 8 and the class cassette to introduce the following phrases:
Ça va? Ça va. Ça ne va pas.

– Salut! Ça va?

– Ça va.

– Non! Ça ne va pas!

- Check and practise understanding of the new language, using drawings of faces and a question mark on the board/OHP. Extend this by introducing the question *Et toi?*

b Ecoute et lis. Ecoute, lis et répète.

AT 1 – 1/2/3, AT 2 – 1/2/3, AT 3 – 2/3

- Play the tape again and encourage students to follow the cartoon in their books while they are listening. Move on to activity B and focus on the pronunciation and intonation of the individual phrases, first directing the class to listen and read and then to listen, read and repeat.

– Ça va?

– Ça va.

– Et toi?

– Ça ne va pas!

- Practise the language by asking individuals how they are and encouraging them to reply and to ask you, gradually moving on to demonstrate and set up pairwork.

c Ecoute et lis.

AT 1 – 1/2/3, AT 3 – 2/3

- Draw attention to the *Ç* and mention briefly its function, before finally directing the class to listen to and read the rhyme '*Bonjour Sophie. Bonjour Yannick.*'

Bonjour Sophie. Bonjour Yannick.

Ça va? Ça va. Et toi?

Salut Louise. Salut Frédéric.

Ça va? Ça va. Au revoir!

- Students could then practise reading the rhyme aloud. This can be done in a variety of ways, for example:
  - They read the rhyme aloud as a class or in groups, in the same rhythm as the original version.
  - They read the rhyme aloud, simultaneously with the cassette. See if the class can maintain the rhythm and speed of the cassette, while you suddenly turn the volume right down. Then turn up the volume again to find out whether or not students have kept pace with the cassette!
  - They practise the rhyme in pairs, taking it in turns to ask and answer the questions.

AT 3 – 2/3   AT 4 – 2/3

- Students could make up their own '*Ça va?*' comic strips for display, adapting the model at the top of page 8.

Differentiation – Extension

AT 2 – 2/3, AT 3 – 2/3

- Some students could be encouraged to say the rhyme by heart. Take time out in English to give them learning strategies, e.g.
  - learning one phrase or one line at a time.
  - using the rhyme as a memory aid.
  - practising with a friend or saying it to a member of the family.
  - recording it and then listening to it and correcting it.
  - trying to remember it while waiting for the bus, before going to sleep etc.

L'alphabet cabaret! (SB p.9)

AT 1 – 2 AT 2 – 2 AT 3 – 2

- Revise the alphabet, using the marine chant and/or the cassette '*On chante l'alphabet*' if appropriate. (See Teacher's Notes page 4.)
- When students are confident, play the song on page 9, set to the tune of the can-can. Encourage students to join in singing as soon as possible, slowly at first (using the first version) and then more quickly (using the second version).

1 Bienvenue!

T: **Ecoutez la cassette. C'est l'alphabet cabaret. Ne chantez pas. (Mime and play the first version.) Ecoutez encore une fois. Et si c'est possible, chantez! (Mime and sing a bar or two, before playing the first version again.) Alors, maintenant chantez plus vite. (Mime and sing at a quicker pace, before playing the second, faster version.)**

- The third, final version is in karaoké style.

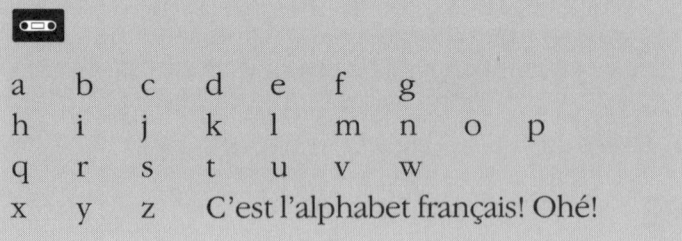

a	b	c	d	e	f	g	
h	i	j	k	l	m	n	o	p
q	r	s	t	u	v	w	
x	y	z	C'est l'alphabet français! Ohé!				

- Play a variety of spelling games to activate the knowledge of the alphabet. (See Number games on Teacher's Notes pages iv – v.) For example:
  - Students give the letters in sequence as you write the alphabet on the board.
  - They point to/circle/wipe off random letters chosen by you.
  - *C'est quelle lettre?* Team game to call out letters you are pointing to.
  - Individuals call out the next letter in the sequence as you throw a soft-ball around the class.
  - *Pendu.* Students play Hangman as a class, in groups or in pairs.

AT 1 – 1, AT 2 – 1

- For final consolidation of the alphabet on an individual basis, direct students to the marine chant on the self-study cassette. Since this is their first encounter with this cassette, spend some time in English explaining how to use it. (See Teacher's Notes introduction, p. iii.) (Additionally, you may wish to point out that some of the material on the cassette is identical to the material which students will have already met in lessons, some material is similar and that some is completely new.)

You will need to look at page 9 in your Students' Book. Listen to the marine chant of the alphabet, *'On chante l'alphabet'*. Echo the chant.

A, B, C, D, E, F, G
A, B, C, D, E, F, G
H, I, J, K, L, M, N
H, I, J, K, L, M, N
O, P, Q, R, S, T, U,
O, P, Q, R, S, T, U,
V, W, X, Y, Z
V, W, X, Y, Z

A, B, C, D, E, F, G
H, I, J, K, L, M, N
O, P, Q, R, S, T, U,
V, W, X, Y, Z

Presentation of: *Ça s'écrit comment?*

Ça s'écrit comment? (SB p.9)

a Ecoute et lis.

AT 1 – 1/2, AT 3 – 2/3

- Students look at Marc's basketball club membership card and read the conversation, whilst listening to the cassette.

– Salut! Tu t'appelles comment?
– Je m'appelle Marc Aubry.
– Aubry? Ça s'écrit comment?
– A – U – B – R – Y.
– Bon, merci.

- Focus on the question *Ça s'écrit comment?* Write it on the board as you say it and check that students understand the meaning.

T: **'Ça s'écrit comment?', c'est quoi en anglais? (Call for a volunteer interpreter.)**

- Use the question to revise the spelling of *Marc* and *Aubry* orally.

b Ecoute et complète.

AT 1 – 1/2, AT 4 – 1

- Explain that the class is now going to listen to the cassette on which the other members of the basketball club spell their names and that, using the damaged form on page 9 as support, they are going to copy and complete the list of surnames in their exercise books/on paper.

T: *Regardez activité B, 'Ecoute et complète'. Voici une liste des membres du club de basket. Alors, regardez ... Marc Aubry est sur la liste ... Mais il y a un petit problème. C'est Françoise Bal... Balfour? Baladin? Balcon?* **(Suggest a variety of** *Bal...* **possibilities and continue the process briefly with** *Martin De...* **etc. to lead pupils through the text.)** *Mais il y a une solution! Il y a une cassette. Ecoutez la cassette. Vous allez écouter un monsieur au club de basket. Par exemple, 'Aubry? Ça s'écrit comment?' Et la réponse: 'A – U – B – R – Y'. Mais regardez ...* **(Point to the damaged form.)** *Marc Aubry, pas de problème, mais Françoise Bal... ? Ecoutez la cassette et écrivez la réponse dans votre cahier, par exemple B – A – L – etcetera.*

- Decide whether to ask students to complete the whole name or the surname only and demonstrate how to write the answer.

Coach:	Marc Aubry.
Marc:	Oui, monsieur.
Coach:	Françoise ...?
Françoise:	Bally, monsieur.
Coach:	Ça s'écrit comment?
Françoise:	B – A – L – L – Y.
Coach:	B – A – L – L – Y, merci. ... Martin ... De ...?
Martin:	Denis, monsieur.
Coach:	Ça s'écrit comment?
Martin:	D – E – N – I – S.
Coach:	... Paul ... ?
Paul:	Jourdain, monsieur. J – O – U – R – D – A – I – N.
Coach:	... Michèle ... ?
Michèle:	Leroux, monsieur. Leroux, c'est L – E – R – O – U – X.
Coach:	... Simon ...?
Simon:	Martel, monsieur. M – A – R – T – E – L.
Coach:	Martel. Oui, je sais. Pas de problème! ... Anne-Marie ... ?

Anne-Marie:	D – R – E – U – X. Dreux, monsieur.
Coach:	Attends ... D – R – E – U – X. Bon, c'est fini. Allons-y!

- Practise the use of the question *Ça s'écrit comment?* with the class, by asking a member of the group, *Tu t'appelles comment? ... Ça s'écrit comment?* Indicate that the student should spell his/her name, giving some support if necessary. Repeat the process with other individuals.
- Then practise class repetition of the question, before encouraging students to produce the question individually. Give them an unknown name or word (N.B. Use a word with no accents) and point to the question on the board to support them in asking *Ça s'écrit comment?* Reply by spelling out and writing the unknown word. Suggested names to use: *Luc, Chantal, Yannick, Xavier, Pauline, Anne-Marie, Marie-Laure, Corinne, Roger, Jeanne.*

c A deux.

AT 2 – 2/3 AT 3 – 2

- Finally, direct students to activity C. Model the example conversation and demonstrate that students should practise the conversation in pairs, using their own and/or well-known people's names.

Presentation of numbers 0 – 20

AT1 – 1, AT 2 – 1, AT 3 – 1

- Revise numbers 0 – 10 and teach the remaining numbers 11 – 20. Write all the numbers in the following grouping on the board/OHP, pointing to the corresponding number as you say it.

0
1 2 3
4 5 6
7 8 9
10 11 12
13 14 15
16 17 18
19 20

- Concentrate on the sequence and encourage students to join in repeating and chanting the numbers.

1 Bienvenue!

- Check understanding of random numbers by playing a variety of number games, e.g. *Effacez!*, *Encerclez,* teacher–class *Loto, Ecoutez et écrivez,* etc.
- Introduce the written forms of the numbers in sequence, either by writing the words on the board or by writing them on A4 or A5 size pieces of paper/card and sticking them onto the board. (The latter method allows them to be rearranged and jumbled more quickly afterwards.)
- Place each word below its corresponding figure. Say the numbers in order in the number groups used previously, point to the words and prompt students to listen, read and repeat.
- Then rub out all the numbers, write a random figure in the middle of the board without saying it, and invite a student to come to the front of the class to select and match the corresponding word. (Initially this task can be simplified by reducing the menu of words, so that the student is given a multiple-choice of only three or four words, rather than the whole list to choose from.)

Radio sport!

AT 1 – 1

- As an additional check of students' comprehension of numbers, play the class cassette and tell students to listen and write down the football and rugby scores.

T: *Ecoutez et écrivez les résultats.*

- Before beginning, show how to write the scores as figures, e.g. 1 – 0. You may also wish to provide a grid (with the names of the teams included) on the board or OHP, for students to copy down and complete with the scores.

Bonsoir. Ici radio sport. Voici les résultats des matchs de football et de rugby. D'abord les résultats de foot ...

Rennes 2	Orléans 3
Calais 1	Boulogne 3
Cherbourg 1	Rouen 6
Tours 4	Dijon 2

Et les résultats de rugby ...

Toulouse 15	Perpignan 12
Marseille 9	Lyon 13
Nice 16	Clermont Ferrand 18
Limoges 14	Bordeaux 11

AT 4 – 1/2

- Allocate one or more of the numbers from 0 – 20 to each student, so that they can prepare a section of a number frieze for display in the classroom. Ask them to draw each figure on an A4-size piece of paper, to decorate it and to clearly write the corresponding French word underneath. Alternatively, this may be word-processed.

Les numéros 0 – 20 (CM 4)

1 Ecoute et répète.

AT 1 – 1, AT 3 – 1

- Students can work independently and use the left-hand column of the copymaster, together with the self-study cassette, to practise and perfect their pronunciation of numbers 0 – 20. They can also keep and use this list of numbers for future reference.

You will need Copymaster 4, activity 1. Look at the list of numbers on the copymaster. Listen to the numbers on the cassette and repeat them, paying careful attention to how they are said.

0			
1	2	3	
4	5	6	
7	8	9	
10	11	12	
13	14	15	16
17	18	19	20

2 Relie.

AT 4 – 1/2

- In the second activity students can practise linking written numbers with corresponding figures.

3 C'est logique! Complète.

AT 4 – 1/2

- Finally, students can demonstrate their powers of logic and their understanding of written numbers by completing the number sequences in activity 3.

Solution

1 zéro, deux, **quatre**, six
2 un, trois, cinq, **sept**
3 cinq, dix, **quinze**, vingt
4 vingt, dix-neuf, dix-huit, **dix-sept**
5 seize, quinze, **quatorze**, **treize**

- Using Copymaster 4 and the self-study cassette as support, students should spend at least two homeworks learning to say and, where appropriate, to spell the numbers 0 – 10 and 11 – 20 by heart.

Differentiation – Extension

AT 4 – 1/2

- Encourage as many students as possible to try tackling the second and third activities on the copymaster without looking at the reference list of numbers on the left-hand side of the sheet.
- Higher attainers could try making up their own logic puzzles in the style of those on Copymaster 4, using the written forms of the numbers 0 – 20. These could form part of a wall display or be exchanged and solved by other members of the class.
- As a further extension activity you may wish to write some simple sums on the board or OHP for students to do orally in French. It is suggested that you limit this to addition only, to avoid teaching new vocabulary for 'minus', 'divided by', etc. Simple addition could be done using simply the new word *font*, e.g. *Deux et trois font …?*

> **Presentation of:** *J'habite à … Tu habites où?*

Tu habites où? (SB p.10)

AT 1 – 2, AT 2 – 2, AT 3 – 2

- Before directing students to page 10, introduce the phrase *J'habite à …* , using your own town, village or district to make the meaning of the phrase clear. Write other place names in your local area on the board/OHP and say *J'habite à …* . Check understanding by calling on an interpreter and asking *J'habite à … ', c'est quoi en anglais?*
- Direct students to page 10 and introduce the question *Tu habites où?* in the title at the top of the page. Combine the question with your initial statement about where you live and then check understanding by again calling on someone in the class to act as an interpreter.
- Play the class cassette which contains the new question and answer within a short conversation. Encourage students to follow the text of the conversation on page 10 as they listen to the tape.

Marc:	Frédéric, tu habites où?
Frédéric:	J'habite à Cordes. Et toi, Marc, tu habites où?
Marc:	J'habite à Albi.

- Clarify the place names by pointing out the map at the top of page 10 and comparing it with the inset map on page 4.
- Focus on the statement *J'habite à …* . Write it on the board and, if appropriate, ask students if it reminds them of anything in English. Practise repetition, highlighting the silent *h*. Underline and stress *J'habite …* and point out the contrasting mispro-nunciation *J'habite …Non!* Ask students around the class where they live and encourage them to volunteer *J'habite à* + their place of residence.
- Use a similar process to focus on the question *Tu habites où?*, linking the spoken and written versions of the phrase and practising repetition, before prompting students to ask the question individually.
- Finally, encourage students to ask *Tu habites où?* and answer *J'habite à …* in pairs or around the class, supplying their own information in the answer. If this is not appropriate because of the lack of variety of places of residence, encourage students to answer imaginatively, using the name of the place where they would most like to live. Alternatively, they could practise the conversation on page 10 in pairs.

Radio Jeunes! (SB p.10)

AT 1 – 2/3   AT 2 – 2/3   AT 3 – 1

- Link this activity to the previous ones by explaining where Frédéric and Marc live.

T: Frédéric habite à Cordes et Marc habite à Albi. Voici Albi … (Point to Albi on the map in the 'Radio Jeunes' activity or on the OHT version of Copymaster 1. If using the latter, number the six locations shown on the map on page 10.) … Et voici Bordeaux. (Point to the map.)

- Explore the map, saying the other place names shown to refamiliarise students with the sounds and locations of these French towns and cities. Also indicate that each location is numbered on this particular map, pointing out the six numbers in succession. Say the place names again and this time ask the students to give the numbers.
- Explain the context of 'Radio Jeunes!'.

T: Vous allez écouter 'Radio Jeunes!'. Vous allez écouter des conversations de téléphone. C'est un quiz. Ecrivez dans votre cahier les lettres A à F. (Write A – F on the board/OHP.) 'A'. Ecoutez bien: 'Salut, Séverine. Tu habites où?' 'J'habite à Nice.' (Point to the letter A and talk through the first conversation from the cassette.) Regardez la carte. Nice, c'est quel numéro? (Point to the map and wait for students to say Six. When they do, say Bravo! and write the number 6 on the board next to the letter A.) Bon. Ecoutez la cassette. A, B, C etc.

- Play the cassette, pausing after the name of the town at the end of each item to allow students time to find and write the appropriate number.

A

| DJ: | Salut, Séverine. Tu habites où? |
| Séverine: | Salut! J'habite à Nice. |

B

| DJ: | Bonjour, Philippe. Tu habites où? |
| Philippe: | Salut! Moi, j'habite à Rouen. |

C

| DJ: | Bonjour, Omar. Tu habites où? |
| Omar: | Bonjour! J'habite à Bordeaux. |

D

| DJ: | Salut, Annette! Toi, tu habites où? |
| Annette: | Moi, j'habite à Orléans. |

E

| DJ: | Salut. Tu habites où, David? |
| David: | Salut! J'habite à Perpignan. |

F

DJ:	Finalement, Catherine. Bonjour! Ça va?
Catherine:	Oui, ça va bien merci.
DJ:	Tu habites où, Catherine?
Catherine:	J'habite à Clermont Ferrand.
DJ	Et voilà. Je vais poser la première question …

Solution

A 6 **B** 1 **C** 4 **D** 2 **E** 5 **F** 3

- Afterwards, the class can work in pairs and make up their own conversations *Tu habites où? / J'habite à* … , using the map on page 10 or chosen French towns. Alternatively, they could use their answers from the previous activity and work in pairs to reconstruct the conversations in 'Radio Jeunes!'.

AT 4 – 2/3

- Students could write some of these conversations. Draw attention briefly to the existence of the grave accent, which occurs in *où* and *à*.

Differentiation – Extension

AT 4 – 3

- Some students could be encouraged to combine the different elements of language learned so far and to write longer interviews based on the material in 'Radio Jeunes!'.

Villes rythmiques (SB p.10)

AT 1 – 2/3, AT 2 – 2, AT 3 – 2/3

- The class cassette can be used for further pronunciation practice and as an aid to remembering the phrases *J'habite à* … and *Tu habites où?* You may also wish to use the rhyme to focus on and to practise nasal sounds.

Moi, j'habite à Perpignan.
Tu habites où? A Rouen?
Nice? Bordeaux? Clermont Ferrand?
Non, j'habite à Orléans!

- Students can also practise the rap version of the rhyme individually or at home using the self-study cassette.

You will need Students' Book page 10. Look at the rhyme, *'Villes rythmiques'* at the bottom of the page. Listen to it on the cassette and see if you can join in the rap.

Moi, j'habite à Perpignan.
Tu habites où? A Rouen?
Nice? Bordeaux? Clermont Ferrand?
Non, j'habite à Orléans!

Moi et toi (CM 5)

AT 3 – 2, AT 4 – 2

- This copymaster gathers together all the personal information language covered so far. Initially, students should match the pairs of phrases before writing the most appropriate exchange underneath each cartoon.

AT 4 – 2/3

- Students can make up their own cartoons and captions.

Differentiation – Extension

AT 4 – 3

- This activity could also be done from memory without the support of Copymaster 5. If so, encourage students to write lightly in pencil first and to have this checked by you before producing their final version in ink, redrafting if necessary. (Suggest that they indicate if they produced their work from memory.)

Au jardin public (SB p.11)

AT 1 – 3, AT 2 – 2/3, AT 3 – 3

- Use page 11 and the class cassette to consolidate all the personal information language encountered so far. Play the tape as support for this first piece of more extended reading, telling students to listen and to follow the story in their books.

Nous les copains

| Sophie: | Salut! Tu t'appelles comment? |
| Marc: | Je m'appelle Marc. |

| Sophie: | Je m'appelle Sophie. |
| Sandrine: | Et moi, je m'appelle Sandrine. |

| Sandrine: | Tu habites où? |
| Marc: | J'habite à Albi. |

| Sophie: | Salut! Ça va? |
| Olivier: | Salut! Oui, ça va. |

| Yannick: | Salut Marc! Tu joues au foot? |
| Marc: | Mais oui! |

Sophie and Sandrine: Chouette! Au revoir les gars!

- Draw attention to the following new language:
  Tu joues au foot?
  Mais oui!
  Chouette!
  les gars
- Point out in particular the spelling of *oui*, which until now has only been encountered aurally. *Chouette* could become the password for the day and *Au revoir, les gars!* could be included in dismissals.
- Discuss briefly in English what 'clues' helped students understand the story (context, cognates, pictures, tone etc.) (See Teacher's Notes p. 5 – Student goals).
- Recap by playing the cassette again while students listen and read the text. Students could then practise reading sections of the text or various characters' parts aloud as a class or in groups.

Differentiation – Extension

- Students could read or act out the whole story in groups of five. (Where the class is not divisible by five, some students could be given more than one role.)

Objectif 2 En classe

New language introduced

un cahier/crayon/livre/sac/stylo
une fiche/gomme/règle/trousse
Tu as/Vous avez/une ... s'il te plaît/s'il vous plaît?

Student goals   (SB p.6)

- Remind students of the second goal for this module. Point to the picture of the second objective on page 6 and say, *Bon. Objectif deux – 'En classe'... .*

Presentation of classroom objects

AT 1 – 1

- Teach the following vocabulary using real objects:
  un cahier
  un crayon
  un livre
  un sac
  un stylo
  un taille-crayon
  une fiche
  une gomme
  une règle
  une trousse
- Present all masculine nouns together and all feminine nouns together and arrange them in two distinct piles according to their gender.

Mes affaires   (SB p.12)

a Ecoute et regarde. C'est quelle lettre?

AT 1 – 1, AT 2 – 1, AT 3 – 1, AT 4 – 1

- Check understanding of this vocabulary using the lettered schoolbag and equipment in the photos on page 12. Begin by revising the letters A – J.

- Demonstrate the activity by writing the numbers 1 – 10 on the board and asking students to copy them down. Explain that they are going to listen to the cassette, look at the picture and write the letter of the object announced each time next to its number. Demonstrate, using the example *Numéro un – un cahier* and writing the letter B next to number 1 on the board.

1	un cahier
2	un stylo
3	une gomme
4	un crayon
5	un sac
6	une trousse
7	un livre
8	un taille-crayon
9	une règle
10	une fiche

Solution

1 B **2** I **3** E **4** G **5** A **6** F **7** C **8** H **9** D **10** J

- Pick up the real classroom objects and use them to revise the new vocabulary and to support repetition.
- Move on to play a *Vrai ou faux?* variation on *Jacques a dit* – hold up one of the classroom objects and say one of the items of vocabulary. If you say the correct item, students repeat it. If you say the wrong item, they must remain silent.
- Then play a guessing game to elicit productive use of the new vocabulary, inviting students to guess the classroom object which you have hidden in your bag. Throughout these activities insist on the use of the correct indefinite article.

b Fais les paires.

AT 1 – 1, AT 2 – 1, AT 3 – 1, AT 4 – 1

- Direct students to activity B. Students copy the lists of vocabulary in the boxes on page 12, look at the photo above and choose the correct letter for each item. They should write the letter next to the word, before drawing the object and/or, if desired, giving the English equivalent.

- Encourage them to line up their work in vertical columns, as this will help to make the list easier to learn from later.
- Students could also work in pairs and match the items of vocabulary with their corresponding objects orally.
- To give themselves more of a challenge they could announce the items in random order, rather than following the alphabetical order of the lists on page 12.

Attention! (SB p.13)

AT 1 – 1, AT 2 – 1, AT 3 – 1

- Ask the class *'Un', c'est quoi en anglais? 'Une', c'est quoi en anglais?* Summarise in English, asking students to say how many words there are in French for 'a' and what they are.
- Write *un* on the board in blue and *une* in red. Explain that in French all things or objects are either *un* which we call masculine or *une* which we call feminine, and stress that we must also learn this whenever we learn a new word for a thing or an object in French.
- Direct students to the *'Attention!'* feature at the top of page 13 and work through this in French, adding examples of other masculine and feminine classroom objects taught previously. Point out afterwards in English that in reality the appearance of an object has nothing to do with whether it is masculine or feminine, and that the objects in the *'Attention!'* feature have simply been stylised to remind students that there are two genders.
- Explain that we can hear as well as see the difference between *un* and *une* and focus on sound discrimination. Say *un, un, un, une, un* etc., telling students to put up their hands when they hear a change in sound. Do a variety of activities of this type, e.g. *une, une, un, une, une* etc., before moving on to more challenging and lively sound discrimination practice such as *un, une, un, une, un* etc.
- Finally, put the sounds back into context and link them with their written forms, by encouraging students to join you in reading aloud through the two lists of vocabulary underneath the photo on page 12.
- In pairs students can now play a game to guess the hidden object in one another's bags, keeping a tally to see who wins with the least number of guesses.

At this point you may wish to use Copymaster 74. Students complete notes on the use of *un/une* and keep them for reference.

Differentiation – Consolidation

Rangez vos affaires! (CM 6)

AT 1 – 1, AT 2 – 1, AT 3 – 1, AT 4 – 1

- Students requiring additional practice of the classroom object vocabulary can use this copymaster in conjunction with the self-study cassette.
- Those requiring pronunciation practice can begin by using the cassette to work through the first activity at their own pace.

You will need Copymaster 6, activity 1. Look at the lists of classroom objects. Listen and repeat.

un cahier
un crayon
un livre
un sac
un stylo
un taille-crayon
une fiche
une gomme
une règle
une trousse

- Students can then practise comprehension and copywriting by labelling the drawings, before finally colour-coding masculine and feminine objects and using this copymaster as a reference sheet.

Differentiation – Extension

AT 4 – 1/2

- Higher attainers could try writing an acrostic of the classroom object vocabulary, fitting in each item of vocabulary horizontally so that it interlinks with the vertical of *un taille-crayon*. They should include the indefinite article with each item and, by careful placement of the vocabulary, should be able to interlink all ten items. For added interest, students could be encouraged to write their acrostic within an appropriate classroom object shape and the results displayed.

- Alternatively, students could produce an interlinking 'Scrabble' version of the classroom object vocabulary, writing all the objects on a grid of squares, again superimposed on an appropriate shape, for example:

```
      u
      n
      s
une trousse
      y
      l
      o
```

Le vocabulaire? Pas de problème!

(SB p.13)

AT 1 – 1/2, AT 2 – 1, AT 3 – 1

- Remind students of the fact that all nouns in French are either masculine or feminine, pointing out again the *'Attention!'* feature at the top of page 13.

- Tell them to cover page 12 and to see how many masculine and then how many feminine classroom objects they can remember.

- In a *pause anglaise*, remind students that whenever they learn a new word in French for a thing or an object (i.e. a noun), they must also try to learn the spelling and gender of the word.

- Explain that there is no easy way to do this, although it may be helpful to point out that nouns ending in *-e* have a tendency to be feminine. Stress, however, that this rule is not 100% reliable; direct students to the list of feminine nouns on page 12 and ask whether or not the rule works; then direct them to the list of masculine nouns and ask if the rule still applies. (N.B. There is no need to mention the existence of *une livre* at this stage.)

- Having established that students need to learn, show how they can go about this. Write a short list of vocabulary on the board and and use it to help you explain the possible learning method illustrated in *'Le vocabulaire? Pas de problème!'*, i.e. how to look

and say, cover and say, try to remember and write and then check and rewrite if necessary.

- Suggest some other simple strategies which students could use to help them learn, e.g. asking another person to test them; doing the learning homework at the beginning of homework time and repeating it again at the end; playing simple word games on the word processor or on paper; recording the phrases onto cassette etc.

- Remind students that it is easier to learn from a list of vocabulary which is set out in vertical columns of French and English or French and pictures, so that one column can be completely covered and the other column can be used as a prompt.

AT 1 – 1, AT 2 – 1, AT 3 – 1, AT 4 – 2

- Set students the task of learning an appropriate number of classroom vocabulary items for a short spelling and comprehension test.

Presentation of:

As-tu/Avez-vous un/une ... s'il te plaît?/s'il vous plaît?

Sortez vos affaires!

(SB p.14)

AT 1 – 2/3, AT 3 – 2/3

- Use the class cassette and page 14 to develop the use of classroom object vocabulary within longer phrases and to establish a body of useful language for classroom situations.

T: Ouvrez le livre à la page 14. Bon, regardez ... Voici une classe ... Regardez les images ... Ecoutez la cassette et regardez attentivement. **(Play the tape through once as students follow the text.)**

La classe d'enfer	
Teacher:	Alors, sortez vos affaires.
Girl 1:	Psst! Tu as un crayon, s'il te plaît?
Boy 1:	Non.

Girl 1:	Vous avez un crayon, s'il vous plaît?
Classmates:	Non!
Girl 1:	Monsieur, vous avez un crayon s'il vous plaît?
Boy 2:	Monsieur, vous avez une règle s'il vous plaît?
Girl 2:	Monsieur!
Girl 3:	Monsieur, vous avez ...?
Teacher:	SILENCE!
Teacher:	Ecoutez ... je fais l'appel ...
Teacher:	Zut!
Teacher:	Psst! Tu as un stylo s'il te plaît?

- Encourage the class to give a brief *resumé* in English and then look at the detail of the text with them. Prompt students to recall the meaning of *Je fais l'appel* and to deduce the meaning of *Zut!*, before focusing on the main teaching point of *Tu as ... ?* and *Vous avez... ?*

- Direct students to *Tu as un crayon, s'il te plaît?* in frame 2 and *Tu as un stylo, s'il te plaît?* in the final frame and check understanding. Then focus on the formal *Monsieur, vous avez un crayon, s'il vous plaît?* in frame 4 and *Monsieur, vous avez une règle, s'il vous plaît?* in frame 5 and again check comprehension.

- Finally, check that students understand the plural *Vous avez un crayon, s'il vous plaît?* in frame 3, before playing the cassette again in full.

Attention!   (SB p.15)

AT 1 – 2, AT 2 – 2, AT 3 – 2

- Direct the class to the pictures and bubbles at the top of page 15 and ask the students to tell you how to ask 'Have you got ... please?', when talking to:
  - a friend/*un copain* ou *une copine*
  - a teacher/*un professeur*
  - a group/*un groupe*.
- Practise thorough repetition of the phrases.
- Finally, explain that to be polite it is important to address people with the correct form and that a student cannot ask a teacher *Tu as ... ?*

At this point you may wish to use Copymaster 75. Students complete notes on the use of *tu/vous* and keep them for reference.

Comment dit-on ...?   (SB p.15)

AT 1 – 2, AT 2 – 2, AT 3 – 2, AT 4 – 2/3

- Check that students understand the different forms of address and that they can use them correctly, by leading them through the activity on page 15 orally, or by creating a similar activity using pictures of pin-figures in combination with actual classroom objects.

T: Regardez l'image. (Point to the picture of the two students at the beginning of the 'Comment dit-on ...?' exercise or draw a pin-picture on the board.) Attention! On dit 'Tu as ... ?' ou 'Vous avez ... ?' (Wait for the response from the class.) Et on dit 's'il te plaît' ou 's'il vous plaît'? (Again, wait for the response.) Très bien. Alors, numéro un. Un(e) volontaire. (Either point to picture number 1 of the pencil or hold up an actual classroom object.)

- Continue cueing *Tu as ..., s'il te plaît?*, using numbers 2 and 3 or other items of classroom equipment. Then repeat the whole process, firstly for the formal use of *vous* and then for the plural form.

- Explain the sequence of the next three activities and write a reminder on the board, before telling students to start working in pairs and individually using *Comment dit-on ...?*

- Students practise the requests orally in pairs.

T: Regardez 'Comment dit-on ...?' avec un(e) partenaire. Numéro 1, personne A; numéro 2, personne B; numéro 3, personne A (etc.).

- Students again work with a partner but this time cue each other by saying a number at random between 1 and 9.

T: Personne A choisit un numéro, par exemple 'trois!' Personne B regarde l'image et dit 'Tu as un livre?' Puis personne B choisit un numéro, etcetera.

- Students draw simplified representations of the pictures of the characters and the relevant classroom equipment in the 'Comment dit-on ...?' activity and write out a representative sample of the nine requests.

T: *Ecrivez les conversations numéros 1, 4 et 7!*

- Encourage students to add others if appropriate. Before they begin, draw their attention to the circumflex î in *s'il te plaît* and *s'il vous plaît*.

C'est à vous! (SB p.15)

AT 1 – 3, AT 2 – 2/3/4, AT 3 – 3, AT 4 – 2/3/4

- When students are confident in using the different register requests, play the tape *'Sortez vos affaires!'* one final time and indicate that they should follow the text on page 14. Go on to explain that now it is their turn to act out *'La classe d'enfer'*.

T: *Maintenant, c'est à vous! Vous êtes la classe d'enfer. Travaillez en groupes de quatre. Alors, 1, 2, 3, 4; 1, 2, 3, 4 etcetera.* **(Count out a couple of groups to demonstrate or sort out all the groups.)** *Personne numéro 1 est le professeur.* **(Point to the silhouette of the teacher at the bottom of page 15.)** *Personnes numéros 2, 3 et 4 sont dans la classe d'enfer.* **(Point to the silhouettes of the pupils at the bottom of page 12.)** *Bon. Le professeur ... Quelles sont les possibilités? 'Bonjour!', 'Sortez vos affaires', 'Silence!'...* **(Suggest a few ideas and encourage the class to think of others, if necessary redirecting them to Copymaster 3 *'Activités'* for help.)** *Et personnes numéros 2, 3, et 4 ... Quelles sont les possibilités? Alors, 'Tu as un crayon?', 'Monsieur/Madame, vous avez un crayon, s'il vous plaît?'...* **(Encourage the class to think of others, before indicating that students should start planning in their groups of four.)**

AT 3 – 3, AT 4 – 2/3/4

- Students either write up their *'Classe d'enfer'* script which they planned in the lesson or prepare a written script for the next lesson, to be used as a basis for their oral work. In the latter instance, each group can use the best ideas from their four scripts and amalgamate them into a group version. Encourage them to use props when acting out their sketch.

Objectif 3 Âge, numéros, dates

New language introduced

Tu as quel âge?
J'ai ... ans
Quelle est la date de ton anniversaire?
C'est le premier/deux (etc.) (+ month)
Mon anniversaire est (+ date)
C'est à moi/toi
Vrai/Faux
J'ai gagné
Numbers 21 – 39
Numbers 40 – 60

Student goals (SB p.6)

- Remind students of the third goal of this module. Point to the picture of the third objective on page 6 and say, *Bon. Objectif trois – 'Age, numéros, dates'...*

Tu as quel âge? (SB p.16)

AT 1 – 2/3, AT 2 – 1/2, AT 3 – 2/3

- Revise numbers 1 – 20 in a series of oral and aural activities. (See Teacher's Notes p. 2, *'Les numéros 0 – 10'* and p. 11, *'Les numéros 0 – 20'*.)
- When students are confident with these numbers again, introduce the phrase *J'ai ... ans*, drawing a birthday cake with a figure 18 on it and stating *J'ai dix-huit ans. Oui ou non?* Repeat the process, changing the figure to 19 and then to 20. Insist that you are this age!
- Having introduced the new statement, direct students to page 16 and tell them to listen to the cassette and follow the cartoon at the top of the page.

Woman:	Tu as quel âge?
Girl:	J'ai douze ans.
Woman:	Tu as quel âge?
Boy 1:	J'ai onze ans.
Woman:	Et toi? Tu as quel âge?
Boy 2:	J'ai douze ans.

- Remind the class *J'ai vingt ans* and then ask individuals *Tu as vingt ans. Oui ou non?* Continue, counting down the age suggested, e.g. *Tu as 18/16/14 ans. Oui ou non?* Finally, give students an appropriate option, e.g. *Tu as douze ans ou onze ans?* to elicit a verbal response. Tell the students who have participated to repeat, saying *Répète: 'J'ai (...) ans.' ... Bravo!,* as you write the statement on the board. Practise class repetition and then encourage students around the class to volunteer their age.

- Next, focus on the question *Tu as quel âge?* Write it on the board, check that students understand what it means and practise pronunciation and intonation in a class repetition activity.

- Combine the question and answer and practise them together, referring to the board for support if necessary, before setting up pairwork. One or two pairs could be invited to perform their mini interviews afterwards.

- Additionally, students could work in fours and act out or adapt the cartoon strip *'Tu as quel âge?'*

Presentation of numbers 20 – 39

AT 1 – 1, AT 2 – 2

- Revise the number 20, writing the figure on the board. Teach numbers 21 – 39. Write all the figures from 20 to 39 on the board/OHP, saying each number as you write it. Encourage students to deduce the pattern and join in saying new numbers as soon as possible. Stress the contrast between *vingt et un* and *vingt-deux* etc. and between *trente et un* and *trente-deux* etc.

- Then concentrate on the full sequence and encourage students to join in repeating and chanting the numbers.

- Check understanding of random numbers by playing a variety of number games. (See Teacher's Notes p. 2 *'Les numéros 0 – 10'* and p. 11 *'Les numéros 0 – 20'.*) Move on afterwards to play Bingo, using Copymaster 7.

Les numéros 20 – 60 (CM 7)

AT 1–1/2, AT 2 – 1, AT 3 – 1

- Direct students to the left-hand side of this copymaster and say the numbers 20 – 39 again.

This time they point to the corresponding word as they repeat the numbers. They can then use the left-hand column of the copymaster to play Bingo. Demonstrate how the game is played, before beginning.

T: *Vous faites une grille comme ça ... (Draw demonstration grid on the board/OHP, using the following format as a guide.) Choisissez huit nombres entre 20 et 39, par exemple ... (Write any eight numbers in the grid on the board.) Bon. Commencez! Vous avez deux minutes. (Wait for students to draw and fill in their grid.)*

- Continue the demonstration using the grid on the board.

- Hold up Copymaster 7 and choose a number between 20 and 39 which is not one of the eight numbers in the demonstration grid. Say the number aloud and tick it in the column on the copymaster.

- Look at the board and show disappointment that it is not one of the numbers in the grid, e.g. *Ah, non. Zut!* Then choose one of the numbers which is in the demonstration grid, saying it aloud and ticking it in the column on the copymaster.

- Look at the board, express pleasure and cross out the number in the grid. Speed up the demonstration of the rest of the game, quickly crossing off the other numbers, until the final number is crossed off with a triumphant *J'ai gagné!*

- Play the game with the class, handing over the game to them afterwards, to play in groups.

- Introduce other group and pair games to practise oral production of numbers from 0 – 39, e.g. 'Buzz' and dice games involving throwing a die twice and adding or multiplying the two numbers to give a total in French.

- Students can use the first part of Copymaster 7 and the accompanying self-study cassette to support them in learning to say and recognise the numbers 20 – 39.

You will need Copymaster 7. Look at the list of numbers 20 – 39. Listen to the numbers and repeat them.

20 21 22
23 24 25
26 27 28 29
30 31 32
33 34 35
36 37 38 39

Now look at the numbers 40 – 60. Listen and repeat.

40 41 42
43 44 45
46 47 48 49
50 51 52
53 54 55
56 57 58 59
60

Presentation of numbers 40 – 60

- Teach numbers 40 – 60, using a similar sequence of activities to previously when teaching 20 – 39. After chanting, repetition and recognition games, use the right hand column of Copymaster 7 to play *Loto* with the higher numbers.

- Finally, use a variety of activities to practise production of numbers 40 – 60 and to revise numbers 0 – 39.

- Revise numbers regularly during lessons, breaking them up and practising them in a variety of short activities at convenient points of lessons.

- Students can use the second part of Copymaster 7 and the accompanying self-study cassette to support them in learning to say and recognise the numbers 40 – 60.

AT 4 – 1

- As an optional activity, you may wish to allot one or more of the numbers from 20 – 60 to each student, so that they can extend the classroom number frieze which they started earlier in the term. (See Teacher's Notes page 11, '*Les numéros 0 – 20*'.) Ask them to draw each figure on an A4-size piece of paper, to decorate it and to clearly write the corresponding French word underneath. Alternatively, this may be word-processed.

J'ai dix-sept ans (SB p.16)

a Ecoute. C'est quel robot?

AT 1 – 2

- Return to ages and remind students of the question *Tu as quel âge?*, giving some the opportunity to answer the question. Move on to the activity '*C'est quel robot?*', to practise comprehension of a selection of numbers between 17 and 60 within the context of ages.

- Students should listen to the interviews, look at the pictures of the robots and decide which robot is giving its age each time.

- Ask students to copy down numbers 1 – 10 from the board. Then play the four dialogues on the cassette.

1 – Tu as quel âge?
  – J'ai 17 ans.
2 – Tu as quel âge?
  – J'ai 41 ans.
3 – Tu as quel âge?
  – J'ai 35 ans.
4 – Tu as quel âge?
  – J'ai 25 ans.

- Check answers around the class before continuing.

- For the remaining six pictures, read out the following text, pausing to allow time for students to note down their answers.

T: Numéro cinq: J'ai vingt-huit ans.
Numéro six: J'ai seize ans.
Numéro sept: J'ai quarante-huit ans.
Numéro huit: J'ai cinquante-trois ans.
Numéro neuf: J'ai soixante ans.
Numéro dix: J'ai vingt et un ans.

Solution
1 C 2 J 3 F 4 A 5 E 6 I 7 B 8 D 9 G 10 H

b A deux.

AT 2 – 2

- Explain to students that they are now going to work in pairs. Use the example to show them how to do this activity.

T: *Personne A pose la question 'Tu as quel âge?' Personne B regarde les robots et dit par exemple 'J'ai dix-sept ans.' Personne A regarde les robots et dit la bonne lettre, par exemple 'C!'*

AT 4 – 2/3/4

- For written practice of the question and assorted answers about ages, students could make up their own cartoon along the lines of the one at the top of page 16. Alternatively, they could write speech bubbles for the robots in activity 2 and/or interviews with some or all of them.

> **Presentation of:**
> *Bon anniversaire*
> *Quelle est la date de ton anniversaire?*
> *C'est le premier/deux* (+ month)

Bon anniversaire! (SB p.17)

AT 1 – 3, AT 2 – 2, AT 3 – 2, AT 4 – 1/2

- Hum a couple of bars of the tune *'Bon anniversaire…'* to establish the birthday context. Then point out the calendar at the top of page 17 and read through the months, before playing the cassette in which Olivier asks Marc the date of his birthday.

T: *Voici un calendrier français. Regardez et écoutez: janvier, février, mars, …* (**Continue reading through all the months.**) *C'est l'anniversaire de Sandrine.* (**Hum a couple of bars of the 'Bon anniversaire' tune again.**) *Alors, regardez la photo et écoutez la cassette.*

Louise:	Salut Sandrine! Bon anniversaire.
Sandrine:	Salut Louise. Merci.

Olivier:	Et toi, Marc, quelle est la date de ton anniversaire?
Marc:	C'est le premier août.
Olivier et Marc:	Salut Sandrine. Bon anniversaire.

- Encourage students to read the shortened text on page 17 as they listen a second time. Then check understanding.

T: *'Bon anniversaire!', c'est quoi en anglais? Et 'Quelle est la date de ton anniversaire?', c'est quoi en anglais? … Très bien.*

- Check understanding of *août*, then refer back to it on the calendar on page 17 and also point out the current month in the French date on the board. Having established the subject matter, write all the months on the board and say them aloud in groups of three, telling students to repeat after you.

- Play a variety of repetition games, varying volume, speed, tone etc. Next, start rubbing out the months three at a time in sequence, until the class can produce them all from memory.

- Days of the week could also be introduced in a similar way, so that full dates can be used from now on when dating work.

AT 1 – 1, AT 2 – 1, AT 3 – 1

- Students can use the self-study cassette for additional support in pronouncing and learning the months.

You will need Students' Book page 17. Look at the calendar showing the months. Listen to the months on the cassette and repeat them.

janvier, février, mars
avril, mai, juin
juillet, août, septembre
octobre, novembre, décembre

- Return to the short dialogue about Marc's birthday on page 17 and read this aloud to the class, checking understanding of *le premier août* afterwards.

- Demonstrate the sequence *le premier août, le deux août, le trois août.* Write these dates and the corresponding figures 1, 2, 3 on the board, saying each date aloud as you write it and pointing to the appropriate figure. Highlight the exception, stressing *Attention! Le premier!*

- Ask the question *Quelle est la date de ton anniversaire?*, rhetorically, giving a selection of random dates in reply, e.g. *C'est le quatre juin, c'est le quinze février, c'est le trente et un octobre,* etc. Stress *c'est le ...* and then start asking individuals in the class *Quelle est la date de ton anniversaire?*

- When students have been asked sufficiently and have practised their answers, focus on the question with the class, practising it thoroughly, before setting up pairwork to practise the question and answer.

- To give added purpose to the latter, students could be encouraged to circulate and find out the dates of as many birthdays in the class as possible, in order to discover which month contains most birthdays. The results could be compiled in a bar graph or pie-chart afterwards, perhaps using I.T.

Presentation of: *Mon anniversaire est* (+ date)

Mon anniversaire est le ... (SB p.17)

AT 1 – 2, AT 2 – 2

- Use this activity to check students' understanding of dates, explaining that they should listen to the birthday dates on the cassette, find the date in the picture on page 17 and follow the line to see who is talking each time.

1	Sophie:	Mon anniversaire est le 21 janvier.
2	Olivier:	Mon anniversaire est le 10 juin.
3	Frédéric:	Mon anniversaire est le 13 avril.
4	Claire:	Mon anniversaire est le 31 janvier.
5	Louise:	Mon anniversaire est le 12 juillet.
6	Yannick:	Mon anniversaire est le 3 avril.

- Return to the title *'Mon anniversaire est le ...'* and ask students what they think the difference is between *C'est le premier août* and *Mon anniversaire est le premier août.* Encourage them to deduce the difference in usage and the fact that *C'est le ...* is used in response to a direct question, whereas the fuller version is needed when offering information.

- Practise the statement *Mon anniversaire est le ...* with the class and then set up a group activity in which students must state the date of their birthday, listen and line themselves up in chronological sequence.

- Demonstrate this lining up activity with a group of three students, before handing it over to be carried out in larger groups of five, six or seven.

- When the students have arranged themselves in chronological order, each member of the group should reel off his or her birthday in succession, whilst the rest of the class listens and checks that the order is correct.

- Alternatively/additionally, the whole class could try to line up in sequence.

AT 4 – 2/3

- Students could now write up full sentences for the characters in the spaghetti diagram on page 17, using the following model:
  Louise: 'Mon anniversaire est le douze juillet.'

- Alternatively/additionally, they could undertake a written task in which they combine ages and birthdays. Explain that they should choose five friends or relatives and complete the following information for each person:
  (Name:)
  J'ai ... ans.
  Mon anniversaire est le ...

- The meaning of each pair of statements could be illustrated with a numbered birthday cake, card, balloon etc. and a calendar tear-off page similar to those shown in the spaghetti diagram on page 17.

- N.B. It might be appropriate at this point to tell students to collect a coat-hanger, card and thread in preparation for the *'Mots-mobile'* activity on page 20.

Comment ça se prononce? (SB p.18)

a Ecoute et lis.

AT 1 – 1/2, AT 3 – 1/2

- Focus on pronunciation of the French *r* sound, encouraging students to listen to the counting rhyme on the class cassette, whilst following it in their books.

Am stram gram
Pic et pic et colégram
Bour et bour et ratatam
Am stram gram!

- Explain quickly that this is a nonsense rhyme. Illustrate the context in which it is used, by saying it as you count out around the class to pick individuals to produce a French word or phrase cued by you, e.g. cue a number with a figure on the board and the question *C'est quel numéro?* Elicit an answer to the question *Tu as quel âge?* etc.

- Emphasize the *r* sounds, encouraging the class to repeat a line of the rhyme at a time. Then play the whole rhyme again and encourage the students to join in.

b Ecoute et lis. Ecoute, lis et répète.

AT 1 – 1/2, AT 2 – 1/2, AT 3 – 1/2

- Having 'loosened up' their throats, they can now undertake detailed practice of this sound in the second activity. They should listen to the cassette, whilst reading the words in their books, and then listen, read and repeat the dates accumulatively.

quatre, février, le quatre février
quatorze, avril, le quatorze avril
trente, septembre, le trente septembre
treize, octobre, le treize octobre

c Lis, prononce et écoute.

AT 1 – 1/2, AT 2 – 1/2, AT 3 – 1/2

- In the third activity, students predict the pronunciation of the words in the illustrations, before listening to the cassette to find out how they compare.

A avril
B février
C trente-trois
D un livre
E Sandrine
F quarante-quatre
G décembre

AT 1 – 1, AT 2 – 1/2, AT 3 – 1, AT 4 – 1/2

- The self-study cassette can be used for extra practice of the *r* sounds.

You will need Students' Book page 18, activity C. Here is another chance to practise the letter '*r*' in French words. Read each word out loud. Check on the cassette after each one to see how well you did, then repeat the word.

A avril
B février
C trente-trois
D un livre
E Sandrine
F quarante-quatre
G décembre

- Students could write out their own set of illustrated words and use this aide-mémoire to practise *r* sounds.
- They could also recite and learn the 'Am stram gram' rhyme for use in future games.

Instructions (CM 8)

AT 3 – 1

- As students now approach the end of the first module of **PASSE-PARTOUT**, it may be appropriate to provide them with a summary of simple rubrics used so far in the Students' Book and on the copymasters. After they have linked each instruction with its corresponding picture, they could keep Copymaster 8 for reference and use it to help them learn the meanings of the instructions.

Entre-temps ... (SB p.19)

AT 3 – 1/2/3

- Encourage students to use this page as independently as possible and to read the selection of texts for interest and enjoyment. Little or no exploitation should be necessary, as virtually all the language should be familiar by now. Some students may, however, need help in deducing the meaning of *Formidable!* in the second secret message. Both this and *Bravo!* can be reinforced when you give praise orally and in your written comments.

SB pages 20 – 22

- The next two and a half pages bring together all the language of the module. After brief explanation and demonstration, they lend themselves to independent and group work and can also be used for assessment purposes.

Une interview! (SB p.20)

a Ecoute. Vrai ou faux?

AT 1 – 3, AT 3 – 2

- Students listen to a longer dialogue containing all elements of personal information covered so far, together with some unfamiliar items which should in no way affect their ability to answer the *vrai ou faux?* questions on page 20.

Interviewer:	C'est le 20 octobre. On est à Paris pour le festival international de jazz. Salut! Ça va?
Musician:	Salut! Ça va très bien merci.
Interviewer:	Tu t'appelles comment?
Musician:	Je m'appelle Yvette Laurent.
Interviewer:	Comment ça s'écrit?
Musician:	Y–V–E–T–T–E L–A–U–R–E–N–T ... Yvette Laurent.
Bierviewer:	Tu habites où?

Musician:	J'habite à Lyon.
Interviewer:	Tu as quel âge?
Musician:	J'ai vingt-cinq ans. Mon anniversaire est le 6 janvier. Encore des questions?
Interviewer:	Non merci. Au revoir.

Solution

1 vrai **2** vrai **3** faux **4** vrai **5** faux

b Ecris les bonnes réponses.

AT 4 – 2/3

- Students write correct answers to the statements which are false.

Solution

3 J'habite à Lyon. **5** Mon anniversaire est le 6 janvier.

Differentiation – Extension

AT 2 – 3/4

- Some students could be encouraged to work in pairs and record a full corrected version of the interview. It may be more appropriate to wait, however, until questions have been revised and practised more thoroughly in other activities on pages 20 – 22.

Mots-mobile (SB p.20)

AT 3 – 2, AT 4 – 2/3

- Students should be able to tackle this activity with little or no explanation, simply using the illustrations as examples of how to make a mobile of questions and answers relating to personal identity or classroom language. Remind them, however, to use the fronts and backs of each part of the mobile and prompt them to think of other shapes.

Jeu de mémoire! (SB p.21)

AT 1 – 1/2, AT 2 – 1/2, AT 3 – 2

- Before pairs start the game on page 21, present and practise the actual game language which they will need and demonstrate how to play. Begin by presenting/revising the following language, demonstrating the meanings with actions or symbols on the board:

C'est à moi!
C'est à toi!
Vrai
Faux
J'ai gagné!

- Check comprehension, write the phrases on the board, say them through again and practise repetition. Finally, use the actions or symbols in random order to cue students to produce the language orally.
- Draw a representative sample of some of the squares from the game on the board and use them to show what to do when landing on each type of square, i.e.
  - A written question = answer the question
  - A classroom object = ask for the object shown
  - A number = say the number
  - A letter = say the letter
- Ask a student to the front of the class and demonstrate how to play the game. Use the counting rhyme '*Am stram gram*' from page 18 to see who starts and use *C'est à moi!* or *C'est à toi!* as appropriate.
- Each person then takes it in turn to roll the die and say the number in French, counting forward the number of squares whilst moving their counter, e.g. *Trois. Un, deux, trois.* (Prompt the student to do this if he/she starts.)
- Show a representation of the square on the board and ask *C'est quoi en français?*, encouraging the class to work out the answer for the player.
- Demonstrate how to monitor the answers, by prompting the class to say whether the answer is *vrai* or *faux* and show how to keep a tally of correct and incorrect answers for use in scoring at the end of the game. The person who finishes first only wins if he or she has the most correct answers!
- Explain that students should now play in pairs and should try to use as many of the expressions at the top of page 21 as possible. Circulate while they are playing and encourage them to maintain the use of the target language.

Differentiation – Extension

AT 1 – 1/2, AT 2 – 1/2, AT 3 – 2, AT 4 2/3

- When students have played the game a few times, they could try making up their own board game, using as much of the language in Module 1 as possible.
- As a quick alternative, requiring no writing, they could simply write out six different numbers and five different letters on pieces of paper and place these over the existing squares to make an 'instant' new version of the game.

Porte ouverte! (SB p.22)
Sommaire (SB pp.22 – 23)

AT 1 – 2, AT 2 – 4, AT 3 – 2/3, AT 4 – 2/3

- All the personal identification language covered in the module is now transferred into a summative mixed-skill activity.
- Go through the instructions with the class to make sure that everyone understands the task. Mention that celebrities' details which are not known (e.g. birthday dates) can be invented. Point out the '*Sommaire*' on pages 22 and 23, showing students how to use it and explaining that it is a useful reference both for now and the future.
- The written tasks can be undertaken as homework or during lesson time, but must all be completed by a certain time, so that the interviews can take place as a final class activity, with students circulating around the class. As an added incentive, their mission can be to find their best 'celebrity partner' – the match can be on the basis of age, place of residence, birthday or actual identity. The written descriptions can be used afterwards for display.

Differentiation – Extension

- Encourage higher attainers to write fuller descriptions or even interviews. If possible, they should try to write a first draft from memory, in pencil or using a word-processor, before checking for spelling and redrafting if necessary.

2 AU COLLEGE

In this module, students learn how to:

Say which school subjects they like and dislike
J'aime le français / Je n'aime pas les maths (etc.)

Ask others whether they like certain subjects
Tu aimes les sciences? (etc.)

Give opinions
C'est intéressant / C'est difficile (etc.)

Ask for classroom objects
Passe-moi le crayon, s'il te plaît / Donne-moi la gomme, s'il te plaît (etc.)

Ask what time it is
Quelle heure est-il?

Give the time, using the 12-hour clock
Il est deux heures et quart (etc.)

Talk about their school routine
J'arrive au collège à ... / Je mange le déjeuner (etc.)

Le premier (etc.) cours commence à ... / commence à quelle heure?

Materials needed
Students' Book pages 24 – 43
Copymasters 9 – 23
Flashcards 1 – 33
Class cassette B
Self-study cassette

Objectif 1 Matières et opinions

New language introduced

le français / le dessin
la musique / la technologie / la géographie
l'anglais / l'informatique / l'histoire /
l'éducation physique
les maths / les sciences
(Extension: *l'allemand / l'espagnol / l'éducation religieuse / l'éducation civique*)

J'aime / j'adore / je préfère / je n'aime pas / je déteste
Tu aimes le / la / l' / les ....?
Et / mais / aussi
C'est super / moche / intéressant / ennuyeux / facile / difficile
(Extension: *C'est fantastique / nul / chic / utile / marrant*)

En classe:
Passe-moi / Donne-moi le / la / l' / les (+ classroom objects), *s'il te plaît*

Revised language
Days of the week
Classroom objects

Student goals (SB p.24)

- Use the top half of the page to introduce the module's goals.

*T: **Voici les objectifs pour ce module, 'Au collège' – c'est quoi en anglais? .... Oui, c'est ça. Regardez** (pointing to relevant part of goals on page 24) **– les matières: le français, les maths, les sciences ... 'matières', c'est quoi en anglais?** (etc.)*

Revision of days of the week
Presentation of school subjects
le français / le dessin
la musique / la technologie / la géographie
l'anglais / l'informatique / l'histoire /
l'éducation physique
les maths / les sciences
(Extension: *l'allemand / l'espagnol /l'éducation religieuse/l'éducation civique*)

Emploi du temps (SB p.24)

AT 1 — 1, AT 3 – 1

- Revise days of the week. Write the date in full on the board, focus on the day and ask students to tell you the other days of the week in French. As you elicit each one, write it on the board and build up a full chronological list. Use this to quickly check understanding.

T: 'Mercredi', c'est quoi en anglais?

- When students are confident, direct them to the timetable on page 24. The class follows in their books as you read out the subjects and breaks for *lundi*.

- Encourage students to <u>deduce</u> the meaning of new items of vocabulary. Cognates, context and previous knowledge of *français* and *anglais* should make this reasonably straightforward. Some help may need to be given with *étude*.

- Work through the other days on the timetable in a similar way, focusing on the subjects not covered previously.

- In a *pause anglaise* ask students to explain which clues helped them to guess the meaning of new vocabulary.

- Finally, ask a variety of simple questions about the timetable, focusing on days of the week and subjects to draw attention to the differences between this timetable and the students' own.

T: Marc a sept cours, mardi? Oui ou non?
Marc a sept cours, mercredi?
Marc a sept cours, samedi?
Marc a l'éducation religieuse?
Marc a la géographie?

- Point out some of the cultural differences, e.g. Saturday school, different arrangements on Wednesdays, no religious education, combined history and geography. Explain that *éducation civique* involves learning about French national and local institutions (e.g. parliament, councils, law, the role of the mayor etc.) and also encompasses PSE.

F **OHT**
Les matières (FC 1–11)
AT 1 – 1
- Use the flashcards to teach the following core school subjects, grouping them according to their definite article:
  1 *le français*
  2 *le dessin*

  3 *la musique*
  4 *la géographie*
  5 *la technologie*
  6 *l'anglais*
  7 *l'informatique*
  8 *l'histoire*
  9 *l'éducation physique*
  10 *les maths*
  11 *les sciences*

- Play games to consolidate understanding and to maximise opportunities for hearing these subjects (see Teacher's Notes introduction, page iv).

- Use Copymaster 9 or an OHT version of the copymaster to introduce the vocabulary in written form before students move on to practise the subjects orally and / or to copywrite.

F
Les matières – Extra! (FC 12–15)
AT 1 – 1
- The following additional flashcards may be presented for passive or productive use:
  12 *l'allemand*
  13 *l'espagnol*
  14 *l'éducation religieuse*
  15 *l'éducation civique*

- If these subjects are taught, provide their written form for students to copy and keep as reference.

Les matières (CM 9)
1 Ecoute et lis. Répète.
AT 1 – 1, AT 2 – 1, AT 3 – 1

- The class cassette and self-study cassette accompanying activity 1 contain identical material, so that students can either use this copymaster as a class or individually / at home.

- Students listen to the cassette item whilst reading the copymaster, in order to relate the spoken and written words, before listening again, reading and repeating.

1 le français
2 le dessin
3 l'anglais
4 la géographie
5 la technologie
6 la musique
7 l'informatique
8 l'histoire
9 l'éducation physique
10 les maths
11 les sciences

You will need Copymaster 9, activity 1. Look at the pictures of school subjects. Listen to the subjects on the cassette and repeat them.

1 le français
2 le dessin
3 l'anglais
4 la géographie
5 la technologie
6 la musique
7 l'informatique
8 l'histoire
9 l'éducation physique
10 les maths
11 les sciences

2 Ecoute. C'est quel numéro?

AT 1 – 1, AT 3 – 1

- Students listen to the cassette and write the number of the visual for each subject they hear.
- Draw a replica grid on the board and demonstrate how to carry out this activity, inviting students to come to the front and enter the number in the grid.

T: Bon. Regardez la fiche et écoutez la cassette. L'éducation physique, c'est quel numéro? Mettez le bon numéro dans la case.

– l'éducation physique
– les sciences
– l'anglais
– l'informatique
– l'histoire
– les maths
– le dessin

You will need Copymaster 9, activity 2. As you hear a subject being said, write the number of the picture that goes with it in the box. The first one has been done for you.

– l'éducation physique
– les sciences
– l'anglais
– l'informatique
– l'histoire
– les maths
– le dessin

Solution

9, 11, 3, 7, 8, 10, 2

- Students then copy the subjects on / from the copymaster.

Loto!

AT 1 – 1, AT 2 – 1, AT 3 – 1

- Afterwards, groups of students could use the copymaster to play subject Bingo. (Revise the phrase *J'ai gagné!*)
- Students tick their copymaster or use small objects to cover an agreed number of school subjects.
- Play the game with the whole class first to remind students of the procedure; after one or two games, it can be handed over to students to play in groups. They can use their copymaster as a mastersheet for calling the subjects.

3 Fais des panneaux pour ton collège.

AT 4 – 1/2

- Using the illustrations on Copymaster 9 as stimulus material, students design their own subject signs for use and display around the school.

T: *Regardez la fiche. Faites des panneaux pour le collège. 'Panneaux', c'est quoi en anglais?*

Differentiation – Extension

4 Jeu de mémoire!   Ecris les matières de mémoire.

AT 4 – 2

- Students could try learning and writing a selection of subjects from memory, covering up the rest of the copymaster before working through this activity.
- Encourage able students to set themselves the challenge of writing other subjects from memory.
- Remind them of the strategies for learning vocabulary in '*Le vocabulaire? Pas de problème!*' on Students' Book page 13.

T: *Regardez la fiche. Couvrez (demonstrate) et écrivez les matières.*

C'est quel jour?   (SB p.25)

AT 1 – 2, AT 3 – 1, AT 4 – 1/2

- Redirect students to the timetable on page 24. Demonstrate how they should listen to the subjects mentioned on the cassette, look at the timetable and deduce which day is being talked about.

T: *Regardez l'emploi du temps et écoutez: 'l'éducation civique'. Alors, regardez. C'est lundi, mardi, jeudi, vendredi ou samedi? Oui, c'est ça. Très bien. C'est vendredi. Bon, écoutez la cassette, regardez l'emploi du temps et écrivez le jour dans votre cahier* (demonstrate on board / OHP).

1 Ah, non! On a l'éducation civique. Bof!
2 – On a deux cours de français ... Oh là, là.
   – Deux! Deux cours de français. Oh là, là.
3 C'est très bien. On a dessin, aujourd'hui!
4 C'est l'éducation physique et puis les sciences.
5 – Paul, on a musique?
   – Mais oui, on a musique, aujourd'hui!
6 – Salut. Ça va?
   – Non, ça ne va pas. J'ai technologie. Je déteste ça.

Solution
1 vendredi **2** lundi **3** mardi **4** mardi **5** jeudi **6** mardi

C'est quelle matière?   (SB p.25)
a Fais les paires.

AT 3 – 1

- Students demonstrate understanding of the written word by matching the subject vocabulary with corresponding illustrations.

T: *Regardez les images et le texte. Numéro un, c'est quelle lettre? Oui, c'est E, le français. Notez dans votre cahier.* (Demonstrate on board / OHP.) *Continuez comme ça.*

Solution
1 E **2** J **3** A **4** I **5** D **6** F **7** K **8** H **9** B **10** C **11** G

Differentiation – Extension
AT 4 – 1/2

- Rather than simply matching numbers and letters, higher attainers could be encouraged to write the subjects in full. They could either use the menu of subjects at the bottom of the activity for support, or could cover this and write from memory.

b Ecoute la cassette et écris la matière.

AT 4 – 2

- Tell students to close their books. Then use the sound effects on the class cassette as a fun activity to encourage them to write the subjects from memory.

T: Fermez les livres. Ecoutez. (Play number 1.) C'est quelle matière? Oui, c'est le français. Notez dans votre cabier.

---

1 Bonjour! Salut!
2 (Sound of piano scales and orchestra tuning up)
3 (Sound of children in gymnasium)
4 (Sound of someone typing on a keyboard, followed by sound of printer)
5 (Sound of sawing and hammering)
6 (Sound of bubbling chemistry experiment that ends in an explosion)
7 (Sound of paintbrush being cleaned in a pot of water)

---

c A deux.

AT 1 – 1, AT 2 – 1, AT 3 – 1

- Remind students of the question *C'est quelle matière?* Check for understanding and then cue repetition practice of this question before demonstrating how to play the guessing game.

T: Regardez les images. Un, deux, trois, quatre ... etc. (Point and count through the illustrations.) Bon. Je choisis un numéro ... (Make a show of secretly writing a number on the board and covering it so that the class cannot see it.) Alors, c'est quelle matière? ... La technologie? ... Non! ... Le dessin? ... Non! (Encourage students to join in guessing and keep a tally of their guesses until they finally guess the subject corresponding to the hidden number on the board.) Oui, bravo! C'est les maths! Encore une fois!

- Repeat the game until students understand how to play, then hand over the activity for them to continue in pairs. As an added incentive they can keep a tally of one another's guesses, to see who wins with the least number of guesses.

AT 4 – 1/2

- Students could adapt the timetable on SB page 24 and write out their own timetable in French. Remind them in particular that they will need to change the days of the week, including *mercredi* and omitting *samedi*.

T: Regardez l'emploi du temps à la page 24. Ecrivez votre emploi du temps. Mais attention! Nous, on a cours mercredi et on n'a pas cours samedi. Vous comprenez?

Giving and asking for opinions

Student goals (SB p.24)

- Refer students again to the visual on the top half of this page and explain that they are now going to learn how to give and ask opinions about school subjects.

T: Maintenant nous allons apprendre à donner et demander les opinions des matières. (Stress the words opinions and matières, whilst pointing to the relevant section of the visual representation of objectives.) ... Par exemple: J'adore le français. C'est super ... (Mime an exaggerated expression of enjoyment.) ... et je déteste l'éducation physique. C'est moche! (Mime an exaggerated expression of dislike whilst jogging on the spot.)

Presentation of opinions

J'aime / j'adore / je préfère/ je n'aime pas / je déteste
(+ school subject)
Tu aimes le / la / l' / les (+ school subject)?

Mes opinions (FC 16–27)

AT 1 – 2, AT 2 – 2, AT 3 – 2

- Use the separate text and picture flashcards to present the following core opinions, linking each written phrase with its appropriate visual:

16 *J'aime*
17 Visual to accompany *J'aime*
18 *J'adore*
19 Visual to accompany *J'adore*
20 *Je préfère*
21 Visual to accompany *Je préfère*
22 *Je n'aime pas*
23 Visual to accompany *Je n'aime pas*
24 *Je déteste*
25 Visual to accompany *Je déteste*
26 *Tu aimes ...?*
27 Visual to accompany *Tu aimes ...?*

- Check understanding by mixing up the phrases and the visuals on the board for students to match.
- When students have matched all the pairs, read the key phrases aloud and ask students to repeat them. Use a variety of speeds, volumes and tones to maximise opportunities for repetition and reading aloud.
- When students are confident, remove the written phrases and use the visual flashcards to cue the appropriate written response.

Les matières et mes opinions
(FC 1–15, 17, 19, 21, 23, 25, 27)
AT 1 – 2, AT 2 – 2

- Use a visual opinion flashcard with a subject flashcard to support a statement about a school subject.

T: *J'adore le français.*

- Then substitute the opinion flashcard with flashcard 27 to support the question:

T: *Tu aimes le français?*

- Repeat and develop the question around the class, varying the subjects and illustrating students' replies by showing the appropriate opinion flashcard.

Tu aimes les maths? (CM 10)

1 Regarde la légende et lis les phrases. Mets la bonne image.

AT 3 – 2

- Use Copymaster 10 or an OHP version of the copymaster to explain to students what to do. Students demonstrate understanding of written opinions by drawing the correct symbol from the *légende* next to the appropriate phrase.

T: *Regardez la légende.* (Point to single heart symbol in key.) *C'est quoi en français? Oui – 'J'aime'. Et ça? ... Oui ... (etc.). Maintenant, mettez la bonne image dans la case.* (Demonstrate.)

Differentiation – Consolidation and / or Extension

AT 3 – 2

- Encourage students who complete this activity quickly to colour in the opinion phrases in the box, using one colour for positive opinions and another for negative opinions. Students could then write their own *légende*, e.g. yellow-shaded box = *positif*, grey-shaded box = *négatif*.

T: *Coloriez les phrases positives et les phrases negatives en deux couleurs différentes.* (Demonstrate.)

2 Ecoute. Mets la bonne image.

AT 1 – 1

- Play the class cassette in which six opinions about various school subjects are given or sought. Students listen and fill in the appropriate symbol for each subject, using the convention shown in the *légende* and activity 1.

1 Je n'aime pas l'éducation physique.
2 J'adore la musique.
3 Je préfère les sciences.
4 J'aime la technologie.
5 Tu aimes les maths?
6 Je déteste l'anglais.

Solution

1 ✕ 2 ♡ ♡ 3 ♡ ♡ ♡ 4 ♡ 5 ? 6 ✕ ✕

3 Ecris les phrases.

AT 4 – 2

- Finally, students complete a series of written opinions, following the clues in the pictures. They use the box at the top of the copymaster as support for the statements and, if possible, write the subjects from memory.

Differentiation – Consolidation

AT 4 – 2

- If necessary, students could refer to Copymaster 9 '*Les matières*' to help complete the statements in activity 3.

Differentiation – Extension

AT 4 – 2

- When students have completed the copymaster, they could do one or more of the following:
  - Make an opinion ladder with the most negative opinion on the bottom rung and the most positive opinion on the top rung.

T: *Faites une échelle des opinions, comme ça.* (Demonstrate on board / OHP.)

  - Learn the key phrases, cover them and write as many as possible from memory.

> **Revision of the alphabet**
> **Introduction of:**
> *et / mais / aussi*

Mes opinions (SB p.26)

a Ecoute et lis.

AT 1 – 2, AT 2 – 2/3, AT 3 – 2, AT 4 – 1

- Before directing students to the contents of the speech bubbles on page 26, you may wish to refamiliarise them with the names of the French teenagers shown below the photos, practising pronunciation and spelling.

T: *Regardez les noms. Ça se prononce comment?*

- Revise the alphabet, with activities such as marine chanting and / or a selection of games.
- Move on to focus on the names of the teenagers, encouraging students to write down the names as you spell them out, without reference to their books.

T: *Fermez vos livres et écrivez les noms des copains. Par exemple,* (demonstrate) *'Louise', ça s'écrit L - O - U - I - S - E.*

- When you have finished, encourage them to spell back the different names.

T: *'Louise', ça s'écrit comment? etc.*

- Students listen to the class cassette whilst following the text on page 26.

Marc:	Je préfère les maths.
Louise:	Je n'aime pas l'éducation physique.
Sandrine:	Je préfère la technologie et les sciences.
Yannick:	J'aime l'anglais et le français mais je n'aime pas la géo.
Olivier:	J'adore l'histoire mais je déteste les maths.
Claire:	J'adore la musique. J'aime aussi le dessin.

- Draw out the meaning of *et*, *mais* and *aussi*.
- Using two school subject flashcards, demonstrate the meaning of *et,* writing the word between the two flashcards on the board as you give an opinion.

T: *J'aime l'histoire* ... (stick history flashcard onto the board) ... *et* ... (write *et* on the board) ... *l'éducation physique* (stick P.E. flashcard onto the board).

- Repeat the pattern with other combinations and invite students to use *et* in a similar way.
- For *mais*, demonstrate as above, but this time pick contrasting visual <u>opinion</u> flashcards and write the word *mais* between the contrasting visuals.

T: *J'adore la géographie* ... (Stick visual opinion and geography flashcards onto the board.) ... *mais* ... (Write *mais* on the board.) *Je déteste les sciences.* (Stick visual opinion and science flashcard onto the board.)

- Repeat the pattern with other combinations and invite students to use *mais* in a similar way.
- For *aussi*, demonstrate in a similar way to *et*, but then mime having a sudden thought.

T: Oh! J'aime aussi les maths. (Add the additional flashcard and write the sentence on the board.)

- Repeat the process and practise with students.
- Replay the class cassette '*Mes opinions*' and encourage students to put up their hands when they hear *et*, *mais* and *aussi*.

T: Ecoutez la cassette. Levez la main (demonstrate) quand vous entendez 'et', 'mais' ou 'aussi'.

b Lis et dessine.

AT 3 – 2, 4 – 1

- Students demonstrate understanding of the text by copying the teenagers' names and drawing an appropriate subject and opinion symbol with the heart(s) / crossed out heart(s) coding, following the example given.

T: Copiez les noms et dessinez une image. (Demonstrate.)

c A deux.

AT 1 – 2, AT 2 – 2/3

- Students now work in pairs, asking and giving opinions about various school subjects, using the visual cues.

Differentiation – Extension

AT1 – 2, AT2 – 3

- Those who have mastered *et*, *mais* and *aussi* can practise giving slightly more complex statements. Students first pronounce the sentences represented visually in '*Extra!*' They can then complete the more complex sentences in 7 and 8.

T: Maintenant, travaillez avec un(e) partenaire. Regardez les images. Posez des questions et répondez. Par exemple, (name) et (name), venez ici ... (etc.).

Solution

J'aime la musique et l'éducation physique.
J'aime les maths mais je n'aime pas l'anglais.
J'aime les sciences. J'aime aussi la géographie.

Jeux de matières (CM 11)

- Students consolidate work on school subjects and opinions by completing the activities on this copymaster.

1 Matières rythmiques

AT 1 – 2/3, AT 2 – 1/2, AT 3 – 1/3, AT 4 – 1/2

- Students listen to the self-study cassette and fill in the missing definite articles in the subjects. This should help provide support for the other activities on the copymaster.

You will need Copymaster 11, activity 1, 'Matières rythmiques'. Listen to the school subjects set to a rhythm. Complete the gaps with le, la, l' or les.

le français et les sciences, le dessin et la musique
l'anglais, la géographie et l'éducation physique

Solution

le français et **les** sciences, **le** dessin et **la** musique
l'anglais, **la** géographie et **l'**éducation physique

- Students listen again and practise reading and repeating the rap. Afterwards this can be learned by heart to support learning of school subjects and their definite articles.

Now listen again and join in the rap. You may need to listen and say it several times to get the rhythm right.

le français et les sciences, le dessin et la musique
l'anglais, la géographie et l'éducation physique

2 Mot caché

AT 4 – 1/2

- Students use visual clues to fill in the definite articles and nouns on the acrostic grid to find the mystery word *le français*.

Solution

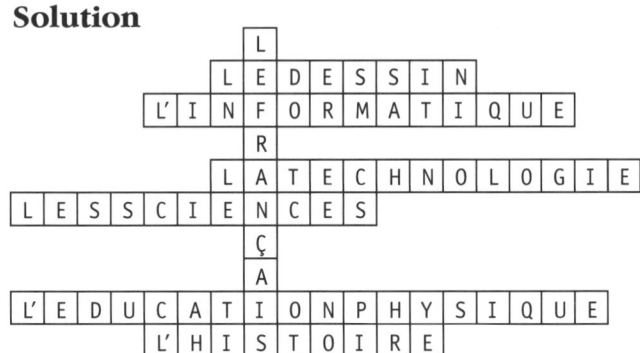

3 Tu aimes tes matières?

AT 4 – 2/3

- Students unscramble the spaghetti diagram to find out the opinion for each subject and write a sentence in French.

T: *Débrouillez et écrivez les phrases.*

Solution

J'adore le français.

Je n'aime pas l'anglais.

J'aime la technologie.

Je déteste les sciences.

Je préfère l'éducation physique.

- Afterwards in a homework activity, students could write their own opinions about school subjects.

AT 3 – 1, AT 4 – 2

- Finally, all students should attempt to learn as many school subjects by heart as possible. (Set a minimum number.) Stress that as they learn the word for the subject, they should learn the *le, la, l'* or *les* which belongs with it and remind them of the learning tips shown in '*Le vocabulaire? Pas de problème*' on page 13 of the Students' Book.

T: *Apprenez par coeur les matières avec 'le', 'la', 'l'' ou 'les'.*

- At this stage, the definite article should simply be learned as part of each item of vocabulary. More detailed explanation can follow after Students' Book pages 28 and 29, when students will encounter the definite article linked to classroom equipment.
- When testing school subjects vocabulary, give students the opportunity of showing what they

know, by asking them to write down as many subjects as possible. Display the subject flashcards to jog their memories, if necessary.

> **Presentation of opinion phrases**
> *C'est super / moche / intéressant / ennuyeux / facile / difficile*
> (Extension: *C'est fantastique / nul / chic / utile / marrant*)

Jeu de cartes (CM 12)

AT 1 – 2, AT 2 – 2, AT 3 – 2

- Transfer the copymaster onto OHT and cut it up into sections for use in presenting the following core French opinion phrases:

  C'est super!

  C'est moche!

  C'est intéressant.

  C'est ennuyeux!

  C'est facile.

  C'est difficile.
- (If no OHP is available, make flashcards by writing the phrases on pieces of A4-size card / paper.)
- Duplicate sufficient numbers of the copymaster onto paper or card, ready for students to cut up and use in twos or threes when playing the pelmanism game later.
- Start the presentation by saying one of the new opinion phrases in context and combining it with a mime.

T: *J'adore la musique. C'est super!* (Mime listening to music on a walkman with exaggerated enjoyment.)

- Then place the phrase *C'est super!* onto the OHP, also showing the English equivalent and repeating the new French opinion phrase *C'est super!*
- Repeat this process with the other core phrases, each time recapping the preceding new vocabulary before presenting the next phrase.

T: *C'est super, ... c'est moche. C'est super, c'est moche, ... c'est intéressant etc.*

- Check understanding by mixing up the French and English phrases. Say one of the French opinion phrases and ask one student at a time up to the OHP / board to select and match the correct English equivalent.

T: Regardez. 'C'est moche!' – c'est quoi en anglais? ... Oui, c'est ça. Continuez comme ça. Trouvez les paires.

- When the class is confident in the meaning of the French phrases, remove the English equivalents and practise pronunciation, varying speed, volume, tone etc.
- Encourage students to produce the French phrases from memory by using the mimes introduced earlier during the presentation phase to cue oral responses.

Differentiation – Extension
Jeu de cartes – Extra! (CM 12)

AT 1 – 2, AT 2 – 2, AT 3 – 2

- Using the same process as for the core opinion phrases, introduce, if appropriate, the additional six *'Extra!'* phrases.

OHT 🎙 F

Jeu de cartes
Pelmanism game (CM 12)

AT 1 – 2, AT 2 – 2, AT 3 – 2

- Using the cut up OHT or the A4-size flashcards from the presentation, demonstrate how to play the game with the core phrases from the top half of the copymaster only.

Demonstration on the OHP:

- Using the OHT version, place the French and English sections on the OHP in random order, saying the French phrase at the same time.
- Cover all the sections with pieces of card and invite a student to the front to take it in turns with you to lift any two pieces of paper to reveal the phrases. Read out the exposed phrases and encourage the student to read out when it is his / her turn.

T: (Name), viens ici. Choisis deux cartes, une en français et une en anglais. Lis les deux phrases, s'il te plaît.

- Each time two cards have been revealed, ask the class, *C'est une paire?* If the phrases do not match, cover them up again and continue this process. Encourage the class to join in expressing

increasingly exaggerated frustration if a match is not easily made.

T: Oh là,là ... , Oh, mais non!, Ce n'est pas vrai! etc.

- When a match is made, remove the pair and mark up *1 point* on the board under the heading *Professeur* or the demonstration student's name.
- When students understand how to play the game, show how it is won and remind them what the winner says, e.g. Write *Professeur 6 points* and *(Student's name) 0 points* on the board. Say this total and exclaim enthusiastically, *J'ai gagné!*, writing this phrase in a speech bubble to highlight it. Then reverse the score and encourage the demonstration student to say, *J'ai gagné!*

Demonstration with the flashcards:

- Use the principles above, sticking the flashcards face down on the board and turning them face up for matching.
- Having demonstrated the game, hand out the top half of the copymasters to students for them to cut up and use to play the game in twos or threes.

Differentiation – Extension

AT 1 – 2, AT 2 – 2, AT 3 – 2

- Hand out whole copymasters to students who can cope with a greater range of phrases.

OHT 🎙 F 🔲

Sondage!
Nos matières et nos opinions (CM 13)

AT 1 – 2/4, AT 2 – 2/4, AT 3 – 2, AT 4 – 2 /3

- Use some visual opinion flashcards and a few school subject flashcards to revise active use of the phrase *Tu aimes ... ?*

T: Hold up flashcard 27 (the visual for Tu aimes ... ?) with a school subject flashcard and ask students the question, e.g. Tu aimes le dessin? Wait for a reply, e.g. Oui, j'aime le dessin or Non, je n'aime pas le dessin and prompt students to suggest a reason, e.g. C'est intéressant?, c'est facile? or C'est ennuyeux?, c'est difficile? etc.

- Use Copymaster 13 or an OHP version of the copymaster. Direct students to the key at the top of the copymaster and familiarise them with the coding in the *légende* which they will need in order to note the responses in the survey. Start with the example conversation shown on the copymaster.

T: *Regardez l'exemple.* (Read the example to the class.) *Alors, j'aime le français. C'est super. Regardez la légende. 'C'est super', c'est quelle lettre? s? i? f? m? e? d? Oui, c'est 's'. Voilà.* (Write *s* on the board, on a replica of the grid, or point to the actual example on the grid in an OHT version of the copymaster.)

- Continue with two or three more examples to elicit a variety of letters.
- Play the class cassette indicating that students are now going to complete the first row of the grid by using the *légende* to record Angélique's opinions about her school subjects. Pause the cassette after each opinion, to allow time to note the responses.

T: *Ecoutez Angélique sur la cassette et notez les lettres dans la grille.* (Demonstrate.)

Teacher:	Bon alors, allez faire votre sondage!
Boy:	Angélique, tu aimes le français?
Girl:	Oui, j'adore le français. C'est super.
Boy:	Et l'anglais?
Girl:	Oui, j'aime l'anglais. C'est intéressant!
Boy:	Et tu aimes les maths?
Girl:	Ben oui. Je préfère les maths. C'est facile.
Boy:	Et les sciences? Tu aimes les sciences?
Girl:	Oui, j'adore les sciences. C'est super.
Boy:	Tu aimes la géographie?
Girl:	Non, je déteste la géographie. C'est ennuyeux.
Boy:	Et l'histoire. Tu aimes l'histoire?
Girl:	Non, je n'aime pas l'histoire. C'est difficile.
Boy:	Mais le dessin. Tu aimes ça?
Girl:	Non, je n'aime pas le dessin. C'est moche.
Boy:	Tu aimes la musique?
Girl:	Mais oui. J'aime les cours de musique. C'est intéressant.

Boy:	Et l'éducation physique?
Girl:	L'éducation physique? Mais non! Je déteste ça. C'est moche.
Boy:	Alors, finalement, tu aimes la technologie?
Girl:	Oui, j'aime la technologie mais c'est difficile.
Boy:	Merci. ... Yannick. Tu aimes le français? ...

Solution

Angélique: s, i, f, s, e, d, m, i, m, d

- Explain that students are now going to carry out their own survey and that they will fill in the grid on the copymaster by using the *légende* in the same way as they did for Angélique's results.
- Use a volunteer and demonstrate how to carry out the survey, recording the replies in a replica of the copymaster grid on the board or OHP. For example, write the name of the demonstration student on the replica grid under the heading *et tes copains?* Then ask the student, *Tu aimes le français?*
- Record the reply using the letter coding shown in the *légende*. Work through one or two more examples before saying, *etcetera* and demonstrating the final survey question, *Tu aimes la technologie?*
- Show how to conclude one person's survey by saying, *Merci, au revoir* etc. before moving on to interview another person.
- Give a realistic time limit and explain that students should now move about the classroom to interview five people.

T: *Vous allez complétez la grille ici.* (Show grid.) *Vous avez __ minutes pour interviewer cinq personnes ... Et on parle en français: Bonjour. Tu aimes ...? Oui, j'aime ... C'est ... etcetera. Bon. Levez-vous ...* (mime that students should stand up) *et circulez.* (Mime that students should move around the classroom.) *Allez-y!*

- Direct students' attention to some of Angélique's opinions which they recorded earlier on the grid.
- Demonstrate the link between the grid and the bubbles, by showing that the opinion in the first speech bubble at the bottom of the copymaster has been converted from the coded response on the grid.

T: Regardez la grille d'Angélique. (Point out the grid.) *Voilà les opinions. Par exemple le français ... 's'...* (Point to the symbol and coded result on the grid.) *'s', qu'est-ce que ça veut dire?* (Consult the key at the top of the copymaster and run your finger through the list of opinions.) *Ah oui, c'est 'super'.* (Write the sentence *J'aime le français. C'est super!* on the board and enclose it in a speech bubble, before showing the link with the copymaster by pointing out the completed example at the bottom of the sheet.)

- Repeat the interpretation process with one or two more examples.
- Finally, explain that students should now complete the empty speech bubbles by writing any five opinions based on the results of the survey which they carried out earlier, giving one opinion per person.

T: Et maintenant, c'est à vous! Ecrivez les noms et cinq opinions de tes copains – une opinion par personne.

Collège extraordinaire! (SB p.27)

AT 2 – 2, AT 3 – 2, AT 4 – 2/3

- Students can read this silently or aloud. They can also use it as a stimulus for producing their own *Collège extraordinaire*. They could, if they wish, change any or all of the following components: opinions, school subjects, context and characters. For example, they could create a school of aliens, celebrities, sports people or popstars, using magazine pictures or their own illustrations.

T: Lisez 'Collège extraordinaire' à la page 27 ... Maintenant, à vous! Dessinez et écrivez ton collège extraordinaire – choisissez votre sujet. Des monstres? (mime) *Des chanteurs de pop?* (mime) *...*

Pas de panique! (SB p.27)

AT 1 – 3, AT 2 – 2/3, AT 3 – 3

- Show flashcards 3, 7 and 9 to elicit *la musique, l'informatique* and *l'éducation physique*.

T: C'est quelle matière? (Wait for response.) *Oui, bien. C'est la musique.* (Stick flashcard onto the board and repeat using the other two flashcards.)

- Then write incomplete words *la mus__, l'informat__* and *l'éducation phys__* on the board underneath the flashcards. Ask for a volunteer to complete these words.

T: Regardez! Qui peut compléter ces mots? (Mime putting up hand.) *Par exemple, la mus__?* (Mime completing the word.)

- When the words have been filled in, underline *-ique* at the end of each word and explain that students are now going to hear other words containing the sound *-ique*.

T: Regardez page 27 'Pas de panique!' et écoutez la cassette. Nous allons écouter le son '-ique'.

- Students listen to the rhyme *'Pas de panique!'* on the class cassette, whilst following the written version in their books.

> 🔲
>
> Pas de panique, Frédéric,
> La musique, c'est fantastique.
> Pas de panique, Dominique,
> L'informatique, c'est très pratique.
> Pas de panique, Véronique,
> L'éducation physique, ça c'est chic!

- Use cognates and visual clues in the accompanying cartoon to help students deduce the meaning of new vocabulary items and the gender of new names in the rhyme.

T: 'Panique', qu'est-ce que c'est en anglais? etc. Regardez l'image. Véronique, c'est le nom d'un garçon ...? (draw stick boy) *... ou c'est le nom d'une fille?* (draw stick girl) etc.

- When students understand the rhyme, encourage them to join in. This can be done in a variety of ways:
  - Split the class into three groups and ask each group to chant or rap two lines.

- Students read the rhyme aloud as a class or in groups, in the same rhythm as the original version.
- They jog on the spot whilst chanting the rhyme.
- Divide the class into groups and conduct them in chanting a round.
- They read the rhyme aloud, simultaneously with the cassette. See if the class can maintain the rhythm and speed of the cassette, while you suddenly turn the volume right down. Then turn up the volume again to find out whether or not students have kept pace with the cassette!

- Encourage the class to point out that the sound *-ique* can be written as *-ic* or *-ique*.

T: *Le son '-ique', ça s'écrit comment?*

- Remind them also of the *-ick* version of this sound, which they have already met in the name Yannick.

AT 2 – 2/3, AT 4 – 2/3/4

- As possible further exploitation and / or homework activities, students can produce their own '*-ique* rhyme' and illustration by switching the subjects and the names of the people, perhaps including Angélique and Yannick.
- Students could then learn their own or the original version of the rhyme by heart.

> **Revision of classroom objects**
> **Presentation of classroom language**
> *Passe-moi / Donne-moi le / la / l' / les*
> (+ classroom objects), *s'il te plaît.*

Vite, vite! (SB p.28)

a Ecoute et lis.

AT 1 – 3, AT 2 – 2, AT 3 – 3

- Students listen to the class cassette, whilst following the text of the cartoon strip. This features classroom language and also introduces the use of the definite article linked to classroom equipment.
- Play the cassette through once continuously, before playing it a second time and pausing the cassette after each frame of the cartoon strip.
- Encourage students to point to the relevant speech bubbles as they hear the language.

T: *Ecoutez encore et indiquez le texte.* (Demonstrate.)

Narrator:	La classe d'enfer
	A la récré
Girl:	Monsieur, le téléphone!
Teacher:	Merci.
Boy:	Regarde les papiers sur l'ordinateur!
	Vite! Passe-moi le sac, s'il te plaît!
	Passe-moi les livres, s'il te plaît!
	Bon! Donne-moi le stylo.
	Non, ça ne va pas.
Girl:	Passe-moi la règle!
	Bon! <u>Vite!</u>
Teacher:	Bonjour! Donne-moi les papiers, s'il te plaît!

- Using appropriate actions, demonstrate the meaning of the following essential phrases from the text:
  ... sur l'ordinateur
  Passe-moi le sac, s'il te plaît.
  Donne-moi le stylo, s'il te plaît.
  Passe-moi la règle, s'il te plaît.
  Passe-moi les livres, s'il te plaît.
  Donne-moi les papiers, s'il te plaît.
- Check understanding of the phrases linked to classroom equipment, by asking students to pass / give you specific items of classroom equipment. These could be lined up on a table in advance, to make the use of the definite article more authentic.
- In particular, check that students understand the difference in meaning between *Tu as un / une ...*, which they met in Module 1 and *Passe-moi / Donne-moi le / la / les ...* featured here. Elicit from them that *un* and *une* mean 'a' and that *le, la* and *les* mean 'the'. (Further explanation will follow on Students' Book page 29.)

T: *'Tu as une règle?' – c'est quoi en anglais? Et 'Passe-moi la règle', c'est quoi? ... Oui, très bien. Alors 'un' et 'une', c'est quoi en anglais? Et 'le, la, l' et les'? ...*

- Students repeat the new classroom language phrases to practise pronounciation.
- Finally, they can produce the language orally in response to you holding up various pieces of classroom equipment, before taking over the activity themselves as a class, in groups or in pairs.

En classe (CM 14)

1 Relie les phrases et les images.

AT 3 – 2

- Students show understanding of the written and spoken form of these classroom language phrases, by linking them to the appropriate visuals.
- Alternatively, this can be done for homework, using the self-study cassette for extra support.

T: *Regardez la fiche. Reliez les phrases et les images.* (Demonstrate.)

You will need Copymaster 14, activity 1. Listen to the cassette and join up the right pictures and sentences.

1 Passe-moi la règle!
2 Donne-moi les papiers!
3 Passe-moi le sac!
4 Passe-moi l'ordinateur!
5 Donne-moi le stylo!
6 Donne-moi les livres!

Solution
1C 2E 3F 4A 5D 6B

2 Ecoute, lis et répète.

AT 1 – 2, AT 2 – 2, AT 3 – 2

- Students listen, read and repeat the phrases on cassette.

Passe-moi la règle!
Donne-moi les papiers!
Passe-moi le sac!
Passe-moi l'ordinateur!
Donne-moi le stylo!
Donne-moi les livres!

- This item is also provided on the self-study cassette for independent practice.

Now read the sentences carefully once more as you listen to them on the cassette. Pause the cassette after each sentence and repeat it.

Passe-moi la règle!
Donne-moi les papiers!
Passe-moi le sac!
Passe-moi l'ordinateur!
Donne-moi le stylo!
Donne-moi les livres!

Vite, vite! (SB p.28)

b Comment dit-on?

AT 2 – 2, AT 4 – 2/3

- Students use the pictures as cues for oral and / or written production of the classroom language. This can be done as a class, group or pairwork activity.

T: *Regardez les images et faites des phrases. Par exemple, numéro 1 …? Excellent! Travaillez avec un(e) partenaire et continuez comme ça.*

Solution
1 Passe-moi le sac, s'il te plaît!
2 Passe-moi la règle!
3 Donne-moi les papiers, s'il te plaît!
4 Passe-moi l'ordinateur, s'il te plaît!
5 Donne-moi le stylo.
6 Passe-moi les livres, s'il te plaît!

Presentation of the definite article and gender

OHT

'The', c'est quoi en français? (SB p.29)

AT 1 – 2, AT 2 – 1, AT 3 – 1

- Read through the *'Attention!'* feature with the class, first highlighting the use of the definite article in expressions such as *Passe-moi le sac, s'il te plaît* and *Donne-moi la règle* and then pointing out *le, la, l'* and *les* and the fact that they all mean 'the'.

- Continue to demonstrate the use of the definite article as follows. Draw three large boxes on the board / OHP, using the following format as a guide:

- Using a biro, a school bag, a ruler and a rubber, quickly revise the vocabulary for these four classroom items. Ensure that students use the definite article by asking, *Comment dit-on* 'Pass me the ...' etc.

- As students identify these items of classroom equipment, write the masculine nouns with their articles in the left hand box on the board and write the feminine nouns with their articles in the middle box. Highlight the genders by outlining the masculine box in blue and the feminine box in red.

- Identify and label the masculine and feminine genders.

T: *'Le', ça c'est masculin ...* (Write *masculin* and *(m)* above the left hand box on the board.) *... et 'la', ça c'est féminin.* (Write *féminin* and *(f)* above the middle box on the board.)

- Then underline the masculine definite articles in blue and the feminine definite articles in red, stressing them at the same time, e.g. *le ...*, (underline in blue) *... la ...*, (underline in red) etc.

- Demonstrate the use of *l'* with a school timetable, a computer and an orange – either real ones or drawings of these items. Again, cue students to ask for these items to be passed to them, prompting them with *l'emploi du temps, l'ordinateur* and *l'orange* if necessary. Add these nouns with their *l'* to the appropriate masculine or feminine gender box on the board.

- Prompt students to spot the fact that the words all begin with vowels.

T: *L'emploi du temps, ça commence avec quelle lettre?* etc.

- Draw attention to the use of *les* for plurals. Using a pile of books, a sheaf of papers and several biros, rules, rubbers etc., cue students to ask for plural items of classroom equipment to be passed. As they do so, add these nouns and their articles to the right hand box on the board.

- Underline the plural 's' in each word and explain.

T: *... les noms se terminent en 's'. 'Les', ça c'est pluriel.* (Write *pluriel* and *(pl)* above the right hand plural box on the board.)

- In a *pause anglaise* explain that all objects in French are either masculine or feminine and that the word for 'a' or 'the' will change depending on the gender of the object. Talk through the concept of singular and plural and explain that if there is more than one object, the word for 'the' is *les*. Tell students that when they learn the words for things in French, they must also learn the word for 'a' or 'the' which belongs with each thing.

- Refer the class back to page 29 of the Students' Book and ask them to read through the *'Attention!'* section again for consolidation of this grammar. Students can use this page as support later when completing Copymaster 14 and / or 15.

- Finally, ask students what other words combined with *le, la, l'* and *les* they have met in this module. Explain that in French it is also important to learn the correct form of *le, la, l'* and *les* with school subjects, even though the word 'the' is not needed with them in English.

At this point you may wish to use Copymaster 76. Students complete notes on the use of the definite article and keep them for reference.

En classe (CM 14)

3 Trouve les objets.

AT 2 – 2, AT 3 – 1, AT 4 – 1/2

- Students revise vocabulary for other classroom equipment and practise the use of the definite article with these items by completing the wordsearch on the copymaster. As they discover each piece of vocabulary, they should write it in their exercise books.

T: Regardez les images et trouvez les objets dans la grille. Par exemple: le crayon (write on board). Notez les mots dans votre cahier avec 'le / la / l' ou les'.

- Some students may like to colour-code their list of vocabulary, underlining masculine nouns in blue, feminine nouns in red and plural nouns in a third colour.

T: Soulignez les mots masculins en bleu, les mots féminins en rouge et les mots pluriels en (violet). (Demonstrate.)

Solution

l	e	s	t	y	l	o	l	e	s	l
e	h	c	i	f	a	l	e	l	a	o
l	e	l	i	v	r	e	s	e	l	r
a	o	a	e	f	è	s	c	c	t	d
g	r	t	g	i	g	c	h	r	r	i
o	g	r	n	n	l	a	a	a	o	n
m	è	o	a	y	e	h	i	y	m	a
m	r	u	r	l	s	i	s	o	m	t
e	c	s	o	o	l	e	e	n	è	e
l	e	s	l'	l	a	r	s	i	v	u
o	d	e	l	e	s	s	a	c	s	r

- Afterwards they can work in pairs and practise asking for the various items to be given or passed. Some students could be encouraged to gradually give up the written support and work solely from the picture cues on the copymaster.

Differentiation – Extension

AT 2 – 2/3/4, AT 4 – 2/3/4

- Working in groups, some students could write, memorise and act out a short scene based in a classroom, using Copymaster 14 and the cartoon strip on page 28 of the Students' Book as stimulus and / or support.

T: Faites une petite scène. Regardez la fiche et la page 28 et changez les détails. Travaillez en groupes de ... personnes.

Le, la, l' ou les? (SB p.29)

AT 3 – 2, AT 4 – 1/2/3

- Having completed Copymaster 14, students should return to page 29 where they have the opportunity to use the definite article within short, familiar constructions.
- Initially, they focus solely on the definite article, copying the sentences and completing them with the correct article.

Solution

Passe-moi **le** crayon.
Donne-moi **les** cahiers, s'il te plaît.
Passe-moi **l'**ordinateur, s'il te plaît.
Donne-moi **la** gomme!

- Afterwards, they should move on to the task *'C'est à toi!'* and produce similar written statements of their own for homework. These could be illustrated and displayed in the form of a classroom language poster.

Differentiation – Extension
Organisation! (CM 15)

1 Mets dans la bonne case.

AT 3 – 1

- Higher attainers could go on to categorise vocabulary into masculine singular, feminine singular and plural groups, transferring vocabulary into boxes similar to those used on the board / OHP in the initial classroom practice of the definite article.

T: Regardez la fiche. Mettez les mots dans la bonne case. Par exemple, 'le cahier', c'est masculin? féminin? ou pluriel? ... Oui, c'est masculin. (Write into correct box on board / OHT.)

Solution

(m)	(f)	(pl)
le cahier	la fiche	les crayons
le taille-crayon	la gomme	les chaises
le stylo	la trousse	les livres
le sac	la règle	les papiers

2 a) Remplis les blancs.
b) Mets dans la bonne case.

AT 4 – 1/2

- Students who can cope with a more challenging task can complete the missing definite article for some of the school subjects, before categorising these items of vocabulary in a similar way.

T: Maintenant, regardez les phrases. Copiez et remplissez les blancs. Par exemple, 'géographie' – c'est __le__ géographie? ou la? ou l'? ou les? ... Oui, c'est 'la', c'est féminin. (Demonstrate copying and filling in missing word.)

Solution

(m)	(f)	(pl)
le français	**la** géographie	**les** maths
le dessin	**la** musique	**les** sciences
	la technologie	

- As an optional extra, students could colour-code their boxes, shading / underlining the masculine nouns in blue, the feminine ones in red and the plurals in a third colour.

T: Coloriez les cases – bleu, rouge ou (violet).

The '*Attention!*' feature at the bottom of the copymaster reminds students of the use of *l'*.

Une lettre de Sophie (SB p.30)

AT 3 – 3

- Students read familiar language from modules 1 and 2 in a short letter. They then demonstrate understanding by looking at the accompanying pictures and deciding whether or not these accurately represent information given in the letter.

T: Lisez la lettre ... Maintenant, regardez les images. Numéro 1, c'est vrai ou faux? Oui, très bien. (Write 1 X on board.) Continuez comme ça. (Draw X on board) – ça, c'est faux et ça, (draw tick) c'est vrai. Notez dans votre cahier.

Solution

1 ✕ 2 ✓ 3 ✓ 4 ✓ 5 ✕ 6 ✕

Differentiation – Extension
Une lettre de Sophie – Extra! (CM 16)

AT 3 – 3/4, AT 4 – 1

- As an alternative to the letter from Sophie on page 30 of the Students' Book, higher attainers read a fuller version of the letter on Copymaster 16. They demonstrate understanding by reading sentences and deciding whether these statements are true or false.

Solution

1 ✕ 2 ✓ 3 ✕ 4 ✓ 5 ✕ 6 ✕ 7 ✓

Quelle catastrophe! (SB p.30)

AT 3 – 2/3, AT 4 – 2/3

- Students reconstruct the damaged letter on page 30 to write a short, supported reply to Sophie.

Differentiation – Extension

AT 3 – 3/4, AT 4 – 3/4

- Rather than copying and completing the damaged letter on page 30, students write their own letter, using either Sophie's letter on page 30 or on Copymaster 16 as support. Encourage those students who can to write from memory and to redraft if necessary. (N.B. Give the word *Cher* to students wishing to write to a boy.)

T: Ecrivez une lettre comme ça. Changez les détails. Par exemple ...

Une interview! (CM 16)

AT 1 – 2, AT 2 – 3/4, AT 3 – 2/3, AT 4 – 2/3

- Hand out the bottom section of Copymaster 16 and demonstrate the task. Using Sophie's letter on page 30 of the Students' Book, ask students to identify the questions in the letter.

T: Regardez la lettre de Sophie et trouvez les questions. (Write question marks on the board / OHP as a prompt.)

- Using these questions as a starting point, encourage students to read the information in the letter and to think of other questions which they already know and which they could now ask Sophie.

T: J'ai onze ans. La question, c'est 'Tu as quel âge?' Je préfère la musique pop. La question, c'est 'Tu aimes la musique pop?' Bon. Je m'appelle Sophie Legrand. La question, c'est …? (Wait for the corresponding question.) J'habite à Paris. La question, c'est …? (Wait for the corresponding question.)

- Show students how to fill in the '*Questions*' section of the copymaster, by writing some of these questions on the board / OHP. Direct students in need of further support to Module 1 '*Sommaire*' on Students' Book pages 22–23.
- Finally, demonstrate how to use these questions for the interview in the pairwork activity by acting out the part of Sophie and using a student to ask the questions listed on the board.

T: Tu es l'interviewer et je suis Sophie. Pose-moi des questions. … Excellent. Merci. Maintenant, travaillez avec un(e) partenaire. Faites une interview avec Sophie comme ça.

Differentiation – Extension
AT 1 – 2, AT 2 – 3/4, AT 3 – 2/3/4, AT 4 – 2/3/4

- Students who have already used '*Une lettre de Sophie - Extra!*' on Copymaster 16 could be asked to develop a more extensive range of questions using the fuller letter for guidance.

Une pendule (CM 17)

- Anticipate teaching 'time' in Objective 2, by issuing Copymaster 17 as homework at some point soon, so that students can use the template to make their own clocks, sticking them onto a paper plate or card and handing them in to you, ready for the planned lesson. (Detach and keep back the list of times at the bottom of the copymaster, so that they can label the clock later.) If required, use the template to make up a teacher's OHT or card clock, ready for the presentation of the new language.

Comment ça se prononce? (SB p.31)
a Ecoute et lis.
AT 1 – 3, AT 2 – 2, AT 3 – 3

- Play the class cassette twice.

Bleuet, le perroquet
Bleuet, le perroquet,
chante en anglais
et parle français!

Bleuet, le perroquet,
Bleuet, le perroquet,
chante en anglais et parle français!
chante en anglais et parle français!

- Check that students understand the meaning of the rhyme and encourage them to join in the marine chant version, if desired. This can be done in a variety of ways:
  - Split the class in half and ask one half to chant the first two lines and the other half to chant the last two lines.
  - Students jog on the spot whilst chanting the rhyme.
  - Divide the class into groups and conduct them in chanting a round.
- This material is also recorded on the self-study cassette for independent learning.

You will need to look at Students' Book page 31, activity A. Listen to the rhyme 'Bleuet le perroquet'. Then listen again and repeat.

Bleuet, le perroquet
Bleuet,
le perroquet,
chante en anglais
et parle français!

Now try saying it as a marine chant.

Bleuet, le perroquet

Bleuet, le perroquet
chante en anglais et parle français!
chante en anglais et parle français!

b Ecoute et lis. Ecoute, lis et répète.

AT 1 – 1/2, AT 2 – 1/2, AT 3 – 1/2

- Students listen to the class cassette whilst reading the list on page 31.
- They then practise their pronunciation by listening, reading and repeating the words and phrases on cassette.

C'est le français
C'est vrai
J'ai un perroquet
Qu'est-ce que c'est, s'il vous plaît?
C'est le français
C'est vrai
J'ai un perroquet
Qu'est-ce que c'est, s'il vous plaît?

- Draw attention to the various spellings representing the sound '*ai*' by asking students to come to the board / OHP and to fill in the missing letters in a selection of the words taken from page 31 as you say them.

T: Write *j* and say *j'ai*. Write *franç* and say *français* etc. (Underline the various alternative spellings at the end of the words, whilst making the phonetic sound.)

- This material is also recorded on the self-study cassette for independent learning.

You will need Students' Book page 31, activity B. Listen and read.

C'est le français
C'est vrai
J'ai un perroquet
Qu'est-ce que c'est, s'il vous plaît?

Now listen again and repeat.

C'est le français
C'est vrai
J'ai un perroquet
Qu'est-ce que c'est, s'il vous plaît?

c Lis et prononce. Ecoute la cassette.

AT 1 – 1/2, AT 2 – 1/2, AT 3 – 1/2

- Students read and pronounce these words, before operating the pause button on the self-study cassette and checking pronunciation after each word. Those in need of further support can rewind the cassette and try again if they so wish.

You will need Students' Book page 31, activity C. Try to pronounce the words, then listen carefully to see how well you have done.

1 Le français
2 Un perroquet
3 S'il vous plaît
4 C'est vrai
5 Qu'est-ce que c'est?
6 Qu'est-ce que c'est, s'il vous plaît?

- This item is also provided on the class cassette should you wish to tackle it as a whole class activity.

1 Le français
2 Un perroquet
3 S'il vous plaît
4 C'est vrai
5 Qu'est-ce que c'est?
6 Qu'est-ce que c'est, s'il vous plaît?

d Copie et complète.

AT 4 – 1/2

- Students copy and complete the *Aide-mémoire* to use for future reference, as part of an ongoing reminder of sounds and spelling.

Solution

ang**l**ais c'**est** franç**ais** j'**ai** perroqu**et** qu'est-ce que
c'**est**? s'il vous pl**aît** vr**ai**

- Finally, students could learn to say and / or write
the rhyme *'Bleuet, le perroquet'* from memory, if
appropriate.

Objectif 2 Quelle heure est-il?

New language introduced

Quelle heure est-il?

Il est midi / minuit / une heure / deux heures (etc.)

Il est midi et demi / une heure et demie (etc.)

Il est midi quart / une heure et quart (etc.)

Il est midi moins le quart (etc.)

*Il est midi cinq / dix / vingt / vingt-cinq / moins
vingt-cinq / moins vingt (etc.)*

Revised language

Numbers 1 – 29

Asking and telling the time

Student goals (SB p. 24)

- Remind the class of the second goal for this
module. Point to the clock in the picture on page
24 and say *Bon. Objectif deux – 'Quelle heure est-
il?'* Mime looking at your watch whilst repeating the
question rhetorically a couple of times and saying
the actual time.

Revision of numbers 1–12
Presentation of:
Quelle heure est-il? Il est midi / minuit / une heure (etc.).

OHT

Une pendule (CM 17)

1 Découpe et attache à la pendule.

AT 1 – 1/2, AT 2 – 1/2

- Before the lesson photocopy the clock face from
the copymaster onto an acetate transparency and
attach card hands with a paper fastener, covering
the sharp back of the fastener with Blu-Tack or
tape. If preferred, stick the photocopied template
of the clock face onto strong card and attach card
hands in the same way. Alternatively, a real or toy
clock with a clear face can be used as a visual aid.

- In addition, students will need their own card
versions of the clock on Copymaster 17 – they
should have prepared these as part of a previous
homework. (See Teacher's Notes page 45.)

- Quickly revise numbers 1 –12. Then ask the
rhetorical question *Quelle heure est-il?*, looking
enquiringly at your watch. Use a clock to
demonstrate the actual time, saying it in French.

- Use the clock to present times on the full hour and
teach the question *Quelle heure est-il?* Progress
through the hours to include *Il est midi / minuit*,
using appropriate mimes or drawings as support.
Ask the question *Quelle heure est-il?* between the
presentation of each time, encouraging students to
repeat the question and then to join in asking it
after they have heard it three or four times. If
appropriate, also encourage them to use the
pattern of the first few time phrases to predict the
French for new times on the full hour.

- Hand out the home-made clocks which the
students prepared in a previous homework and
demonstrate the next activity.

***T: Regardez votre pendule. Ecoutez bien. Il est
deux heures … (Demonstrate moving the
hands on a clock to the correct time.) Il est
trois heures … etc. (Move clock hands
appropriately.) Bon. Allez-y! Il est …***

- Check students' understanding by saying a
random selection of times on the full hour and
encouraging them to move their own clock hands
to the appropriate times. After each example they
should hold up their clocks and compare their
time with the correct time on your clock.

- Encourage the class to repeat the times, first in
sequence and then in random order. Write up the
phrases for the following times as they do so, to
show the structure of the phrase and to start
linking the spoken and the written word:

Il est une heur<u>e</u>.

Il est deux heure<u>s</u>.

Il est trois heure<u>s</u>.

Il est <u>midi.</u>

Il est <u>minuit.</u>

- Students now work in pairs, playing a game to
guess the times on one another's clock.

- Demonstrate this first with the class. Set a time on
your clock and keep this hidden from the class.
Ask *Quelle heure est-il?* and encourage students
to guess the time. Keep a tally of how many
guesses they take to find the correct time.

- Ask the student who guesses the time to set his or her own clock for the class to guess, replying *oui / non*. Again keep a tally and encourage the class to see if they can 'beat' their last score.

- Hand over the game for students to continue in pairs, encouraging them to reply *oui / non* and to keep a tally of their guesses.

2 Mets la bonne heure.

AT 3 – 2, AT 4 – 2

- As a final optional activity, issue the jumbled list of times from the bottom section of Copymaster 17, to support students in writing the full hours on their clock face.

*T: **Regardez les phrases. Copiez les bonnes phrases sur la pendule.** (Demonstrate.)*

> **Presentation of:**
> *Il est midi quart / une heure et quart (etc.)*
> *Il est midi et demi / une heure et demie (etc.)*
> *Il est midi moins le quart (etc.)*

Vrai ou faux?

AT 1 – 2, AT 2 – 2

- Use the clock from Copymaster 17 or an alternative clock to present and teach times a quarter past the various hours. Present *Il est —— heure(s) et quart*, varying the hours in sequence and encouraging students to build up and use the pattern after a few initial examples.

- Proceed in the same way, first presenting 'half past' and then 'a quarter to' and 'a quarter past' the hour.

- Check understanding by means of a *vrai ou faux?* activity. Demonstrate this by holding up the clock set at one of these times (e.g. half past nine), saying a time and asking whether this statement is true or false.

*T: **Il est neuf heures et demie. Vrai ou faux?***

- Continue the process with as many examples as necessary. Students can either respond orally or with ticks and crosses on a piece of paper. Check their comprehension throughout by giving the correct answer after each example.

- Encourage the students to practise pronunciation by repeating a selection of these new times in a variety of chanting games.

Quelle heure est-il? (CM 18)

1 Lis et écris l'heure.

AT 3 – 2, AT 4 – 2

- Students build up a reference page of times by matching time phrases to clock visuals and copying each phrase beneath its corresponding clock.

*T: **Regardez les pendules et les phrases. Numéro 1, c'est quelle phrase? ... Oui, très bien. Copiez la bonne phrase pour chaque image.***

Differentiation – Extension

2 Complète.

AT 4 – 3

- Students complete the time phrases cued by the additional four clocks in activity 2.

3 C'est à toi!

- Some may progress to activity 3 – drawing their own clocks in their exercise books / on paper and labelling them from memory. They could be encouraged to design varied and / or humorous clock faces and could also include times which are exceptions to the rule, as shown in the *'Attention!'* section of the copymaster.

Jeux de l'heure (CM 19)

1 Jeu de morpion

AT 1 – 2, AT 2 – 2

- Transfer this copymaster onto acetate for demonstration and class games on the OHP. (Retain section 2 for later use.) Cut the acetate sheet into individual clocks and draw a noughts and crosses grid on a second acetate sheet or the white board.

- Quickly revise pronunciation of times taught so far. Divide the class into two teams and play the *'Jeu de morpion'* noughts and crosses game on the OHP, using combinations of any nine 'quarter past', 'quarter to' and 'half past' times.

- Lay the acetate clocks on the noughts and crosses grid. Students should say the correct time to win the square. As they do, replace the clock with a nought or cross, depending on the team.

T: C'est le jeu de morpion. C'est quoi en anglais? Oui, 'noughts and crosses'. On joue en deux équipes. Equipe A, ici (indicate group) – quelle heure est-il? ... Oui, super! (Fill in cross or nought on board / OHT grid.) Alors, équipe B ...

- When students are confident, hand over this activity for them to play in groups or pairs. They should cut up paper or card versions of the *'Jeu de morpion'* and draw their own grids on a piece of paper. Afterwards each game can be collected in a separate envelope and stored for future use. In order to facilitate classroom organisation, you may wish to photocopy each set on to a different coloured piece of paper or card. (Alternatively, students can <u>draw</u> clocks on their grids.)

T: Maintenant, faites le jeu de morpion en paires / en groupes de ... personnes.

> **Revision of numbers 1–29**
> **Presentation of:**
> *Il est midi cinq / dix / vingt / vingt-cinq / moins vingt-cinq / moins vingt / moins dix / moins cinq*

Une pendule (CM 17)

AT 1 – 1/2, AT 2 – 1/2

- Revise numbers 1–29, using a selection of oral and aural games. (See Teacher's Notes introduction, 'Games' page iv.)
- Use the OHT / card clock from Copymaster 17 or an alternative clock to present minutes 'past' and 'to' the hour. Choose any hour and give the time in five-minute intervals, demonstrating the times on the clock as you work through the complete hour.

T: Il est une heure cinq, il est une heure dix, ... , il est deux heures moins dix, il est deux heures moins cinq, il est deux heures.

- Focus first on teaching times past the hour. Choose another hour. Start telling times past the hour and encourage students to join in giving the time. Then repeat the process and teach times to the hour.
- Check students' understanding by saying random times and encouraging them to set their home-made clocks to these times. Then practise pronunciation of these new times and recognition of the written forms. (Cf. Teacher's Notes page 47 earlier in the teaching of this objective.)

L'heure précise (CM 20)

1 Ecoute et répète.

AT 1 – 2, AT 2 – 2, AT 3 – 2, AT 4 – 2

- Students use this copymaster to support their learning of times involving minutes past and to the hour. The copymaster can either be used in the lesson in conjunction with the class cassette, or can be used for independent work with the self-study cassette.
- Initially, students should listen to the cassette whilst reading the copymaster, in order to relate the spoken and written times.
- They then listen, read and repeat the times. In addition, they can, if desired, copywrite the times afterwards.

1 Il est une heure cinq.
2 Il est une heure dix.
3 Il est une heure vingt.
4 Il est une heure vingt-cinq.
5 Il est deux heures moins vingt-cinq.
6 Il est deux heures moins vingt.
7 Il est deux heures moins dix.
8 Il est deux heures moins cinq.
9 Il est deux heures.

You will need Copymaster 20, activity 1. Listen and repeat the times.

1 Il est une heure cinq.
2 Il est une heure dix.
3 Il est une heure vingt.
4 Il est une heure vingt-cinq.
5 Il est deux heures moins vingt-cinq.
6 Il est deux heures moins vingt.
7 Il est deux heures moins dix.
8 Il est deux heures moins cinq.
9 Il est deux heures.

Differentiation – Consolidation

2 Ecoute et complète les pendules.

AT 1 – 2

- Where appropriate, students can have further practice of listening to and demonstrating understanding of times involving minutes past and to the hour. They listen to the class cassette and draw hands on the six clocks.

1 Il est trois heures cinq.
2 Il est six heures vingt.
3 Il est deux heures moins dix.
4 Il est huit heures vingt-cinq.
5 Il est quatre heures moins vingt.
6 Il est cinq heures moins cinq.

- This can alternatively be carried out independently by using the self-study cassette.

You will need Copymaster 20, activity 2. Listen and draw the correct time on the clocks.

1 Il est trois heures cinq.
2 Il est six heures vingt.
3 Il est deux heures moins dix.
4 Il est huit heures vingt-cinq.
5 Il est quatre heures moins vingt.
6 Il est cinq heures moins cinq.

Jeux de l'heure (CM 19)

2 Jeu de Kim

AT 1 – 2, AT 2 – 2

- Cut up section 2 of the acetate version of this copymaster and play 'Le jeu de Kim' on the OHP with the class. This activity allows students to practise the full range of times within a single hour. Shuffle the clocks, arrange them on the OHP and then remove a clock, asking *Quelle heure manque?* to elicit the missing time. (See 'Games', Teacher's Notes page iv for the rules.)

- When students are confident, hand over the activity for them to play in groups or pairs. Students cut up the paper or card versions of section 2 of the copymaster and play as demonstrated.

Les heures sonores (SB p.32)

a Ecoute. Ecris les lettres dans le bon ordre.

AT 1 – 3, AT 3 – 2

- Students listen to the class cassette featuring eight short conversations in which the time is mentioned. They should focus on the detail of the times, look at the photos of the clocks in their books and note the letters in the correct order.

- Emphasise the need to listen for the times only and not to worry about other details in the conversations.

T: Vous allez écouter des conversations. Ecoutez bien l'heure. Par exemple ... **Talk quickly in French and emphasise** *Il est huit heures et demie.* **Then talk again, give another time clearly amidst the redundant language and ask,** *Quelle heure est-il?* **(Wait for the response.)** *Oui! Très bien. Alors, écoutez la cassette, regardez les photos et écrivez les lettres dans le bon ordre.*

1 – Quelle heure est-il, maman?
   – Il est onze heures et quart.
2 – Oh, non. Ce n'est pas possible! Il est déjà six heures vingt. Zut, alors!
3 – Madame, je veux du pain, s'il vous plaît!
   – Désolée, on est fermé. Il est midi cinq.
   – Oh, s'il vous plaît madame.
4 – Le train en provenance de Paris arrive au quai numéro onze.
   – Pardon, monsieur, quelle heure est-il s'il vous plaît?
   – Il est dix heures vingt-cinq.
5 – Il est onze heures moins cinq. Ici la météo pour jeudi le vingt-deux novembre. Dans le nord de la France ...

6 – Merci!
– A demain!
– Hé oh! Vous exagérez, quoi. Il est trois heures moins vingt. Taisez-vous ou je vais téléphoner à la police.

7 – Oh, les pauvres petits. Il est sept heures moins dix.
– Que vous avez faim. Voilà!

8 – Il est sept heures moins le quart. Vous avez encore dix minutes!

Solution

1D 2G 3A 4H 5E 6B 7F 8C

Differentiation – Extension

AT 1 – 3, AT 3 – 2

- Higher attainers could alternatively listen to the cassette with their books closed. They could try drawing / noting the times without using the support of the photos on page 32.

T: *Fermez les livres.* (Demonstrate.) *Ecoutez et notez les heures.*

- Some follow-up work on gist listening could be done in a *pause anglaise* afterwards. Encourage the class to say what, in addition to the times, they understood in the cassette conversations.
- Move on to highlight simple listening strategies, asking them for example to say what clues (e.g. sound effects) and what language (e.g. cognates and key words) helped them to understand the additional information.

b Relie la phrase et la photo.

AT 2 – 2, AT 3 – 2

- Students link the written phrases with the photos. The photos could also be used to cue oral pairwork.

T: *Reliez les phrases et les photos. Par exemple, 1 ...? Oui, c'est ça, 1–A.* (Note on board.)

Solution

1A 2H 3D 4G 5C 6F 7B 8E

Differentiation – Extension

AT 4 – 2/3

- Rather than simply matching numbers and letters, higher attainers could be encouraged to write the time in full for each photo. They could either use the

menu of times at the bottom of the page for support, or could cover this and write from memory.

Jeu de collège (SB p.33)

AT 1 – 2, AT 2 – 2, AT 3 – 2

- Prepare students for the board game which encourages comprehension and productive use of language encountered in this and the previous module.
- Write the following phrases on the board / OHP: *avance d'une case; n'avance pas; recule de deux cases;* and *passe un tour.* Point to each phrase and mime an appropriate action, moving one pace forwards, standing still, moving two paces backwards or sitting down. Encourage students to join in and to repeat the phrases.

T: *Nous allons faire un jeu – Le jeu de collège. Ecoutez et regardez. 'Avance d'une case', c'est ça* (mime or demonstrate). *Maintenant à vous. Avance d'une case. Oui, excellent ... (etc.). Maintenant, écoutez et répétez.*

- Point to the instructions in random order and say them aloud. Students demonstrate understanding by repeating and miming the appropriate action. Hand over the activity so that a student then gives the class directions.
- Leave these phrases on the board. Next, draw a clock on the board / OHP, similar to one from the board game. Mime throwing a die and landing on a clock square.

T: *Quatre. Un, deux, trois, quatre ...*

- Land on the square and mime a thinking expression. Say the correct time on the clock and appeal to the class.

T: *C'est correct, oui ou non?*

- Show that your counter remains on the square as a reward for getting the time right. Then give an action replay, but this time say the <u>wrong</u> time. Ask *C'est correct?* and this time point to the *n'avance pas* phrase, encouraging students to say this.
- Show that your counter has to go back to its previous position as a penalty for not getting the time / classroom phrase right. Mime appropriate disappointment!
- Remind the class of the game language on Students' Book page 21 and also of the *'Am stram gram'* rhyme on page 18, which they can use to see who starts the game.

- Having established the principles of the game, organise students to play in groups of two or three.

T: Maintenant c'est à vous. Travaillez en groupes – il y a un minimum de deux personnes et un maximum de trois personnes dans chaque groupe.

Objectif 3   Cours et activités

New language introduced

J'arrive au collège à ... / je mange / je quitte le collège à ... / je parle avec mes copains / je reste au lit / je joue au volley (foot)

Le premier / deuxième (etc.) / dernier cours / la récréation / le déjeuner commence à ... / commence à quelle heure?

Student goals   (SB p.24)

- Remind students of the third goal for this module. Point to the picture of the third goal on page 24 and say *Bon. Objectif trois – 'Cours et activités'.*
- Cross-refer this to the corresponding visual at the top of page 34, before moving on to *'La vie scolaire'*.

Presentation of:
J'arrive au collège / je mange / je quitte le collège / je parle avec mes copains / je reste au lit / je joue au volley (foot)

La vie scolaire   (SB p.34)

AT 1 – 3, AT 3 – 3

- Students listen to the class cassette and read the short descriptions about aspects of school routine in France.
- They then match the photos to the corresponding descriptions. Their choices will involve reading for detail and gist and will be based on detailed understanding of time and deduction of broad meaning, using cognates, photos and context for help.

T: Reliez le texte avec la bonne photo. Par exemple, numéro un, c'est quelle photo?

1 J'arrive au collège à huit heures vingt. Le premier cours commence à huit heures et demie. Aujourd'hui, c'est l'éducation physique. Je n'aime pas ça.
2 Le mercredi, c'est super. Le matin je reste au lit et l'après-midi je joue au volley!
3 A midi et demi c'est le déjeuner. Je mange à la cantine avec mes copains.
4 L'après-midi à quatre heures, c'est la deuxième récréation. Je parle avec mes copains.
5 Je quitte le collège à cinq heures et quart. Aujourd'hui le dernier cours est la musique.
6 J'adore le samedi. Je quitte le collège à une heure moins vingt-cinq!

Solution
1C 2F 3A 4E 5B 6D

- When students have completed the matching activity, encourage them to deduce the meanings of the verbs *j'arrive, je quitte, je mange, je joue, je parle, je reste* and *commence*.

T: Alors, 'j'arrive au collège à huit heures vingt' – 'j'arrive', c'est quoi en anglais? (etc.)

- Discuss associated words in English which helped them to reach their conclusions and point out the meaning of the 'faux ami' *je reste*.
- Delay discussion of other unknown vocabulary in *'La vie scolaire'* until after the class has completed the dictionary skills work on page 35.

Le glossaire, c'est clair!   (SB p.35)

AT 1 – 2, AT 2 – 2/3, AT 3 – 1/2, AT 4 – 1

- The activities on this page are designed to encourage simple dictionary skills and to promote the use of the French – English glossary. Before students begin, familiarise them with the concept of alphabetical ordering by playing some preliminary games as a class or in groups:
  - Write each letter of the alphabet on a separate piece of card / paper. Shuffle them and ask students to arrange them in alphabetical order whilst they say the letters in French.

T: *Mettez les cartes en ordre alphabétique. Alors, A ... Oui, c'est ça ...*

- Students arrange themselves in a line according to the alphabetical order of their first names and / or surnames. Encourage students to ask and give this information in French.

T: *Bon, levez-vous, tout le monde. (Gesture.) Rangez-vous en ordre alphabétique. Quelle est la première lettre de l'alphabet? ... Oui, c'est 'A'. Alors, qui a un nom qui commence avec 'A'? Oui, toi, (name). Et toi, (name). Mettez-vous là. Et 'B'? ... C'est à vous. Demandez: Tu t'appelles comment? Ça s'écrit comment?*

a Ecris dans l'ordre alphabetique.

- Demonstrate the alphabetical ordering activities in exercise A on page 35 by writing some simple familiar French words on A4-size pieces of paper / card for students to arrange alphabetically on the board.

T: *Voici quelques mots, par exemple stylo, règle, histoire, collège, maths. (Stick word cards onto the board in a vertical list in non-alphabetical order.) Mettez les mots dans l'ordre alphabétique, par exemple ... (Move the card labelled collège to the top of the list.) ... collège, ça c'est le premier mot. Et le deuxième, ça c'est ...? (Wait for the correct answer and then ask the student who gave it to come to the board and move the card labelled histoire.) Bien. Viens ici. etc.*

Solution

1 collège, emploi du temps, image, matière, professeur, récréation, technologie

2 copie, cours, déjeuner, madame, mathématiques, musique, premier

b C'est quoi en anglais?

- Write the word *collège* on the board / OHP.

T: *'Collège', c'est quoi en anglais? ... Vous êtes certains? Regardez dans vos glossaires.*

- Show students the French – English glossary at the back of the Students' Book, explaining, *C'est dans l'ordre alphabétique* and waiting for them to check the answer.

- Repeat the process with some unknown words such as *cheval* and *souris*. Point out the fact that there are in fact two glossaries at the back of the book, one which contains *vocabulaire français – anglais* and one which contains *vocabulaire anglais – français*. Stress that at the moment students only need to use the French – English glossary.

T: *Activité B. C'est quoi en anglais? Regardez dans votre glossaire!*

c Lis 'La vie scolaire' encore une fois.

- Finally, explain that when students have completed activity B, they should reread *'La vie scolaire'*, using their answers to help them understand the texts better.

Ma routine scolaire (FC 28–33)

AT 1 – 2

- Use the following flashcards to focus in detail on the limited number of present tense verbs first encountered in *'La vie scolaire'* on page 34:

  28 *J'arrive*
  29 *Je mange*
  30 *Je quitte le collège*
  31 *Je parle avec mes copains*
  32 *Je reste au lit*
  33 *Je joue au volley*

- A variety of games can be played to consolidate understanding and to maximise opportunities for hearing these verbs:

  - Hold up a flashcard and say one of the verbs. Ask whether the picture is *vrai ou faux*.
  - Stick the flashcards on the board and number them. Call out a verb and ask students to write or say the number of the card.

- Move on to practise repetition of the verbs in a series of chanting activities and a *'Jacques a dit'*- type game. In this you hold up a flashcard and say an activity; students repeat if the activity is the one shown on the card and remain silent if it is not. Finally, cue individual oral responses to the flashcards.

- Using Copymaster 21, the written word can then be reintroduced as an aid to comprehension, before students move on to individual pronunciation and copywriting practice.

2 Au collège

Ma routine scolaire (CM 21)

1 Ecoute, lis et prononce.

AT 1 – 2, AT 2 – 2

- Students listen to the self-study cassette item, whilst reading the copymaster, in order to relate the spoken and written phrases. They then listen again, read and repeat.

You will need Copymaster 21, activity 1. Look at the pictures and sentences. Listen and repeat.

J'arrive au collège.
Je mange.
Je quitte le collège.
Je parle avec mes copains.
Je reste au lit.
Je joue au volley.

2 Lis et copie.

AT 3 – 2, AT 4 – 2

- In this activity students copy the phrases, before returning to page 36 of the Students' Book.

Les copains au collège (SB p.36)

AT 1 – 2

- Activities are now combined with times in sentences such as *Je mange à une heure*.

a Ecoute la cassette. Qui parle?

- Students listen to the cassette and decide which of the six friends shown in the photo is giving each statement.

T: Regardez la page 36. Qui parle? C'est Claire? Ou Marc? Ou …?

Louise: J'arrive au collège à huit heures vingt.
Olivier: A deux heures et quart je joue au volley.

Sophie: Je mange à une heure cinq.
Marc: La récré commence à dix heures vingt. Je parle avec mes copains.
Yannick: Je quitte le collège à cinq heures vingt.
Claire: Le mercredi c'est super. Je reste au lit jusqu'à onze heures et demie. Et toi?

b Ecoute la cassette. Ecris l'heure.

- Demonstrate how to use the notation 8h05, 8h10, 8h15 etc., or, if this is too complex at this stage, explain how you would like students to note / draw the times.
- Students then listen to the cassette again and note the six times mentioned.

T: Ecoutez encore et notez les heures. **(Play the first one)** *C'est quelle heure? … Oui, excellent.* **(Note 8h20 on board).** *Continuez comme ça.*

Louise: J'arrive au collège à **huit heures vingt**.
Olivier: A **deux heures et quart** je joue au volley.
Sophie: Je mange à **une heure cinq**.
Marc: La récré commence à **dix heures vingt**. Je parle avec mes copains.
Yannick: Je quitte le collège à **cinq heures vingt**.
Claire: Le mercredi c'est super. Je reste au lit jusqu'à **onze heures et demie**. Et toi?

F
Attention! (FC 28–33, SB p.36)

AT 1 – 2, AT 3 – 2

- Work through the example in the *'Attention!'* feature with the class.

T: Regardez – 'Je mange à une heure'. C'est quoi en anglais? … Alors, 'at', c'est quoi en français?

- Demonstrate other examples of your own, using the school routine flashcards in combination with *à* … and drawings of clocks on the board to consolidate understanding of 'verbs + *à* + clock time'.

C'est à quelle heure? (SB p.36)

AT 2 – 2, AT 4 – 2 /3

- Students use the pictures to cue oral work, combining verbs and times. Some may be able to write the sentences in full, using Copymaster 21 for support if necessary.

Solution

1 Je joue au volley à deux heures.

2 J'arrive au collège à huit heures et demie.

3 Je parle avec mes copains à dix heures et demie.

4 Je quitte le collège à cinq heures et quart.

Ma routine scolaire (CM 21)

3 Et ta routine scolaire? Complète et écris.

AT 4 – 2/3

- In this final activity on Copymaster 21, students personalise simple language covering aspects of school routine. First, they fill in the clocks to show the times of their own school routine and complete corresponding sentences, using the top section of the copymaster for support if necessary. They could then add a sentence or two about the weekend, e.g. *Je reste au lit, je joue au volley / foot.*

Presentation of:

Le premier / deuxième (etc.) / dernier cours / le déjeuner / la récréation commence à ... / commence à quelle heure?

Le premier cours commence à quelle heure? (SB p.37)

AT 1 – 2 /3, AT3 – 2 /3, AT4 – 2 /3

- Revise / teach and practise the time notation 8h05, 8h10, 8h15 etc. and focus on *le premier cours, le deuxième cours, le dernier cours* etc. as follows:

- Use a clock to cue responses to the question *Quelle heure est-il?* and as students give the

answers write them down using the convention outlined above. When they are confident, remove the support of the clock and ask volunteers to the front to convert various times given by you into written abbreviations on the board.

T: 'Huit heures cinq', ça s'écrit comme ça. (Write it on board. Then write another time, using the same convention.) Et ça? Quelle heure est-il? ... Oui, très bien.

- Finally, say about half a dozen times and give the whole class the opportunity to write these as abbreviations in a quick 'quiz'. Write up the correct abbreviation immediately after they have written each answer, so that the times are still fresh in their minds.

- Next, draw an outline timetable on the board, without subjects, simply showing seven numbered lesson slots, *récréation(s)* and *déjeuner*. Use this to demonstrate *le premier cours, le deuxième cours, le dernier cours* etc. Work through all the lessons first and then through break(s) and lunch, to highlight the pattern of the ordinal numbers. After *le troisième cours* encourage students to deduce how to refer to the other lessons.

T: Voici un emploi du temps. Voici le premier cours, le deuxième cours ... Et ça, c'est ... ? Oui, excellent – le troisième cours ... Et ça, c'est le dernier cours. 'Dernier', c'est quoi en anglais?

- When they understand this pattern, invent some statements about the timings of lessons and ask volunteers to write the abbreviations for these times on the board.

T: Le premier cours commence à neuf heures dix. (Name), écris l'heure, s'il te plaît.

a Ecoute la cassette. Vrai ou faux?

- The class should now be ready to begin page 37, '*Le premier cours commence à quelle heure?*' Point out the timetable at the top of the page and tell students to listen to the cassette.

- They should then read the six statements and listen to the cassette again in order to decide whether each sentence is true or false.

⊟

1 Le premier cours commence à huit heures trente.

2 Le deuxième cours commence à neuf heures vingt-cinq.

3 La récréation commence à dix heures vingt.

4 Le troisième cours commence à onze heures vingt-cinq.

5 Le déjeuner commence à midi et demi.

6 Le dernier cours commence à quatre heures et quart.

Solution

1 ✕ 2 ✓ 3 ✓ 4 ✕ 5 ✕ 6 ✓

b Et à ton collège?

- Draw attention to the ordinal numbers in the 'Attention!' feature 'Le marathon', before encouraging students to answer activity B.
- Show them how to write their own information by adapting the six sentences at the top of the page. These can then be practised orally, before moving on to the 'Interview scolaire!' activity.

Interview scolaire! (SB p.37)

AT 1 – 2, AT 2 – 2/3, AT 3 – 2, AT 4 – 2/3

- Focus on the question *Le premier / deuxième / troisième cours commence à quelle heure?* Check understanding and practise repetition of these questions, using numbers on a timetable outline on the board as cues.
- Develop the question, showing how to substitute alternatives to ask *La récréation / le déjeuner / le dernier cours commence à quelle heure?* and practise in a similar way.
- The class can now have concentrated oral practice of these questions and of appropriate responses by playing a Beetle-style game in pairs. For this each pair will need a die and each individual will need a piece of paper numbered 1 – 6 and the written sentences about his or her own timetable prepared earlier in response to 'Et à ton collège?' Students then take it in turns to ask the question ... *commence à quelle heure?*, cued by the

number on the die and the *légende* on page 37. In each case their partner must give an answer ... *commence à ...* , based on his or her own sentences. The questioner can then tick off the corresponding number written on their piece of paper and fill in the time alongside. The winner is the person who manages to tick off all six numbers and collect all six times first. (Cf. the illustrations on page 37 of the Students' Book.)

- Before setting up the game, ask a student to come to the front of the class to help demonstrate how to play.

T: Nous jouons maintenant à deux 'Interview scolaire!' Nous commençons! C'est à moi!

- Shake the die and announce the number, e.g. *Deux!* Write the number on the board, point out the *légende* on page 37, repeat the number and say the question.

T: Le deuxième cours commence à quelle heure?

- Indicate that the demonstration student should reply using his or her sentences. Demonstrate on the board how to tick off the appropriate number on a piece of paper and to draw a clock showing the time which the student gave. Then swap, saying *C'est à toi!*
- Prompt the student to shake the die and announce the number. Point out the *légende* on page 37 again and this time encourage the class to work out what the question should be. Give the appropriate reply and demonstrate that the student should tick off the corresponding number on his / her piece of paper and draw a clock showing the time you gave.
- Continue the demonstration for as long as is necessary, showing how students should aim to win by ticking off all the numbers and filling in clocks on their piece of paper. Stress that students should always ask a question and give a full response, even if they have already ticked off a particular number. (A penalty system of missing goes could be introduced to ensure full responses!) Finally divide the class into pairs and hand out dice so that they can play.

Differentiation – Extension

Toi et moi! (CM 22)

AT 3 – 4, AT 4 – 4

- Higher attainers could now read an extract of a letter from Marc, detailing aspects of his school routine. They should then write a reply giving parallel information about their own routine.

- Afterwards they could perhaps underline similarities and / or differences between the two routines in different colours.

- Finally, they should consider the two school days and decide whether or not they prefer Marc's day to their own, deleting the final sentence at the bottom right of their copymaster as applicable.

T: Vous préférez votre routine ou la routine de Marc? Moi, je préfère ma routine. (Name) – qu'est-ce que tu préfères?

Collège des vampires! (SB pp.38–39)

a Ecoute et lis.

AT 1 – 3/4, AT 3 – 3/4

- Students listen to the class cassette, whilst following the cartoon strip and reading the accompanying text on page 38.

Narrator:	Il est onze heures et demie. Dracula reste au lit. Il est professeur au collège des vampires.
	Dracula mange un sandwich à minuit moins vingt. Le premier cours commence à minuit.
	Le premier vampire arrive au collège à minuit moins le quart.
Pupil vampire:	Bonjour, Monsieur le Comte. Le premier cours, c'est la musique?
Dracula:	Non, le deuxième cours, c'est la musique. Le premier cours c'est l'éducation physique.
Narrator:	Le deuxième vampire arrive à minuit moins dix. Puis le troisième, le quatrième, le cinquième … .

	Le dernier? Le dernier vampire joue au foot.
Dracula:	Dépêchez-vous mes petits vampires, le premier cours commence.
	Il est une heure. Le deuxième cours commence. C'est la musique. Sortez vos instruments, s'il vous plaît.
	Bravo! Il est deux heures. Le déjeuner commence. Bon appétit!

b Ce n'est pas vrai!
Ecris les bonnes phrases.

AT 4 – 1/2

- Students demonstrate understanding by correcting a series of incorrect statements.

Solution

1 Dracula mange un sandwich à **minuit moins vingt**.
2 Le premier cours commence à **minuit**.
3 Le premier vampire arrive à minuit **moins** le quart.
4 Le premier cours, c'est **l'éducation physique**.
5 Le deuxième vampire arrive à minuit **moins** dix.
6 Le deuxième cours commence à **une heure**.
7 Le **déjeuner** commence à deux heures.

c C'est quel mot?

AT 4 – 1/2

- Students complete a cloze text which practises verbs and ordinals.

Solution

A mange **B** commence **C** premier **D** arrive
E dernier **F** joue **G** deuxième

Differentiation – Consolidation and Extension

d Mets dans le bon ordre.

AT 3 – 2/3/4

- Activity D on page 39 consolidates students' understanding of times, ordinals and a small number of verbs. Initially, they should use the text on page 38 to help resequence the sentences in chronological order. Some students may wish to copy the six sentences in the correct sequence within an imaginative shape.

Solution

4, 1, 6, 3, 5, 2

e C'est à toi!

AT 4 – 2/3/4

- Where appropriate, as an additional or alternative activity, students could invent and sequence their own sentences by substituting the coloured words in the original sentences. Again, these could be written within an imaginative shape connected with the context, e.g. a bat, haunted castle, Dracula, pumpkin, cobweb, owl, etc. Suggest a few possibilities and encourage students to think of their own ideas. The results could be made into a wall display afterwards.

T: *Maintenant à vous! Ecrivez une histoire de Dracula!*

Mes découvertes! (CM 23)

AT 3 – level(s) determined by texts, AT 4 – 1/2

- This copymaster can be used in conjunction with any text, to help students understand and develop the skills involved in reading and to give them a framework for recording and learning new vocabulary. Additional copies can be issued as the need arises.

- Show students that the copymaster can remind them of four possible strategies for understanding new language. Explain how to build up a written record of new vocabulary using the sheet, demonstrating how to note new vocabulary in the grids and discussing possible ways of learning it afterwards. Where appropriate, students could be encouraged to transfer their new vocabulary to an ongoing database.

Entre-temps ... (SB p.40)

AT 3 – 1/2/3/4, AT 4 – 1/2

- Students should read the selection of articles on this page for personal interest and enjoyment. Copymaster 23 *'Mes découvertes!'* can be used in conjunction with this page, to help students develop reading skills and widen their vocabulary.

Solution 'Qu'est-ce que c'est?'
cantine

Zut alors! (SB p.41)

AT 1 – 4, AT 3 – 4

- The *'Nous les copains'* cartoon story brings together some of the previous strands of the module in a different context. It can help promote independent reading and more extended listening, and again Copymaster 23, *'Mes découvertes!'*, can be used to support the acquisition of new vocabulary. The story also provides a framework for the *'Porte ouverte!'* activity on page 42.

Narrator:	Nous les copains Chez Olivier
Olivier:	Oh non! Mon cahier de français?
Father:	Olivier! Il est sept heures et demie!
Olivier:	Zut! J'ai raté le bus! ... Papa ... ?
Narrator:	Au collège
Olivier:	Merci. Au revoir!
Louise:	Salut!
Marc:	Salut!
Louise:	Alors Marc, tu aimes les maths?
Marc:	Oui. C'est facile!
Olivier:	Les maths?! Mais le premier cours, c'est le français!
Louise:	Idiot! Aujourd'hui, c'est vendredi. Le premier cours, c'est les maths!
Olivier:	J'ai un problème ... Alors, Marc ...?
Narrator:	Dans la salle de maths
Prof de maths:	Regarde Olivier! Tes devoirs sont excellents, mais ... tu as les mêmes erreurs que Marc ...
Narrator:	A la récré
Olivier:	Zut alors! Moi je déteste les maths.

Porte ouverte! (SB p.42)
Sommaire (SB pp.42–43)

AT 1 – 2/3/4, AT 2 – 2/3/4, AT 3 – 2/3/4, AT 4 – 2/3/4

- In this summative activity students work in groups to produce and act out their own playlet *'Une journé au collège'*, (with sound effects and props if possible), based on a situation at school.

- Talk through the instructions on page 42, pointing out the 'faux ami' *journée* in the title and making sure that students understand the task.

- Help them with the organisation of the activity and show them how to use the support provided by the story and cassette from page 41. Also spend some time talking through the summary of the module's language on pages 42 and 43, showing that this is a useful and important reference.

- Where appropriate, encourage students to learn rather than read their lines. The final playlets can be acted out in front of the rest of the class and perhaps recorded on cassette or video.

Differentiation – Consolidation and Extension

- You may wish to allocate roles to some students; the father, for example, has considerably less to say in the original version of the story.

- Encourage higher attainers to adapt the original text as much as possible and to incorporate their own ideas. Show how to substitute some of the phrases as indicated in the instructions on page 42, eliciting suggestions for possible changes from the students.

- Some students could write up their playlet afterwards. They could be encouraged to redraft their work by word processing it or writing it in pencil first. Rather than producing a script, they may wish to present the playlet in the form of a picture story, using their own drawings. Alternatively, if they have sufficient pictures of the same people, they could produce a photo story using magazine photos.

At this point you may wish to assess students by using the Assessment Copymasters for Modules 1 and 2 (Assessment Test 1, Copymasters 88–91). Teacher's notes and solutions can be found on Copymaster 92 onwards in the Copymasters book.

3 VIVE LES PASSE-TEMPS!

In this module students learn how to:

Talk about their pastimes
Je joue au foot / Je fais de la natation.
Je lis (etc.)

Ask others about their pastimes
Que fais-tu comme passe-temps?
Tu regardes les vidéos? (etc.)

Say what they do not do
Je ne vais pas au cinéma. (etc.)

Understand and use numbers 61 – 100

Buy tickets for a raffle
Un billet s'il te plaît. (etc.)

Ask for help in class
Répétez, s'il vous plaît / Je ne comprends pas /
Comment dit-on ... en anglais? (etc.)

Materials needed
Students' Book pages 44 – 63
Copymasters 24 – 34
Flashcards 34 – 53
Class cassette C
Self-study cassette

New language introduced
Je joue au tennis (de table)/
basket/foot/rugby/hockey
avec l'ordinateur/aux cartes.

Je fais du vélo/patin à roulettes
de la natation
des promenades
Que fais-tu comme passe-temps?
Tu joues ...? / Tu fais ... ? (etc.)
Je regarde la télé / les vidéos
J'écoute de la musique
Je lis
Je vais au cinéma / à la pêche / chez les copains /
en ville.
Je reste au lit
Qu'est-ce que tu préfères comme passe-temps?

En classe:
Comment dit-on ... en anglais/français?
Répétez, s'il vous plaît.
Ça s'écrit comment?
J'ai un problème
Lentement, s'il vous plaît
Je ne comprends pas
C'est quoi en anglais/français?

Revision of
Je/Tu habite(s)/mange(s)/quitte(s)/arrive(s)/
parle(s)

Objectif 1
Que fais-tu comme passe-temps?

F

Student goals   (SB p.44, FC 34 – 45))

- Use the top half of the page to familiarise students with the module's main teaching points and goals. Look at the first objectif and use flashcards 34 – 45 to present the following activities.

T: Bon alors. Objectif un. Que fais-tu comme passe-temps? Regardez bien.

Presentation of activities in 1st person singular: *Je joue .../Je fais ...*

- Use flashcards 34 – 41 to present activities using *Je joue*. Use mime to reinforce meaning.

34 *Je joue au tennis.*

35 *Je joue au tennis de table.*

36 *Je joue au basket.*

37 *Je joue au foot.*

38 *Je joue au rugby.*

39 *Je joue au hockey.*

40 *Je joue avec l'ordinateur.*

41 *Je joue aux cartes.*

- When students feel confident, present flashcards 42 – 45 using *Je fais*. Support these also with mime.

42 *Je fais du vélo.*

43 *Je fais du patin à roulettes.*

44 *Je fais de la natation.*

45 *Je fais des promenades.*

- Use a variety of games to consolidate understanding and to maximise the opportunity for hearing these activities. Pupils can also be asked to respond with a mime. (See Teacher's Notes Introduction page iv.) Using Copymaster 24, introduce the written word as an aid to comprehension, before students move on to practise the subjects orally and/or copywrite.

Les passe-temps   (CM 24)

1 Ecoute et regarde les images. Répète.

AT 1 – 2, AT 2 – 2, AT 3 – 2, AT 4 – 2

- The class cassette and self-study cassette accompanying this activity contain identical material so that students can either use this as a class or individually/at home. They listen to the cassette item, whilst looking at the pictures on copymaster. They then listen again and repeat.

1 Je joue au tennis.

2 Je joue au tennis de table.

3 Je joue au basket.

4 Je joue au foot.

5 Je joue au rugby.

6 Je joue au hockey.

7 Je joue avec l'ordinateur.

8 Je joue aux cartes.

9 Je fais du vélo.

10 Je fais du patin à roulettes.

11 Je fais de la natation.

12 Je fais des promenades.

You will need Copymaster 24, activity 1. As you listen to young people talking about their hobbies on the cassette, look at the pictures.

1 Je joue au tennis.

2 Je joue au tennis de table.

3 Je joue au basket.

4 Je joue au foot.

5 Je joue au rugby.

6 Je joue au hockey.

7 Je joue avec l'ordinateur.

8 Je joue aux cartes.

9 Je fais du vélo.

10 Je fais du patin à roulettes.

11 Je fais de la natation.

12 Je fais des promenades.

Now rewind the cassette and listen again. This time pause the cassette after each sentence and repeat it.

2 Ecoute. C'est quel numéro?

AT 1 – 2

- Students listen to the cassette, presenting brief conversations about pastimes, and write the number of the appropriate picture for each extract.
- They should now be familiar with this activity but, if needed, demonstrate the activity by working through the example.

T: *Je joue au basket. C'est quel numéro?* (Wait for the correct number and then write the number 3 in a replica grid.) *Bravo! Alors, écoutez la cassette. Mettez le bon numéro dans la case.*

– Je joue au basket.

– Je joue aux cartes.

– Je fais de la natation.

– Je joue au tennis de table.

– Je joue avec l'ordinateur.

– Je fais des promenades.

You will need Copymaster 24, activity 2. Listen to the cassette and write the number of the picture that goes with each hobby in the box. The first one has been done for you.

– Je joue au basket.
– Je joue aux cartes.
– Je fais de la natation.
– Je joue au tennis de table.
– Je joue avec l'ordinateur.
– Je fais des promenades.

Solution

3, 8, 11, 2, 7, 12

3 Copie ou mets la bonne phrase.

AT 3 – 2, AT 4 – 2

- Students copy/select and write appropriate sentences from a menu at the bottom of the copymaster.
- Afterwards the copymaster could be used for playing class or small group Bingo. Remind them of games language e.g. *J'ai gagné.*

> **Presentation of:**
> *Que fais-tu comme passe-temps?*
> Activities in 2nd person singular
> *Tu joues … ?/Tu fais … ?*

Que fais-tu comme passe-temps?

(SB p.44)

AT 1 – 2

- Ask *Que fais-tu comme passe-temps?*, then give some possible suggestions with the emphasis on the activity. On receiving a response, repeat the phrase.

T: Que fais-tu comme passe-temps? Tu joues au tennis? Tu fais du vélo? Très bien.

- Repeat the process before asking *'Que fais-tu comme passe-temps?' C'est quoi en anglais?* If there is no answer, give one or two silly suggestions in reply e.g. Do you come to school by plane? but include the correct meaning i.e. What do you do in your free time?

- Repeat the French and ask students to open their books to page 44.

T: Regardez la section 'Que fais-tu comme passe-temps?' Vous allez écouter neuf français parler de leurs passe-temps. (Write numbers 1 – 9 on the board.) *Ouvrez les cahiers et écrivez les numéros 1 – 9.* (Students write the numbers down.) *Trouvez la bonne image.* (Play the first item and check the letter, writing it next to number 1.)

- Students are now ready for the activity.

1 – Que fais tu comme passe-temps?
  – Je joue au foot.
2 – Que fais-tu comme passe-temps?
  – Je fais du vélo.
3 – Que fais-tu comme passe-temps?
  – Je joue avec l'ordinateur.
4 – Que fais-tu comme passe-temps?
  – Je fais du patin à roulettes.
5 – Que fais-tu comme passe-temps?
  – Je joue au basket.
6 – Que fais-tu comme passe-temps?
  – Je joue au tennis.
7 – Et toi, que fais-tu comme passe-temps?
  – Je fais des promenades.
8 – Et toi, Yvette, que fais-tu comme passe-temps?
  – Je fais de la natation.
9 – Et finalement, toi, Michel, que fais-tu comme passe-temps?
  – Moi, je joue aux cartes.

Solution

1 F **2** B **3** H **4** E **5** C **6** A **7** G **8** I **9** D

Et les copains? (SB p.45)

a Lis les passe-temps. Trouve les bonnes images à la page 44.

AT 3 –2

- Students read simple handwritten descriptions of the hobbies of five young people and demonstrate understanding of the written word.

They look at the pictures on page 44 to find the appropriate images for each person, writing the name and the letters of the pictures.

- If students are experiencing difficulty in coping with the handwritten text, read the items aloud. Demonstrate the first item, by reading it aloud and agreeing on which pictures it refers to.

T: Marc, quelles lettres? Oui c'est ça. F et B. Allez.

Solution

Marc F, B   Olivier E, G, H   Louise I, A   Sophie C, H Frédéric D, B, I

b A deux.

AT 1 – 2, AT 2 – 2

- Students use the information about the pastimes as the basis for oral pairwork. They choose and say the name of any of the young people as a prompt for their partner to describe the appropriate pastimes.

T: A deux. Vous allez travailler avec un partenaire. Partenaire A et partenaire B. Par exemple: Partenaire A (Make show of looking for Olivier.) Olivier, que fais-tu comme passe-temps? Partenaire B (Make show of finding the information.) Je fais du patin à roulettes, je fais des promenades et je joue avec l'ordinateur.

- Referring to the page on learning strategies, Module 1 Students' Book page 13, students learn the vocabulary for homework. Test by putting several flashcards on the board as a visual clue. Alternatively invite students to write down a specific number of phrases e.g. any 10.

L'écriture française   (CM 25)

AT 3 – 2, AT 4 – 2

- Students use the upper and lower case alphabet on the copymaster as reference. Draw attention to the French *r* and *s* as this is probably where the main difficulties in reading handwriting occur. Ask students if there are any other letters that seem unusual.
- Students then copy the letters *r* and *s*. They then proceed to single familiar words for pastimes and

then to copying and illustrating simple familar sentences on the theme. Students try their hand at writing their own name in French style.

- Encourage students to work independently but check that they understand the instructions on the copymaster. Mime an artist painting or drawing to make the meaning of *dessine* clear. To explain *Et ton nom?*, demonstrate by writing up the name of a member of the class in English, then in French handwriting.

Differentiation – Extension

- Encourage students, as appropriate, to decipher and use the glossary to look up the handwritten new vocabulary in activity 5, to extend their range of pastimes language. They write the meaning in English.

> **Presentation of further activities in 1st person singular:** *Je regarde .../J'écoute .../Je lis/ Je vais ...*

Encore des passe-temps!
(SB p.46, FC 46 – 53)

AT 1 – 1

- Present flashcards 46 – 53.

   46 *Je regarde la télé.*
   47 *Je regarde les vidéos.*
   48 *J'écoute de la musique.*
   49 *Je lis.*
   50 *Je vais au cinéma.*
   51 *Je vais à la pêche.*
   52 *Je vais chez les copains.*
   53 *Je vais en ville.*

- Use mime to accompany the flashcards to reinforce understanding. Check understanding either by playing *Jacques a dit*, when students respond with a mime or by pointing to/putting on or taking the flashcards from the board. Introduce the written form and continue with activities matching spoken/visual with the written form.

3 Vive les passe-temps!

a Ecoute. Qui parle?

AT1 – 2, AT3 – 3, AT4 – 3

- Students listen to the cassette and demonstrate understanding of the new pastimes by matching the speaker with a visual, presented in the form of a spaghetti diagram.

1 Je vais au cinéma.
2 Je lis.
3 Je regarde la télé.
4 Je vais chez les copains.
5 Je vais en ville.
6 Je vais à la pêche.
7 J'écoute de la musique.

Solution

1 Sophie   2 Olivier   3 Sandrine   4 Marc   5 Claire
6 Yannick   7 Louise

b Vrai ou faux?

AT 3 – 3

- Students demonstrate understanding of written sentences about the pastimes shown in the spaghetti diagram at the top of the page.

Solution

Sandrine – vrai Yannick – faux Claire – vrai
Louise – faux Olivier – faux

Jeu de passe-temps   (CM 26, 2 pages)

AT 1 – 3, AT 2 – 3/4, AT 3 – 3, AT 4 – 3/4

- Students use the first sheet of Copymaster 26 to revise the first set of pastimes.
- They use the second sheet to reinforce their pronunciation of the pastimes, flashcards 46 – 53 by listening to the cassette and repeating.

- Je regarde la télé.
- Je regarde les vidéos.
- J'écoute de la musique.
- Je lis.

- Je vais au cinéma.
- Je vais à la pêche.
- Je vais chez des copains.
- Je vais en ville.

- Students then move on to copywrite these phrases.
- They then use the cut up pages to play Pelmanism using the full range of pastimes, matching visuals to the written word, working in groups of four. It is helpful to photocopy each group's set on to a different coloured card or to ask each group to store their cards in separate envelopes to ease storage.
- Draw their attention to the games vocabulary on the top of sheet I and encourage them to use it. Retain the cut cards to support the oral activity (described below) based on Students' Book, page 46, 'C'est quel mot?'
- Using the days of the week in the section 'Extra!' students, working individually or in pairs, can arrange the cards with the written language to describe their ideal week of activities either orally or in writing. They can also express an opinion of those activities.

Differentiation

AT 2 – 4, AT 4 – 4

- Encourage appropriate students to speak/write from memory by using the visual prompts only.

C'est quel mot?   (SB p.46)

AT 3 – 3, AT 4 – 3

- Return to the Students' Book. Students select words from a menu to complete sentences about pastimes.

Solution

A regarde   B vais   C écoute   D musique   E lis
F livre

Differentiation – Extension

AT 4 – 4

- Encourage students, as appropriate, to write out the sentences without looking at the menu.
- For further practice ask students to write down their top five activities, using the sentences on the

page for support. Alternatively students could work from Copymaster 26, '*Jeu de passe-temps*' for a full menu. They then interview five or six people. Demonstrate the activity on the board/OHP.

T: Ecrivez les numéros 1 – 5. (Write on the board.) Qu'est-ce que tu préfères comme passe-temps? (As if talking aloud to yourself.) Moi, je préfère … (State your preference within students' known language) … Je vais au cinéma. Ça, c'est numéro 1. (Write it at the top of your list. Continue until the students are sure of the task.)

- Then invite them to exchange their information by interviewing at least four others. Students who work more quickly will be able to circulate as soon as they have written up their preferences and can be encouraged to report either in writing or orally what one other person has said.

Differentiation – Extension

- Encourage appropriate students to speak/write from memory by using the visual prompts only.

- Remind students of strategies for learning by heart. Students learn either a limited range of language from Students' Book page 46 or the full range from the first uncut section of Copymaster 26.

Comment ça se prononce? (SB p.47)

a Ecoute, lis et chante!

AT 1 – 1/2, AT 2 – 1/2

- Engage the students in some initial fun practice of the sounds *-ain, -in, -on, -an, -en* to raise awareness of nasal sounds. They then go to Students' Book page 47, where they relate the nasal sounds to the different written forms to the tune of 'Twinkle, twinkle, little star'.

in, in, on, on
in, en, in
ain, ain, an, an
ain, en, ain!

- This is also provided on the self-study cassette for extra practice and enjoyment.

You will need Students' Book page 47, activity A. First listen and look at the sounds in your book. Then listen as many times as you like, joining in. Then close your book and try joining in.

in, in, on, on
in, en, in
ain, ain, an, an
ain, en, ain!

b Ecoute et lis. Ecoute, lis et répète.

AT 1 – 1/2, AT 2 – 1/2

- Students listen and read, then listen, read and repeat the words and phrases on cassette. They are first presented with single known words containing the nasal sounds in their different written forms before using them within familiar sentences on the theme of pastimes.

patin copain
natation Lyon
en Sandrine
Je fais du patin avec mon copain.
Je fais du patin avec mon copain.
Je fais de la natation à Lyon.
Je fais de la natation à Lyon.
Je vais en ville avec Sandine.
Je vais en ville avec Sandrine.

Now look at Students' Book page 47, activity B. First listen and read the words. Then listen and read the words, pause the cassette and repeat them carefully.

patin copain
natation Lyon

en Sandrine

Je fais du patin avec mon copain.

Je fais du patin avec mon copain.

Je fais de la natation à Lyon.

Je fais de la natation à Lyon.

Je vais en ville avec Sandine.

Je vais en ville avec Sandrine.

c Lis et prononce. Ecoute la cassette.

AT 1 – 1, AT 2 –1

- Students anticipate pronunciation cued by visual prompts then check their pronunciation with the cassette.

A Pardon?

B Alain

C Fantastique!

D Intéressant!

E le trente janvier

You will need Students' Book page 47, activity C. Say the words then check your pronunciation, listening to the cassette to see how well you managed.

A Pardon?

B Alain

C Fantastique!

D Intéressant!

E le trente janvier

C'est la vie! (SB p.48)

a Ecoute et lis.

AT 1 – 4, AT 3 – 4

- Before going into the cartoon story of Robinson on his island, revise the activities using flashcards 34 – 53.
- Direct students to the story which they follow frame by frame, supported by the cassette (including sound effects) and the visuals. They

will probably need to hear the tape twice and then have an opportunity for quiet reading to familiarise themselves with the text.

Salut! Je m'appelle Robinson. J'ai quarante-deux ans. J'habite à Waikiki.

Lundi, je fais de la natation à six heures.

A sept heures, je mange le petit déjeuner et je lis.

Le matin, je fais du vélo et je joue au rugby avec mes copains.

Je mange le déjeuner à midi et je regarde la télé. J'adore la télé.

Puis je reste au lit et j'écoute de la musique.

L'après-midi à trois heures, je fais des promenades et je vais chez mes copains.

Le soir, je joue au basket ou je vais à la pêche.

Et mardi, mercredi, jeudi ...?

b Vrai ou faux?

AT 3 – 3

- Students demonstrate understanding of the written language on page 48 by completing the 'Vrai ou faux?' activity on page 49.

Solution

1 faux **2** vrai **3** faux **4** faux **5** vrai **6** faux

c Trouve le bon mot.

AT 3 – 3, AT 4 – 3

- Students show understanding of the text, focusing on verbs, by completing sentences from a menu of verbs. They may either write the letter of the correct verb for each sentence or rewrite the complete sentences in their exercise books.

Solution

1 A Je **vais** chez mes copains.

2 F J'**écoute** de la musique.

3 E Je **mange** le déjeuner.

4 D J'**habite** à Waikiki.

5 C Je **joue** au rugby.

6 G Je **fais** du vélo.

7 B Je **regarde** la télé.

Attention! (SB p.49)

- Draw attention to the regular verb ending *Je ...-e* and also to the three verbs students have met with the ending *...-s*. Students may find a *pause anglaise* helpful for this discussion. Ask students if they can remember other verbs, cueing them with an example e.g. *Je quitte*. Make a note of their suggestions on the board and compare them with the words in the *'Rappel'* box. Students can hunt for and make a note of where the verbs occur in other parts of their book.

T: Tournez à la page 34 'La vie scolaire'. (Alternatively direct different students to different pages e.g. 'Nous les copains', Module 1 page 11/'Collège des vampires', Module 2 page 38.) Trouvez les verbes e.g. je mange. Faites une liste. (Add any 'new' finds to their list on the board.)

Differentiation – Extension

- Encourage some students to make up their own grammar reminder notes and to read them out to the rest of the class. Their explanation can further support the understanding of others.

> Alternatively, you may wish to use Copymaster 77. Students complete notes on the 1st person singular and keep them for reference.

Sondage (SB p.50)

AT 1 – 3, AT 2 – 3, AT 3 – 3, AT 4 – 3 / 4

- Remind students of the question *Que fais-tu comme passe-temps?* and elicit individual responses. Direct students to the model conversation at the top of Students' Book page 50. Students can read the question and listen to you read the response.

T: Regardez la question, 'Que fais-tu comme passe-temps?' Répétez la question ... (Pause for class to repeat, then read the answer.) Je fais du vélo, je vais au cinéma et je joue avec l'ordinateur.

- Ask for two volunteers to take over the two roles. Ask for further volunteers to establish the pattern for all members of the class, before the students work with a partner using the text. Prepare students for the limited *sondage* to be carried out in groups of five.

- Students look at the photo of the five *copains* and study how the results of this survey were recorded by jotting down a significant word and making a tally. Alternatively select a number of flashcards, displaying them on the board. Put the question to an appropriate individual. Write up the abridged response(s) and put a tally mark beside the response.

- Students then make groups of five and can either use the flashcards as a visual cue or can refer to the model on the page. After a set time limit, ask each group, *Quel est le passe-temps numéro un de ton groupe?* Write the result on the board and find out which is the most popular pastime.

Grimaud (SB p.50)

AT 1 – 3/4, AT 3 – 4

- Students listen to the cassette featuring Grimaud. Draw attention to the additional unknown language e.g. *Spectreville*. Encourage students to guess what *Spectreville* might mean. Invite students to listen again and to read the description in pairs.

> Je m'appelle Grimaud.
> J'habite à Spectreville.
> Je joue au basket avec mes copains et je fais du vélo – oh – oh!
> Le soir je fais des promenades.
> Je vais chez mes copains et je mange ... !
> Le matin je reste au lit.

AT 4 – 3/4

- Students can use Grimaud as a model, and draw and write their own version, simply changing the pastimes.

Differentiation – Extension

AT 4 – 3/4

- Encourage others to make up their own picture description, based on Grimaud. Alternatively students can use drawings or photos of famous people and magazine cuttings but with the health warning to use a full range of known language as they are not able to manipulate the use of *je joue au ... etc./je fais du ... etc./je vais au ... etc.*

J'ai un problème (SB p.51)

a Ecoute et lis.

AT 1 – 4, AT 2 – 3/4, AT 3 – 4

- Students listen to the class cassette, whilst following the text of the *'Classe d'enfer'* cartoon strip in their books. This features classroom language 'Asking for help'.

Teacher:	Numéro 1. Comment dit-on 'pen' en français?
Girl:	Répétez, s'il vous plaît, monsieur.
Boy:	Lentement, s'il vous plaît, monsieur.
Teacher:	Comment dit-on 'pen' en français?
Girl:	Monsieur, je ne comprends pas.
Teacher:	Silence! 'Pen', comment ca s'écrit?
Girl:	Répétez, monsieur!
Boy:	J'ai un problème, monsieur!
Girl:	Lentement, monsieur!
Teacher:	Oh là, là! Cette classe! … er … un moment … Oh, pardon!

- Play the cassette through once continuously. Then play it a second time, pausing the cassette after each frame of the cartoon strip. Demonstrate the linking of the text to the cassette and encourage students to point to the relevant speech bubbles as they hear the language.
- Use appropriate actions to support understanding e.g. slow tortoise-like movement for *lentement*/ scratching of head for *J'ai un problème*. Use British and French flags to assist understanding of the question *Comment dit-on …?* This approach will relate to the visuals used on Copymaster 27.
- Referring to the visuals in the cartoon strip, encourage students to work out the meaning of the following phrases:

Comment dit-on en français / anglais?
Répétez, s'il vous plaît. (Students should be familiar with this from Module 1.)
Lentement, s'il vous plaît.
Je ne comprends pas.

Comment ça s'écrit?
J'ai un problème.

- Play the cassette through once more to consolidate understanding.

Au secours! (CM 27)

1 Ecoute, lis et répète.

AT 1 – 3, AT 2 – 3

- Students first listen to the classroom language on the tape, whilst reading the items. They then repeat the phrases and check their pronunciation with the cassette.

1 Comment dit-on 'ruler' en français?
2 Répétez, s'il vous plaît.
3 Ça s'écrit comment?
4 J'ai un problème.
5 Comment dit-on 'règle' en anglais?
6 Lentement, s'il vous plaît.
7 Je ne comprends pas.
Extra!
C'est quoi en anglais?
C'est quoi en français?

You will need Copymaster 27, activity 1. Look at the phrases that you have already met in *'La classe d'enfer'*. Listen to the phrases on the cassette. Pause the cassette and repeat each phrase, paying careful attention to how it is said.

1 Comment dit-on 'ruler' en français?
2 Répétez, s'il vous plaît.
3 Ça s'écrit comment?
4 J'ai un problème.
5 Comment dit-on 'règle' en anglais?
6 Lentement, s'il vous plaît.
7 Je ne comprends pas.
Extra!
C'est quoi en anglais?
C'est quoi en français?

- Remind students of the use of *C'est quoi en anglais?* as an alternative to *Comment dit-on ...?*

2 Relie les phrases et les images.

AT 3 – 3, AT 4 – 3 / 4

- Students check understanding by matching the written sentences to the appropiate visual.

J'ai un problème (SB p.51)
b Comment dit-on?

AT 1 – 3, AT 2 – 3, AT 4 – 3

- Students use the pictures as cues for oral/written production of the classroom language. This can be done as a class, group or pairwork activity.

Au secours! (CM 27)
3 A toi! Fais ta classe d'enfer.

AT 4 – 3/4

- Students complete the speech bubbles in the cartoon pictures.

T: Regardez les deux images. Voilà le professeur qui parle. (Mime, then give some examples.) Comment dit-on 'bicycle' en français? ou bien, Comment dit-on 'patin' en anglais? Il y a d'autres possibilités? (Students give other suggestions. Repeat the process with the pupil's empty speech bubble.) Alors, c'est à vous. Imaginez et écrivez.

Differentiation – Extension

AT 4 – 3/4

- Students can make up their own more extensive 'Classe d'enfer' cartoon strip, referring to Students' Book page 51 for support.

Je parle et je comprends! (CM 28)

AT 1 – 2/3, AT 2 – 3, AT 3 – 2

- Students use this summative copymaster as support for classroom language. Draw their attention to all the classroom language that they have met so far, with special emphasis on the earlier language. Revise each section. Return to

the appropriate 'Classe d'enfer' cartoon strips in modules 1 and 2 to refresh students, pausing to exploit the language in the following way:

Section 1: Actions
Students respond physically to the commands in this section. Encourage students to take over the role of giving the instructions. This can be played in a *Jacques a dit* game.

Section 2: Sortez vos affaires / Passe-moi ...
Expand the language in the first box by using other classroom objects e.g. *Tu as une règle?* and encourage students to ask one another. Contrive situations to provoke the language in the second box, *Passe-moi ...* for example ask for a pencil to complete the register. Alternatively individual students can respond to a visual prompt such as the visuals in 'Classe d'enfer, Comment-dit on?', Module 2. Encourage other students to join in a 'Classe d'enfer' situation.

Section 3: Au secours!
Draw attention to the latest classroom language.

- Students may keep a copy of this page for easy reference in class. Give it a name that they will easily identify e.g. 'Rappel. En classe' and insist on use of this language in the classroom. An A3 copy or copies could be on permanent display around the classroom for easy reference. Set up a system of reward to encourage consistent attempts to use the language.

Objectif 2
Questions et réponses

New language introduced:
*Tu regardes ...?/Tu écoutes ... ?/Tu lis?/Tu vas ... ?
Je ne joue/fais/vais (etc.) pas.*

Revision of opinions

Student goals (SB p. 52)

- Remind students of the second goal for this module.

Presentation of activities in 2nd person singular: *Tu regardes/écoutes/lis/vas?*

Questions, toujours des questions!

(SB p.52)

a Ecoute et lis.

AT 1 – 3, AT 2 – 3

- Use the cartoon strip, supported by the class cassette to introduce questions in the *tu* form. Play the cassette through continuously, then play it again asking the students to follow and to point to the relevant speech bubbles.

> – Thérèse, tu joues avec l'ordinateur?
> – Non, maman!
> – Tu regardes la télé?
> – Non, maman!
> – Tu écoutes de la musique?
> – Tu lis?
> – Non, maman. Je reste au lit!

- Pick up the three questions *Tu joues?, Tu regardes?, Tu écoutes?* and exploit them using the activity flashcards. Concentrate on one verb at a time. Write on the board *Tu + verb + flashcard + ?* to give the construction of the question. Say the question. By changing the flashcard, show how the questions can vary within the established sequence of the sentence.
- Now teach the three irregular verb forms *Tu fais?, Tu lis?, Tu vas?* by the same method.

b Retrouve et copie les bonnes questions.

AT 3 – 3, AT 4 – 3

- Students demonstrate their understanding of the questions by matching split sentences and copying them out in full. Read out the correctly matched questions and encourage students to read out their completed/corrected questions after you.

Solution

1 Tu joues avec l'ordinateur?
2 Tu lis un livre?
3 Tu fais du vélo?
4 Tu vas au cinéma?
5 Tu regardes les vidéos?
6 Tu écoutes de la musique?

- Students may then ask their neighbour those same questions, accepting a *Oui/Non* answer.

Attention!

- Look at the questions in the split sentences again and encourage students to note the endings of *joues/regardes/écoutes* and to say what the endings have in common. Then ask them what the other verbs, *lis/fais/vas* have in common. Whilst exploring the patterns, students will probably welcome the use of a *pause anglaise*.
- Then look at the *'Attention!'* section and point out that there are other verbs that share the ending *-es* with *tu*, drawing attention to the examples given. Stress that it is *tu* that is controlling the endings, by underlining or using colour to highlight the connection.
- Explore verbs that are familiar to the students from previous modules in addition to *habites/manges* e.g. *Tu quittes? Tu arrives? Tu parles (français)?*
- Then practise the full range of *-er* verbs and the three irregular verbs provided in the *'Attention!'* box, cueing with questions and flashcards to remind students of the structure.

> At this point you may wish to use Copymaster 78. Students complete notes on the 2nd person singular and keep them for reference.

c A deux.

AT 1 – 3, AT 2 – 3, AT 3 – 3, AT 4 – 3

- Working in pairs, students write down as many different questions as possible within a time limit. Emphasise the importance of checking the endings of the verbs. Extend the activity into oral work by asking one pair to work with another pair to ask and answer one another's questions. Alternatively, where a time limit is unhelpful, students can prepare their questions as homework ready for use in the next lesson.
- The questions form support for the 'Happy families' game on Copymaster 29.

Jeu de questions! (CM 29, 2 pages)

AT 1 – 2, AT 2 – 2, AT 3 – 2

- Prepare students for the *Jeu de questions!*, 'Happy families' game, that requires students to ask the full range of known questions. Either transfer the copymaster onto OHT or make a quick sketch of any card e.g. *Je fais du vélo* and demonstrate how to play.

- Write up the question *Tu fais ...?* Work with a volunteer student who is given another card in the *Je fais* family, preferably the last one on the card i.e. *Je fais du patin à roulettes*. Point to *Je fais du vélo* on your sketch.

T: **(Pointing to yourself.) *Je fais du vélo*. (As if you have a good idea, ask the volunteer.) *Tu fais des promenades?* (The student answers *Non*. Ask the second question on the card.) *Tu fais de la natation?* (The student continues, *Non*. Then ask the final question.) *Tu fais du patin à roulettes?* (The student hands over his/her card, saying *Oui*.)**

- With the OHT version, show the range of the families, writing up the questions to use for each family, i.e. *Tu vas ...?* etc. Alternatively, direct students to Students' Book page 52, '*Attention!*' for the full menu of questions.
- Explain how the game is won.

T: Imaginez j'ai quatre familles. J'ai gagné!

- Students now form groups of four, each student has five cards. Remind students of their games language, *C'est à moi* etc. and if appropriate introduce them to the new phrases *Tu triches!* and *J'en ai marre* at the top of sheet I. To ensure equal participation, students can play in rotation i.e. play passes to the next person after each question.

Differentiation – Extension

AT2 – 3

- Students use the '*Extra!*' family, that features eating at different times, and uses familiar vocabulary in a new context. Remind students of the necessary question form, *Tu manges ...?*

Mots croisés (CM 30)

AT 3 – 3, AT 4 – 2

- Redirect students to Students' Book page 49 to revise verbs in the *je* form and draw out the difference with verbs using *tu* on Students' Book page 52 i.e. *je* + regular -*e* and irregular -*s* and *tu* + regular -*es* and irregular with special attention to *vas*.

- Direct students to the crossword on Copymaster 30 to give extra practice in recognition of the verb forms and endings. Here they complete the crossword by using cloze sentence clues. A menu of words supports them.

Solution

1 MANGE **2** LIS **3** VAS **4** REGARDES
5 ECOUTES **6** FAIS **7** JE **8** HABITE
9 HABITES **10** FAIS **11** AIMES **12** VAIS
13 TU **14** ECOUTE **15** AIME

Differentiation – Extension

- Encourage some students to cover the menu and complete the crossword totally or as far as possible from memory.

> **Presentation of activities with negative in 1st person singular:** *Je ne joue pas (etc.)*

Ce n'est pas vrai! (SB p.53)

a Ecoute la cassette. C'est quelle image?

AT 1 – 3

- Use the cassette item to present negative sentences. Students follow the taped conversation between an interviewer and a very negative 'person' about pastimes. They hear questions and replies using the negative, until a positive statement is made in the punch line. They are supported, as they listen, by mini flashcard visuals which are slashed through to indicate the negative. The visuals are in the same order as on the tape.
- Play through once continuously, then encourage students to point to the visuals as they hear them. Play a third time.

A – Salut! Que fais-tu comme passe-temps? Tu joues au foot?
   – Non. Je ne joue pas au foot.

B – Tu joues au tennis?
   – Non. Je ne joue pas au tennis.

C – Tu fais du vélo?

– Non. Je ne fais pas de vélo.

D – Tu fais du patin à roulettes?

– Non. Je ne fais pas de patin à roulettes. Je ne fais pas de sport!

E – Alors, tu vas chez les copains.

Non, je ne vais pas chez les copains.

F – Tu lis?

– Non, je ne lis pas.

– Alors, que fais-tu comme passe-temps?

– Moi, je regarde la télé ... et je mange!

b Regarde les images. Mets dans le bon ordre.

AT 3 – 2

• Students demonstrate understanding by matching the written sentences to the mini flashcard visuals above.

Solution

1 F **2** A **3** D **4** E **5** C **6** B

Positif ou négatif? (CM 31)

1 Ecoute et lis. Ecoute, lis et répète.

AT 1 – 2/3, AT 2 – 2/3, AT 3 – 2/3

• Students use the self-study cassette with the copymaster, that combines questions, positive and negative replies to the tune of 'We shall not be moved'. They listen and read before joining in the three verses.

You will need Copymaster 31, activity 1. As you follow the words on the cassette, you will probably recognise the tune that goes with them. Listen again and this time, try to join in. You may want to try again, clicking your fingers or clapping and stamping to the rhythm.

| Tu vas? | Je vais | Je ne vais pas |
| Tu vas? | Je vais | Je ne vais pas |

| Tu vas? | Je vais | Je ne vais pas |

Je ne vais pas au cinéma!

Tu fais?	Je fais	Je ne fais pas
Tu fais?	Je fais	Je ne fais pas
Tu fais?	Je fais	Je ne fais pas

Je ne fais pas de vélo!

Tu écoutes?	J'écoute	Je n'écoute pas
Tu écoutes?	J'écoute	Je n'écoute pas
Tu écoutes?	J'écoute	Je n'écoute pas

Je n'écoute pas la radio!

2 A toi! Ecris.

AT4 – 3

• Students then fill in a positive and negative face, supported by a menu of words.

Differentiation – Extension

AT4 – 4

• Encourage some students to use a wider range of verbs referring to Students' Book pages 48/49/53.

Attention! (SB p.53)

• Return to Students' Book, page 53 to practise the negative orally. Students needing a high level of support can read the sentences. Most students can respond to the slashed visuals A – F.

• When they are confident, invite them to look at the visual representation in 'Attention!', drawing out the structure of the sentence.

• Give students the opportunity to practise the structure. Write the parts of the verb on separate pieces of paper to be put up on the board e.g. *je + regarde*. Use different coloured paper for the negative, writing *ne/pas* on two separate pieces. Write possible ends of sentence e.g. *la télé/les vidéos* on further pieces of paper. Put up all the pieces of paper in random order. Focus on one verb at a time.

T: ***Je ne regarde pas la télé.*** **(Invite students to arrange the parts of the sentence in the correct order.)**

- Then use *Je ne lis pas/Je ne vais pas*. Introduce *Je fais du/Je ne fais pas de* as a separate issue to highlight that *du* changes to *de*. If appropriate, demonstrate by using a different coloured card with *de* that a further change is needed with *Je ne fais pas*.

- Draw attention to '*Extra!*' at the bottom of the page. A number of students will learn the negative as a lexical item and it is important to let them enjoy the sentence manipulation rather then making it into a heavy grammatical activity. Encourage higher attaining students to add to their own 'grammar' rules notes.

> At this point you may wish to use Copymaster 79. Students complete notes on the use of the negative and keep them for reference.

A deux   (SB p.53)

AT 1 – 3, AT 2 – 3

- Direct students to the pairwork activity, which practises using question and negative forms. Quickly revise the question forms or direct students to Students' Book page 52. Encourage appropriate students to make up further questions.

C'est impossible!   (SB p.54)

AT 1 – 4, AT 2 – 4, AT 3 – 4

- Use page 54 and the class cassette to consolidate all the questions, positive and negative statements in a '*Nous les copains*' cartoon strip about the *copains* looking after a small child. Play the cassette as support, asking students to follow the story in their books.

Chez Marc

Louise:	Oh, non, Annie arrive.
Marc:	Salut, Annie. Ça va?
Marc:	Annie, tu joues au foot?
Annie:	Non, je ne joue pas au foot!
Louise:	Tu fais du vélo, Annie?
Annie:	Non, je ne fais pas de vélo. C'est moche!

Olivier:	Alors Annie, tu joues avec l'ordinateur?
Annie:	Non, je ne joue pas avec l'ordinateur. C'est nul!
Marc:	Tu lis?
Louise:	C'est impossible!
Annie:	Non, je ne lis pas.
Marc, Olivier, Louise:	Tu regardes la télé?
Annie:	Oui, je regarde la télé!
Annie:	J'adore ça. C'est super.

- Pull out the threads of the language e.g. How many questions? How many negative statements? Point out the opinions and in particular the new *C'est impossible!* This could be the password for the day.

- Revise opinions from Module 2, Copymaster 12 including those in the '*Extra!*' section e.g. *C'est fantastique/marrant/nul*.

- Redirect students to page 54 '*Nous les copains*' and encourage students to think of alternatives to those opinions expressed by the characters in the story.

- Play the cassette again for further familiarisation before asking students to read out the story in parts as a class/in groups or to act it out in groups of four.

Differentiation – Extension

- Encourage appropriate students to extend the dialogue by asking more questions and replies and by expressing more opinions.

Passe-temps et opinions   (CM 32)

AT 1 – 3, AT 2 – 4, AT 3 – 3, AT 4 – 4

- Prepare students for the oral pairwork on the copymaster by using a selection of significant flashcards to elicit:
  - questions by writing a question mark above the flashcard
  - positive answers by writing a tick
  - negative answers by putting a cross.

- Look at the copymaster, where students will meet the same conventions.

  Practise one or two of the questions from the visuals that head the columns. Write the question on the board for further support. Then ask the class what the next visual represents and continue the process for revision and to ensure understanding.

- Then look at the *Légende* to remind students of the conventions used to record their answers. Read through the opinions column and demonstrate the abbreviations.

T: *C'est super ... s.* **(Write the letter on the board.)** *C'est chic ...?* **(Cue student response.)** *... c.*

- Now demonstrate the activity by using the first column, working with an appropriate student. Cue the student by pointing to the visual at the top of the first column. If necessary prompt the student. As you reply, mark up *Moi* with a tick or a cross and the abbreviation and point to the corresponding opinions section. Now ask the student, *Tu lis?* Wait for a reply and write *toi* with a tick or a cross and the abbreviation, pointing to the corresponding opinions section.
- Draw attention to the written support at the bottom of the copymaster, before students work independently in pairs.
- Extend the activity by suggesting that students either use a selection of their results as the basis for a recorded interview or for a written version.

Lettre d'un corres.   (SB p.55)

AT 3 – 4, AT 4 – 3/4

- Students read a penfriend letter containing information about freetime activities and preferences, consolidating the language of the module. To support students in reading the full text, read it aloud.
- Encourage students to look at and deduce the meaning of the new language e.g. *une équipe/l'entraînement/c'est sérieux*. Ask in English what helped them work out the meaning, cf reading skills, Module 2, Copymaster 23.

a Vrai ou faux?

AT3 – 3

- Students now have an opportunity to read the letter for themselves, before they demonstrate understanding by completing the '*Vrai ou faux?*' activity.

Solution

1 faux **2** faux **3** vrai **4** faux **5** faux

b Ecris une lettre à Michel.

AT 3 – 2, AT 4 – 3/4

- Read out the addressed envelope and the half hidden reply. Encourage students to complete the reply orally. Explain that they are going to write a reply.
- Direct them to Michel's letter and draw attention to the date and the use of *cher/chère,* as some students may wish to write to a girl. Also remind them how to finish the letter off, looking at Michel's ending.
- Raise awareness of the questions that Michel has asked. Remind students to look carefully at Michel's letter and the sentences in the '*Vrai ou faux?*' section and to look back at the previous pages, picking out language from the various texts.
- (Some students may find it more appropriate to complete and write out the half hidden extract from the letter on page 55.)

Differentiation – Extension

AT4 – 3/4

- Encourage appropriate students to write as far as possible from memory. They can write their first draft in pencil or on word processor, prior to checking and redrafting.

Entre-temps ...   (SB p.56)

AT 3 – 2/3/4

- Encourage students to use this page as independently as possible and to read the selection of texts for interest and enjoyment. Little or no exploitation should be necessary as most of the language is familiar by now. Students should use Copymaster 23, '*Mes découvertes*' to help them develop reading skills and widen their vocabulary.

Solution

'Qu'est-ce que c'est?' karaté

Objectif 3   Rendez-vous

New language introduced

Numbers 61 – 100

Mon numéro est … /Le numéro de mon billet est …

Un billet, s'il vous plaît

Voilà

Bonne chance!

Revision of:

Tu t'appelles comment?

Student goals   (SB p.57)

- Remind the class of the third goal for this Module. Point to the third *objectif* on page 57 and say, *Objectif trois – Rendez-vous.*

- Revise numbers 1 – 60 with a variety of board games e.g. *Effacez, Encerclez le bon numéro*, or team games: hearing a number and writing it in a figure and/or writing a number on the board in response to a written number.

Presentation of numbers 61 – 100

Nombres toréadors   (CM 33)

AT 1 – 1, AT 2 – 1

- Play the first verse of the class cassette item *'Nombres toréadors'*, set to the Toreadors' song from Carmen. Write up numbers 61 – 72 in the sequence shown in the tapescript. Students listen whilst looking at the numbers.

- Play the cassette a second time before encouraging the students to join in the verse.

- Then write the numbers in words alongside the figure or replace the figure. Students listen again but this time following the written words. *'Nombres toréadors'* is also recorded on the self-study cassette and students can use it in conjunction with Copymaster 33 for individual study/homework.

soixante et un, soixante-deux,
soixante-trois, soixante-quatre,
soixante-cinq, soixante-six,
soixante-sept, soixante-huit,

soixante-neuf, soixante-dix,
soixante et onze, soixante-douze

You will need Copymaster 33. Look at the numbers 61 to 72 as you hear them. They are set to music that you will probably recognise. Listen as many times as you need to get the rhythm, then join in. See if you can make up your own verse or verses with another batch of numbers.

soixante et un, soixante-deux,
soixante-trois, soixante-quatre,
soixante-cinq, soixante-six,
soixante-sept, soixante-huit,
soixante-neuf, soixante-dix,
soixante et onze, soixante-douze

- Draw attention to 70/72. Revise numbers 11 – 19. Invite students to anticipate what 73 is and continue through to 79.

Les nombres du loto   (CM 33)

AT 1 – 1, AT 2 – 1, AT 3 – 1

- Direct students to the first column of numbers 60 – 79. Call out the numbers. Students point to the corresponding word and repeat the numbers. They can then use the first column to play Bingo. They are familiar with the game and should be able to start playing without any further explanation than an invitation to make their grid and choose an agreed amount of numbers e.g. *Choisissez neuf numéros.* Play as a class, before handing the activity over to be played in small groups.

- Present numbers 80 – 100 using the second column of the copymaster, to follow, as they listen to the remaining verses of *'Nombres toréadors'*.

soixante-treize, soixante-quatorze,
soixante-quinze, soixante-seize,
soixante-dix-sept, soixante-dix-huit,
soixante-dix-neuf, quatre-vingts,
quatre-vingt-un, quatre-vingt-deux,
quatre-vingt-trois, quatre-vingt-quatre

quatre-vingt-cinq, quatre-vingt-six,
quatre-vingt-sept, quatre-vingt-huit,
quatre-vingt-neuf, quatre-vingt-dix,
quatre-vingt-onze, quatre-vingt-douze,
quatre-vingt-treize, quatre-vingt-quatorze,
quatre-vingt-quinze, quatre-vingt-seize

quatre-vingt-dix-sept, quatre-vingt-dix-huit,
quatre-vingt-dix-neuf, cent

- To help students to become familar with the numbers, call out any number between 80 – 100 and ask students to point to or to write down the figure. Check understanding, then write up some numbers in the written form for students to give the number in figures.

- Encourage students to discover the different way of counting 60 + 10, 60 + 11 and to look across the columns at the similarities between 60 + 12 = 72 and 80 + 12 = 92. This will help some students who are numerically inclined to remember the sequence. Say the sequence through rhythmically inviting students to clap along, before they chant the numbers and clap.

- Students should be able to play Bingo, first making a grid and choosing an agreed number of numbers from the second column.

- At the end of the lesson, leave just enough time before the bell to see how high students can count before the bell goes. Accompany the counting with tones and gestures of despair, as the counting gets higher and higher. Adopt this way of ending the lesson for the next few sessions.

- Students use the self-study cassette and Copymaster 33 to learn a selection of key numbers (either/and oral/written production) to include 61/70/71/72/80/81/90/91 using the learning skills page 13, Module 1.

Messages secrets (CM 34)

AT 1 – 1/2, AT 2 – 1/2

- Cut this copymaster in half and prepare students for the information-gap exercise, showing them how to work in pairs to solve the four coded messages. For the demonstration write the following code in a box on the board/OHP:

60 = R
63 = A
74 = N
79 = U
86 = E
91 = S
100 = P

- Demonstrate how to decode a letter.

T: Soixante-trois, c'est quelle lettre? **(Point at the box on the board and wait for the answer 'A'. Insist on use of the French alphabet. Repeat the process with another number e.g.)** *Et soixante-quatorze?*

- When students understand the principle, tell them to look at the code on the board and to use it to write down the letter corresponding to each number which you are going to call out. Then read the following sequence of numbers slowly in French: 91, 79, 100, 86, 60, giving the students time to decode the mystery word *Super*. Some students may need to use Copymaster 33 as support.

- Show students how to apply this procedure to working in pairs, so that they can solve the four secret messages on Copymaster 34.

T: Vous comprenez les messages secrets? Alors, travaillez à deux. Par exemple personne A, personne B, personne A, personne B etc. **(Show how roles will be divided.)** *Ça va? Personne A commence … par exemple …* **(Call out random numbers e.g. 90, 66, 69 … Also explain how to announce the slash denoting the end of a word by saying** *Pause.***)** *Personne B regarde le code et écrit les lettres, par exemple: A, B, C … etc.* **(Mime searching for and writing down letters.)** *Puis changez de rôle. Bon. Allez.* **(Give out one A sheet and one B sheet to each pair.)**

Solution

A **1** Moi/je/déteste/le/lundi!
     3 Je/n'ai/pas/de/devoirs!
B **2** Tu/manges/un/sandwich?
     4 Rendez-/vous/à/midi/dix!

Casse-tête! (SB p.57)

AT 3 – 1

- When students are familiar with the higher numbers, they can move on to the activities on page 57. This first activity tests comprehension of the written form of numbers, as students convert the numbers to figures, before using their logic to complete the sequences.

Phrases fantastiques! (SB p.57)

AT 1 – 2/3, AT 2 – 2/3, AT 3 -2/3

- Students can practise the tongue twister as a class, in groups or individually, with or without the cassette support.

six saucissons secs
seize saucissons secs
soixante saucissons secs
soixante-six saucissons secs
soixante-seize saucissons secs
cent saucissons secs
six cent soixante-six saucissons secs!

Mots en image (SB p.57)

AT 3 – 1

- Draw attention to these visual reminders of how higher numbers are formed in French.

Differentiation – Extension

C'est à toi! (SB p.57)

AT 2 – 2/3, AT 3 – 1/2/3, AT 4 – 1/2/3

- Encourage students to use higher numbers to invent their own 'Casse-têtes' or 'Mots en image' for display in the classroom. Higher attainers could also experiment with writing and saying their own 'Phrases fantastiques', although they should be steered away from using adjectives which necessitate agreement.

> **Presentation of:**
> *des cadeaux/le premier (etc.) prix/une télévision/*
> *un baladeur/des CD/des T-shirts/des pin's*
> *Bonne chance!*

La tombola! (SB p.58)

a Ecoute et lis.

AT 1 – 4, AT 3 – 3

- Students listen to the class cassette whilst looking at the poster on page 58. Check understanding and clarify the raffle context and the new vocabulary.

Club sportif
Samedi le 24 février
Grande tombola
30 cadeaux à gagner!
1er prix = une télévision
2ème prix = un baladeur
3ème prix = CD ou cassettes
Aussi à gagner: 4 T-shirts, 4 vidéos, 3 livres, 3 trousses, 5 paquets de 10 crayons, 5 pin's.
Tirage au sort au collège à 16h 00
Bonne chance!

- Select a student capable of demonstrating a simple conversation in which a ticket is bought for the raffle. A name is given as a reference for the ticket stub.

T: (Hold up an A4 size 'replica' of a raffle ticket, folded in half with a dotted line down the middle and a large identical number on each half. Indicate the student and mime throughout to clarify.) *Tu achètes un billet pour la tombola? Oui? Voilà.* (Tear the replica ticket in half along the dotted line and hand over one half to the student. Ask the student,) *Tu t'appelles comment?* (As the student gives his or her name, write the name on your half of the replica ticket. Hand over the ticket, saying the number.) *Voilà, numéro …*

3 Vive les passe-temps!

> **Presentation of:**
> *Mon numéro est .../Le numéro de mon billet est ...*

b Ecoute. Qui parle?

AT 1 – 3, AT 3 – 3

- Explain that students are now going to hear six conversations in which teenagers buy raffle tickets and that they must look at the speech bubbles on page 58 and decide who is speaking each time.

T: ***Ecoutez les six conversations à la tombola au club sportif et regardez les textes.* (Point to the speech bubbles.) *Qui parle? Conversation numéro 1 est Sandrine, Jérôme, Monique, Marie-France, Nicolas ou Olivier?* (Pointing to the appropriate photos.) *Ecoutez et lisez.* (Play the first conversation on the cassette.) *Le numéro du billet est le 64 .* (Write the number on the board) *C'est le numéro de Sandrine?* (Wait for students to contradict and give the correct answer. Confirm the answer.) *Oui, c'est ça. C'est le numéro d'Olivier. Ecrivez 1 – F.* (Draw attention to the example on the page to demonstrate how to set down the answer.)**

- Tell students to write down numbers 1 – 6 in readiness for the task. Then play the rest of the cassette for students to tackle individually.

---

1 Salut! J'ai le billet numéro 64.

2 Salut! J'ai le billet numéro 79 et toi?

3 – Quel est le numéro de ton billet?
  – J'ai le billet 85 ... et toi?

4 – Tu as un billet pour la tombola?
  – Oui, j'ai le billet numéro 90.

5 – Salut! Tu as un billet pour la tombola?
  – Oui, j'ai le billet 95 ... Je vais gagner la télé!

6 – Quel est le numéro de ton billet?
  – Un moment ... oui, c'est numéro 76. Et toi, tu as un billet?

Solution

1 F **2** A **3** E **4** B **5** C **6** D

- Practise the phrase *Le numéro de mon billet* or *Mon numéro est le ...* with the class. Show how the students can use the texts on page 58 to play a comprehension game in pairs.

T: ***Travaillez à deux. Personne A regarde les textes et donne le numéro de billet. Par exemple, Mon numéro est le 90. Personne B regarde les textes et donne le nom. Par exemple, Tu t'appelles Jérôme.***

J'ai gagné! (SB p.59)

AT 1 – 4

- As further practice of higher numbers within a longer conversation, students listen to the draw and note the numbers of the winning raffle tickets.

- C'est le grand moment. Le premier prix ce soir, c'est la télévision. Qui va gagner le premier prix? ... C'est le billet numéro 72, 72.
- C'est moi!
- Et le deuxième prix, le baladeur ... c'est le billet 81 ... 81.
- C'est pas vrai. C'est moi!
- Et le troisième prix ... les CD ou les cassettes ... Qui va les gagner? ... et voilà, c'est le numéro 94 ... 94 ... Qui a le 94?
- C'est moi. Super ... . Merci, madame!
- Bon alors, quatre T-shirts à gagner... et ce sont les numéros 69 ... 69; 78 ... 78; 99 ... 99 et 82 ... 82. Je répète ... 69, 78, 99 et 82.
- Oui.
- C'est moi!
- C'est toi!
- Regarde, c'est toi!'
- Et les trois livres? Quels numéros? Voilà ... 66 ... 66, 90 ... 90, et ... 95 ... 95.
- J'ai gagné!
- C'est moi!
- C'est toi, Monique!

Solution

TV: 72   Baladeur: 81   CD/cassettes: 94
T-shirts: 69, 78, 99, 82   Livres: 66, 90, 95

Presentation of:
Un billet, s'il vous plaît.
Voilà
Bonne chance!
Revision of: *Tu t'appelles comment?*

C'est à vous! (SB p.59)

AT 1 – 3, AT 2 – 3, AT 3 – 3

- Play the model conversation on the cassette and tell students to listen and to follow it in their books.
- Practise the key phrases with the class, before telling the students to work in groups and to act out a short scene in which they buy their own raffle tickets. Encourage them to use props and draw their attention to the picture of the raffle ticket on the page which they can use as a model for their own scene.

– Bonjour!
– Bonjour!
– Un billet, s'il te plaît.
– Voilà. Tu t'appelles comment?
– Michel Blanc.
– Voila Michel, numéro 84.
– Merci.
– Merci. Bonne chance!

Differentiation – Extension

AT 1 – 3, AT 2 – 3/4, AT 3 – 3

- Higher attainers could include additional language which they have learned previously, e.g. *Où habites-tu?, J'habite à …* . They could also extend the playlet by acting out the actual draw and by announcing the prizes and/or winning ticket numbers using the *'Résultats Tombola'* at the top of page 59 for support.

Grande Tombola (SB p.59)

AT 2 – 2/3/4, AT 3 – 2/3/4, AT 4 – 2/3/4

- As a final activity, students could design their own poster advertising a raffle, by adapting the one on page 59. Some students could alternatively or additionally record this onto a cassette in the style of an advert.

J'écoute – pas de panique! (SB p.60)

AT 1 – 3/4, AT 3 – 2/3, AT 4 – 2/3

- This item aims to introduce students to basic listening skills. Students listen to Martin talking about his hobbies on the class cassette. Play the tape through continuously, before looking at page 60.

Martin: Salut! Je m'appelle Martin. Qu'est-ce que je fais comme passe-temps? Je préfère faire du vélo. J'ai un vélo tout terrain. Je fais du vélo avec les copains surtout le dimanche. Je quitte la maison à huit heures et demie et je prends la piste cyclable qui mène à la rivière. J'arrive à la rivière à neuf heures où je fais de la pêche avec les copains. C'est super! Nous passons deux bonnes heures au bord de la rivière. Je quitte la rivière à onze heures pour arriver à la maison à onze heures et demie. Maman a déjà préparé le déjeuner. Vive le dimanche!

- Direct students to Students' Book page 60. In a *pause anglaise* explain that there are ways to help understanding of a spoken text. Reassure the students that they cannot expect to understand everything at once and that the main thing is not to panic! Explain the importance of getting the gist, giving the word *Thème* and pointing to the section *'Thème'* on the page. Then convey that having established the gist, students listen for key details. Point to the section *'Détails. Note le bon détail.'* Then explain that the final step is to listen for finer details, indicating the section *'Encore des détails. Note le bon détail.'*
- As this is the first time that students have used this approach, play the tape through, concentrating on and checking each section at a time. Accept oral feedback and write the answers up on the board.

Solution
Thème: 3
Détails: **1** c **2** b **3** b

3 Vive les passe-temps!

Encore des détails: **1** neuf heures **2** s **3** onze heures et demie

- Play the cassette through a final time for students to listen without being engaged in any task.

[cassette icon]

Radio Jeunes (SB p.61)

a Ecoute et lis.

AT 1 – 3/4, AT 3 – 3/4

- Students combine their listening skills with skimming and scanning texts of advertisements in a magazine, where young people are seeking penfriends. The adverts combine the language of the unit.
- As students listen to the cassette, they take notes. Demonstrate how they can do this. First draw a large cross shape on the board with ample room to enter notes. Number the spaces 1 – 4. Refer to your own diagram, saying *Faites une croix et écris les numéros 1 – 4.* When they have done this, tell students to listen for the *Thème* and play the introductory part of '*Radio Jeunes*'.

[cassette icon]

– Salut les copains. Dans votre magazine 'Radio jeunes – coin correspondance', vous allez voir des jeunes qui recherchent des correspondants. Vous voulez correspondre? Ecoutez!

- Check that students have understood the theme. Prepare students for their note-taking by giving an example that does not feature on the cassette e.g. *Je joue au basket. Je fais de la natation. J'adore ça.* Enter just the hobbies in the space marked 1 on your diagram in note form or abbreviations, entering just the nouns, e.g. *bas./nat.* Give a second example, if it is needed and again enter just the hobbies, this time in space numbered 2. Simulate at top speed filling in the remaining two spaces.
- Now direct students to their diagrams and tell them to listen for the hobbies only and to make notes in the appropriate spaces.

T: *Ecoutez les quatre jeunes qui cherchent un(e) correspondant(e). Notez leurs passe-temps.* **(Point to your example on the board.)**

- Play the cassette through, pausing after each item to allow students to make notes. Play through

again or as many times as is needed for students to complete the task.

- Now encourage students to add finer detail to their notes in the appropriate numbered spaces. Refer to '*Encore des détails*', page 60.

[cassette icon]

– Notre premier correspondant dit :
'Je fais du patin à roulettes. Le soir je joue aux cartes ou j'écoute de la musique. Je ne regarde pas la télé!'
Notre deuxième correspondant dit:
'Je joue au badminton et je lis beaucoup. J'écoute de la musique mais je préfère la musique pop. Le soir je regarde la télé!'
Notre troisième correspondant dit:
'Je fais de la natation et je joue au tennis. J'adore le sport!'
Et notre dernière jeune personne dit:
'Je joue avec l'ordinateur. Je joue au tennis et je fais du vélo.'
Trouvez tous les détails de nos correspondants à la page 61, 'Radio Jeunes'.

b Qui parle?

AT 3 – 4

- Direct students to page 61 to match the letters with the notes that they have made from the cassette.

T: *Qui parle?* **(Read the first advert from Dorothée aloud, checking the statements with your notes on the board.)** *Qui parle?* **(Look at your notes on the board and say:)** *Non, mais ...* **(Pointing to the first advert on page 61)** *c'est Dorothée? C'est Luc? C'est Coralie? C'est Jean? Qui parle? Allez, lisez les textes, regardez vos notes et trouvez qui parle.* **(Support with mime if necessary.)**

- Give a time limit and then check the first answer. Students may work in twos sharing the reading and the decision-making.

Solution

1 Jean **2** Luc **3** Coralie **4** Dorothée

- Explore some of the new language used in the adverts e.g. *Je (re)cherche un(e) correspondant(e)*. Encourage students to work out why there are the two forms *un/une*. Write up *entre 11 – 13 ans* and ask the students to name the young people who use that expression. Ask what other expression is used instead i.e. *de mon âge*. Ask the students if there is any other language e.g. *musique classique* that is unfamiliar and encourage them to deduce the meaning.

Porte ouverte!   (SB p.62)
Sommaire   (SB pp.62-63)

AT 1 – 2/3/4, AT 2 – 2/3/4, AT 3 – 2/3/4, AT4 – 2/3/4

- Return to the *objectifs* section on page 44 to show how all the language is leading to the *'Porte ouverte!'* activity – *'Trouve la bonne personne'*. Remind students of the language they have learned by referring to each goal in turn and looking at the relevant pages together in class. Also refer students to the *'Sommaire'* for help in completing the activity.

- Students reread selected pages in the module and revise key pages on copymaster. Alternatively direct them to the *'Sommaire'* to remind them of the range and depth of the language in the module. Remind them in English that the *'Porte ouverte!'* activity should show up their knowledge and be a cause for celebration.

- Students take part in an open-ended muti-skill activity that revolves around finding the identity of a class member, who has written true information on an advert looking for a penfriend. Explain the sequence of activities by using the visual representation on page 62, emphasising the key instructions *Ecris. Lis. Interviewe!*

- First students write their own *'Cherche corres.'* basing it on the models on page 61. Read through the instructions written in the first section, clarifying what information to include: *correspondant, tes passe-temps, et tes opinions.*

- Encourage students to word process their advert to conceal their identity and to produce a drafted,

correct script. Ideally students prepare the first part of the activity for homework to save time in class and to preserve anonymity.

Differentiation – Extension

- Encourage higher attainers to write fuller descriptions. If possible, they should try writing a first draft from memory, in pencil or using a word processor, before checking for spelling and redrafting if necessary.

- Pointing to the second phase of the visual representation on page 62, ask students to report to you before putting up their adverts on the wall. Check that the student has not left his/her name on the advert. Have numbers, written on pieces of paper, to correspond to the number of students in your class. Give the student a number to put up beside his/her advert and take a note of both the number and the student's name. If students have prepared the advert for homework, the management of this phase can be more efficient. Keep a note of names and numbers and encourage willing students to come before the lesson to put the adverts up. To avoid the density of students crowding around a small area, designate a different part of the classroom wall for every six adverts. Make sure that the adverts are well spaced and clearly numbered.

- Encourage students to start reading the adverts making a note of the number and of the details that lead them to possible identification of a fellow student. Draw the attention of the students to the lead language in the section *'Interviewe!'* on page 62. Students then interview possible 'authors' to confirm their suspicions. If the students have forgotten which was their advert, they can check their number with you! Give students who work more slowly the opportunity to take part in all the phases, lending support where needed. Give those students who have successfully made an identification a challenge e.g. how many people can they identify, or encourage them to support a fellow student who is experiencing difficulties in completing the task.

4 EN FAMILLE

In this module students learn how to:

Talk about their brothers and sisters
J'ai une sœur / Je suis fils unique

Ask others about their brothers and sisters
Tu as des frères ou des sœurs?

Talk about their pets
J'ai un chien / Je n'ai pas d'animal (etc.)

Introduce members of the family
Voici ma mère (etc.)

Ask about family members' and pets' names and ages
Il s'appelle comment? / Ils ont quel âge? (etc.)

Ask what family members and pets are like
Elle est comment? / Ils sont comment? (etc.)

Describe family members and pets
Elle est grande / Ils sont verts (etc.)

Seek permission in class
Je peux aller aux toilettes? / ouvrir la fenêtre? (etc.)

Materials needed
Students' Book pages 64 – 83
Copymasters 35 – 50
Flashcards 54 – 65

Class cassette D
Self-study cassette

New language introduced

J'ai un (deux) frère(s)/une (trois) sœur(s)/un demi-frère/une demi-sœur (etc.)
Je suis fils/fille unique
Tu as des frères et des sœurs?
Il/Elle s'appelle ...
Ils/Elles s'appellent ...
Il/Elle a ... ans
Ils/Elles ont ... ans
Il/Elle s'appelle comment?
Ils/Elles s'appellent comment?
Il/Elle a quel âge?
Ils/Elles ont quel âge?
Voici mon frère/père/grand-père/oncle
ma famille/sœur/mère/grand-mère/tante
mes (demi-) frères/sœurs/parents

Revision of
Je m'appelle ...
J'ai ... ans
J'habite à ...
Numbers 0 – 84

Objectif 1   Famille

Student goals   (SB p.64)

• Use the top half of the page to familiarise students with the module's main teaching points and goals.

*T: **Voici les objectifs pour ce module. Alors, voici ma famille.** (Draw pin-figures on the board, whilst describing your own or an imaginary family.) ... **Et voici mes animaux:***

***J'ai un chien, j'ai un chat ...** (Show a few pet flashcards.) **Regardez .**(Direct students to the third objective.) **Alors, descriptions ... Voici mon frère.** (Point to the pin-figure drawn earlier.) **Il est grand.** (mime) ... **Et voici mon chien.** (Show flashcard.) **Il est petit** (Mime).*

Presentation of:

J'ai un frère/une sœur/un demi-frère/une demi-sœur

Je suis fils/fille unique

Tu as des frères et des sœurs?

(SB p.64)

AT 1 – 2, AT 2 – 2, AT 3 – 2

- Remind students again of the first section of the goals visual at the top of the page.

T: *Bon. Objectif un – 'Famille'.*

- Introduce the five core statements about siblings, using the cassette and directing students to follow the text and photos in their books whilst they listen.

Sandrine:	J'ai un frère.
Marc:	J'ai une sœur.
François:	J'ai un demi-frère et une demi-sœur.
Sébastien:	Je suis fils unique.
Nicole:	Je suis fille unique.

- Check that students understand the meaning of these statements, before playing the cassette again and encouraging repetition.
- Move on to check sound discrimination and to practise linking the spoken and written phrases in a teacher-led *Qui parle?* activity, giving statements in random order and asking the students to identify the speaker.
- This can be developed into a *Vrai ou faux?* activity to practise linking the spoken and written statements and reading aloud.

T: *Regardez les photos et les phrases et écoutez bien: 'Sandrine: J'ai une sœur.' Vrai ou faux?* **(Wait for response, faux, before eliciting the correct statement.)** *Alors, que dit Sandrine?* **etc.**

- When students are confident with the five core statements, introduce the plural *J'ai ... (demi-) frères* and *J'ai ... (demi-) sœurs*, drawing pin-figures on the board to support the meaning. Check understanding and practise pronunciation, before moving on to Copymaster 35.

Presentation of: *Tu as des frères et des sœurs?*

Mes frères et mes sœurs (CM 35)

1 Ecoute et remplis la grille.

AT1 – 2/3

- Students listen to the cassette and after each conversation complete the appropriate column of the grid at the top of the copymaster, to show understanding of the statements about siblings.
- Introduce the activity briefly and demonstrate what students have to do before playing through the cassette as many times as necessary, pausing after each conversation.

1

– Tu as des frères et des sœurs, Monique?

– J'ai un demi-frère.

– Un demi-frère?

– Oui. J'ai un demi-frère.

2

– Et toi, Paul? Tu as des frères et des sœurs?

– Oui. J'ai un frère et une sœur.

– Pardon?

– J'ai un frère et une sœur.

3

– Tu as des frères et des sœurs, Martin?

– Ah oui, j'ai deux frères et une demi-sœur.

4

– Et toi, Julie? Tu as des frères et des sœurs?

– Non, je suis fille unique.

5

– Bonjour, Françoise. Tu as des frères et des sœurs?

– Oui, j'ai un frère et deux sœurs.

– Un frère et deux sœurs?

– Oui.

6

– Et toi? Tu t'appelles comment?

– Je m'appelle Frédéric.

> – Alors, Frédéric, tu as des frères et des sœurs?
> – Non, je n'en ai pas. Je suis fils unique.

Solution

	frère	demi-frère	sœur	demi-sœur	fils unique	fille unique
1 Monique		1				
2 Paul	1		1			
3 Martin	2			1		
4 Julie						✓
5 Françoise	1		2			
6 Frédéric					✓	

- Play the first conversation on the cassette again, pause it after the question *Tu as des frères et des sœurs?*

T: ***'Tu as des frères et des sœurs', c'est quoi en anglais?***

- Having confirmed the meaning, move on to thoroughly practise this question. Gradually begin to develop a question and answer session, asking the class the question and cueing their responses with labels on the board.

2 A deux!

AT 1 – 1, AT 2 – 2

- Direct students to the summary of the question and answers below the grid on the copymaster and show how to use the information on the grid to reconstruct the interviews in the pairwork activity. Use a student to demonstrate the task, before setting up pairwork.

3 Regarde la grille et complète.

AT 4 – 2

- Students should now be ready to complete the sentences in Paul's, Martin's and Sandrine's speech bubbles, using the information in the grid, together with support from the phrases provided in the summary box.

Solution

Paul: J'ai un frère et une sœur.

Martin: J'ai deux frères et une demi-sœur.

Julie: Je suis fille unique.

4 Et toi?

AT 4 – 2

- Finally, students write a sentence about whether or not they have any brothers or sisters.

Differentiation – Extension

AT 4 – 2

- Some students could use the information from their grid to also write speech bubbles for Monique, Françoise and Frédéric. Alternatively, they could write up some or all of the conversations practised earlier in the 'A deux!' activity.

> **Presentation of:**
> *Il/Elle s'appelle … Ils/Elles s'appellent …*

Fais des paires (SB p.65)

a Ecoute et lis. Fais des paires

AT 1 – 2, AT 3 – 2

- Statements about siblings are now linked to the 3rd person singular and plural forms of *s'appeler*. Students listen to the cassette, whilst following the statements on page 65 in order to make the link between the spoken and written forms of the pronouns and verbs.
- They then match the appropriate visual to each pair of sentences. This matching is based on comprehension of the vocabulary covered so far; the *s'appeler* element is introduced but is not essential for completion of the task.

1 J'ai un frère. Il s'appelle Joël.
2 J'ai une sœur. Elle s'appelle Véronique.
3 J'ai deux frères. Ils s'appellent Eric et Thomas.
4 J'ai deux sœurs. Elles s'appellent Nathalie et Isabelle.
5 J'ai un demi-frère et une demi-sœur. Ils s'appellent Stéphane et Karine.

Solution

1 C 2 E 3 D 4 B 5 A

- Having completed the matching activity, direct students' attention to the statements about the brothers' and sisters' names and check that they understand the meaning of *il/elle s'appelle ...* and *ils/elles s'appellent ...* . Write the full forms of these four parts of the verb *s'appeler* on the board and ask questions such as *Comment dit-on 'Il s'appelle Joël' en anglais?* Also point out that *ils s'appellent ...* is used to mean 'they are called ...' when talking about a mixed collection of brothers and sisters.

- Practise repetition and pronunciation with the class, using the written forms of the verb on the board as cues. Stress the fact that although the singular and plural forms are spelt differently, they sound exactly the same. Move on to use combinations of pin figures and names to cue other oral statements and point out the *'Attention!'* feature which summarises the forms of *s'appeler* covered here.

> At this point you may wish to use Copymaster 80. Students complete notes on the use of *il/elle* and *ils/elles* and keep them for reference.

b A deux.

AT 1 – 2, AT 2 – 2

- Revise the question *Tu as des frères et des soeurs?*, before demonstrating how students should conduct questions and answers in pairs, responding to the question by reading aloud the appropriate statement from page 65.

c Et toi?

AT 2 – 2

- When they are confident, students can move on to respond to one another's question, giving their own information.

Ils s'appellent comment? (CM 36)

AT 3 – 2, AT 4 – 2/3

- This copymaster is designed to give concentrated practice of the 3rd person singular and plural pronouns and forms of *s'appeler*. Students should first practise comprehension by matching the sentences about siblings with the appropriate statements about their names.

- In the second task they complete the gapped speech bubbles, using the linked sentences above

as support if necessary. To show that they have understood the meaning of what they have written, they should then draw appropriate pin figures to accompany the speech bubbles.

Solution

1

J'ai un frère. Il s'appelle Marc.

J'ai une sœur. Elle s'appelle Claire.

J'ai deux frères et un demi-frère. Ils s'appellent Richard, Martin et Nicolas.

J'ai deux sœurs. Elles s'appellent Nadia et Carole.

J'ai deux frères et une demi-sœur. Ils s'appelle Paul, Luc et Louise.

2

A J'ai un frère. Il **s'appelle** Eric. (+ drawing of a brother)

B J'ai deux **(demi-) sœurs**. Elles **s'appellent** Marie et Anne. (+ drawing of 2 sisters)

C J'ai un demi-frère et une demi-soeur. **Ils** s'appellent Olivier et Hélène. (+ drawing of a brother and a sister)

D J'ai une **(demi-) sœur**. **Elle s'appelle** Suzanne. (+ drawing of a sister)

E J'ai deux frères. **Ils s'appellent** Thomas et Patrick. (+ drawing of 2 brothers)

Differentiation – Extension and Consolidation

- Some students could invent other speech bubbles in the style of those on Copymaster 36 and illustrate them in a similar style. Alternatively or additionally, they could return to the *'Et toi?'* task at the bottom of page 65 of their books and write a statement about whether or not they have any siblings and, if so, what they are called.

> **Presentation of:**
> *Il/Elle a quel âge? Ils/Elles ont quel âge?*

Ils ont quel âge? (SB p.66)

a Ecoute la cassette et regarde les photos. Ecris la bonne lettre!

AT 1 – 2

- Revise *Tu as quel âge?* and *J'ai ... ans* by asking questions around the class. Then demonstrate that students are going to find out about the ages of brothers and sisters, by pointing to the photos on page 66 and asking rhetorically, *Et les frères et les soeurs ici, ils ont quel âge?* Explain what the class is going to do in the first activity.

T: *Alors, nous écoutons les âges des frères et des soeurs. Bon. Regardez les photos des frères et des soeurs. Ecoutez la cassette, par exemple 'J'ai une soeur. Elle a sept ans.' C'est quelle photo? A, B, C, D, E ou F? Alors, écoutez la cassette, regardez les photos et écrivez la bonne lettre!*

- Students listen to the cassette and decide which photo is being described. (NB It is important that students understand in advance that the speaker is not in the photograph.)

---

1 J'ai une soeur. Elle s'appelle Coralie. Elle a sept ans.

2 J'ai un frère. Il s'appelle Richard. Il a onze ans.

3 J'ai une soeur et un frère. Mélanie a cinq ans et Robert a douze ans.

4 J'ai deux frères, Franck et Pierre. Ils ont seize ans et quatre ans.

5 J'ai un frère et une soeur. Ils ont quinze ans et treize ans.

6 J'ai deux soeurs. Elles ont quatorze ans et dix-sept ans.

Solution

D, A, F, B, C, E

- Having completed the activity, check that students understand the meaning of *il/elle a ... ans* and *ils/elles ont ... ans.* Write the full forms of these four parts of the verb *avoir* on the board and ask questions such as *Comment dit-on 'Il a ... ans' en anglais?*
- Move on to use combinations of pin figures and ages to cue other oral statements.

b Relie la phrase avec la bonne photo.

AT 2 – 2, AT 3 – 2, AT 4 – 2

- Students now read the sentences about ages and match each with the appropriate photo above. This can be done as an oral, letter-matching or written activity.

Solution

1 A   **2** D   **3** F   **4** B   **5** E   **6** C

- Copymaster 37 and/or Copymaster 38 may now be issued.

Differentiation – Support and Consolidation

Les âges des frères et des soeurs
(CM 37)

- This copymaster is intended for students requiring further oral, reading and written practice of the 3rd person singular and plural pronouns and forms of *avoir*. The activities are intended for independent work at home or in the classroom.

1 Ecoute, lis et répète.

Lis, prononce et écoute.

AT 1 – 2, AT 2 – 2, AT 3 – 2

- Students listen to the self-study cassette, whilst reading the copymaster, in order to relate the written and spoken statements about ages, before repeating them. They then practise independently reading the phrases aloud, checking their pronunciation by using the cassette.

You will need Copymaster 37, activity 1. Look at the six pictures at the top of the page. Listen to the cassette as you read the sentence underneath each picture. Pause the cassette after each sentence and repeat it.

1 Il a cinq ans.

2 Elle a huit ans.

3 Sophie a onze ans et Alain a neuf ans.

4 Ils ont trois ans.

5 Elles ont douze ans.

6 Ils ont six ans et sept ans.

In a moment, rewind the cassette to the beginning of *'Les âges des frères et des soeurs'.* Look again at the six pictures and sentences. This time, read the sentences out loud. After each sentence listen to the cassette to check your pronunciation. Pause the cassette after each sentence.

2 Lis et copie.

AT 4 – 1

- Students read and copy the captions below each cartoon frame.

3 C'est quel mot?

AT 3 – 2, AT 4 – 1

- Students then complete the cloze sentences, choosing the correct word from the menu alongside.

Solution

1 a **2** ont **3** ont; et **4** Il **5** a

4 Complète.

AT 3 – 2, AT 4 – 2/3

- Finally, students complete the sentences about three more sets of brothers and sisters, using the support provided by the accompanying pictures.

Solution

J'ai un frère. Il s'appelle Luc et il a **douze ans**.

J'ai une **(demi-) soeur**. **Elle** s'appelle Nicole et elle **a trois** ans.

J'ai **deux (demi-) frères. Ils** s'appellent Paul et André. Ils **ont dix** ans et **sept** ans.

Differentiation – Extension

Noms et âges   (CM 38)

1 Ecoute. C'est quelle lettre?

AT 1 – 2, AT 4 – 2

- Students capable of coping with descriptions of names and ages simultaneously can move on to this copymaster. In the first activity, they listen to the class cassette and select the appropriate cartoon for each statement.

1 Il s'appelle Antoine.
2 Elle s'appelle Annette.
3 Ils s'appellent Alain et Eric.
4 Elles s'appellent Anne et Elizabeth.
5 Il a sept ans.
6 Elle a sept ans.
7 Ils ont cinq ans.
8 Elles ont cinq ans.

Solution

1 E **2** G **3** D **4** B **5** A **6** H **7** C **8** F

2 Ecris la bonne phrase.

AT 2 – 2, AT 4 – 2

- Students then write the correct phrase beneath each cartoon. This could also be done as an oral activity.

Solution

A Il a sept ans.

B Elles s'appellent Anne et Elizabeth.

C Ils ont cinq ans.

D Ils s'appellent Alain et Eric.

E Il s'appelle Antoine.

F Elles ont cinq ans.

G Elle s'appelle Annette.

H Elle a sept ans.

Differentiation – Extension

AT 3 – 2

- Higher attainers could write/say the captions from memory by folding back or covering the menu of phrases at the top of the sheet.

Ils ont quel âge?   (SB p.66)

c Regarde les images et fais des phrases.

AT 2 – 2/3, AT 4 – 3

- Point out the 'Attention!' feature, which summarises the use of the 3rd person singular and plural forms of *avoir*, before directing students to describe the names and ages of the figures shown in the pictures at the bottom of the page. This could be an oral or a written task.

Solution

A (J'ai un frère.) Il s'appelle Marc. Il a onze ans.

B (J'ai une soeur.) Elle s'appelle Carole. Elle a dix ans.

C (J'ai un frère et une soeur.) Ils s'appellent Franck et Nadia. Franck a treize ans et Nadia a trois ans.

D (J'ai deux soeurs.) Elles s'appellent Sylvie et Sandrine. Elles ont douze ans.

E (J'ai deux frères.) Ils s'appellent Martin et Claude. Martin a dix-huit ans et Claude a quinze ans.

Differentiation – Consolidation or Extension

- For some students it may be more appropriate to focus solely on describing the ages indicated. Higher attainers, however, could be encouraged to preface each description with a statement about the number of brothers and sisters shown, e.g. *J'ai un frère. Il s'appelle … Il a … ans.* etc.

Des détails, s'il te plaît! (SB p.67)

a Ecoute et lis.

AT 1 – 3, AT 3 – 3

- Students listen to the class cassette, whilst following the text of the cartoon strip which introduces the questions *Il s'appelle comment?* and *Il a quel âge?* Play the cassette through continuously and then play it again and ask students to follow it and point to the relevant speech bubbles.

> – Tu as des frères et des soeurs?
> – Oui, j'ai un frère.
> – Le quatorze février … La Saint Valentin …
>   … Il s'appelle comment? Il a quel âge?
> – Il s'appelle Georges et il a cinq mois.

- Before proceding to the next sequence of activities, photocopy Copymaster 39, '*Questions et réponses*' onto acetate for use on the OHP and cut the acetate into 10 questions and 10 answers. It may also be helpful to prepare a second acetate and cut it up into segments in order to demonstrate the more challenging version of the game which follows later.
- To make an optional game, also photocopy the copymaster onto card, to allow for one copy between two students. Cut these up into questions and answers and store each cut up copymaster in an envelope. N.B. lower attainers will find it easier if the questions are kept intact, but for a more challenging version of the game each question can be cut into three segments.

Presentation of:

Il/Elle s'appelle comment?
Ils/Elles s'appellent comment?
Il/Elle a quel âge?
Ils/Elles ont quel âge?

Questions et réponses (CM 39)

AT 1 – 2, AT 2 – 2, AT 3 – 2

- Use the OHT version of Copymaster 39 to focus on the questions *Il s'appelle comment?* and *Il a quel âge?* Show the two questions and check that students understand their meaning.

T: 'Il s'appelle comment?', c'est quoi en anglais? etc. (If no OHP is available, the questions can be written on the board instead.)

- Encourage repetition of the French questions and then stress the pronoun.

T: Il s'appelle comment? Ça veut dire 'What is he called?' Alors, comment dit-on 'What is she called?' Oui, très bien, Elle s'appelle comment?

- Repeat this process with *Il a quel âge?* and encourage students to deduce how to ask *Elle a quel âge?*
- Next draw a male pin figure on the board, point to it and ask *Il s'appelle comment? Il a quel âge?* Place the acetate answers *Martin* and *10 ans* on the OHP and encourage students to respond to the questions. Repeat this process, drawing a female pin figure, asking the questions *Elle s'appelle comment?* and *Elle a quel âge?* and using the acetate answers *Carole* and *11 ans* to cue the responses. The questions and answers can be chorused backwards and forwards around the class until students can use them confidently.
- Point to individual students and ask *Il/Elle s'appelle comment?* etc. to elicit an answer and encourage students to 'test' one another's knowlege of the names and ages of their classmates.
- When the class is confident in the use of the singular questions, present and practise the plural equivalents, using a similar method to that outlined above and remind students that *ils* is used for a mixed group of boys and girls.

- As an optional activity, the class can then be divided into pairs and given the task of matching the cut up questions and answers from the card versions of Copymaster 39, before practising them orally.

Differentiation – Extension

- Higher attainers can be given a more challenging version of the game, in which the questions are cut up into segments. They should first reconstruct the questions and then match the answers. This can be demonstrated first, using the alternative version of the OHT prepared earlier.

Solution

Il s'appelle comment? Martin.
Elle s'appelle comment? Carole.
Ils s'appellent comment? Paul et Robert./Luc et Louise.
Elles s'appellent comment? Sophie et Sandrine.
Ils s'appellent comment? Luc et Louise./Paul et Robert.

Il a quel âge?	10 ans./11 ans.
Elle a quel âge?	11 ans./10 ans.
Ils ont quel âge?	13 ans et 15 ans.
Elles ont quel âge?	3 ans et 7 ans.
Ils ont quel âge?	16 ans et 17 ans.

Des détails, s'il te plaît!   (SB p.67)

b Copie les questions et trouve les bonnes réponses.

AT 3 – 2, AT 4 – 2

- When students are confident in the use of the questions and answers about other people's names and ages, they can reread the cartoon strip on page 67, before copying and matching the jumbled questions and answers in the second activity on the page.

Solution

1 H **2** A or F **3** D **4** A or F **5** G **6** E **7** B **8** C

Cherche corres.   (CM 40)

AT 1 – 2, AT 2 – 3

- Tell students that they are going to work in pairs and interview their partner to find out information about possible penfriends.

- Write the questions shown on the copymaster on the board and quickly draw a blank grid underneath and a completed grid diagonally opposite and below.

T: Vous posez des questions pour compléter cette grille, par exemple … (**Point to the blank grid and ask the first question.**) *Votre partenaire regarde cette grille et répond, par exemple …* (**Point to the other completed grid and give a statement about brothers and sisters.**) *Bon. Vous écoutez et vous dessinez, par exemple …* (**Show how to fill in the grid.**) *Alors, vous continuez …* (**Show how to ask the next question.**) *Votre partenaire regarde cette grille et répond et vous notez ici …* (**Show how the partner gives information from the completed grid and how to add his/her response to the first piece of information recorded in the blank grid.**)

- Continue the demonstration and show how to swap roles and then use the completed grid printed on the copymaster to answer the partner's questions. Involve a student in the demonstration to clarify how the information is being exchanged.

- Explain that when both students have exchanged all their information and completed their blank grid, they should look at the two grids on their sheet and try to find the best pairs of partners.

T: Alors, finalement, vous avez deux grilles comme ça. Bon. Regardez les grilles et cherchez les paires! Reliez les partenaires, par exemple … (**Demonstrate how to link the best matched pairs.**)

- Divide the class into pairs, give part A of Copymaster 40 to one member of each pair and part B to the other member and tell the class to start their interviews.

Des détails, s'il te plaît!   (SB p.67)

c Continue la conversation.

AT 2 – 3, AT 3 – 2, AT 4 – 3

- Students can now use their imagination to continue the conversation between the two toddlers shown in the illustration at the foot of the page. This could be in the form of a cartoon or acted out as an actual conversation.

- Remind students of the cartoon at the top of the page and encourage them to think of a humorous twist, e.g. one toddler might have a large number of brothers and sisters or could be holding on to a much larger and older brother or sister, etc.

Presentation of:

Voici mon frère/père/grand-père
ma famille/sœur/mère/grand-mère
mes (demi-) frères/sœurs

Ma famille (SB p.68)

a Ecoute et lis.

AT 1 – 1/2, AT 3 – 1/2

- Use the cassette item and the labelled picture of Delphine's relatives on page 68 to introduce vocabulary for other members of the family in combination with *mon, ma* and *mes.* Play the class cassette through twice and encourage students to look at the pictures of the different relatives and read the labels as they listen.

Delphine:	Salut! Je m'appelle Delphine. Voici ma famille! … Voici mon grand-père, … ma grand-mère, … mon père, … ma mère, … mon frère, … ma soeur, … et mes demi-frères!

- Check that the meaning of the new vocabulary is understood, before encouraging repetition and practising pronunciation of the new items.

b Copie, écoute et complète.

AT 1 – 3, AT 4 – 1

- Revise numbers from 0 to 84 with a selection of games (see Teacher's Notes introduction, page iv) and the 'Nombres toréadors' song used in Module 3.
- When students have been reminded of the numbers again, direct them to Delphine's list of names and tell them to quickly copy down the list. (If preferred, in order to save time, suggest abbreviations for the names.)

- Explain that the class is now going to listen to a series of conversations with Delphine and that they should listen carefully, look at the picture at the top of page 68 and note the letter of each relative next to his or her name. They should then note the age of each relative – some students will find it easier to concentrate solely on the relatives during the first playing of the cassette and to listen for the ages during the second playing.

1

Delphine:	Voici ma sœur. Elle s'appelle Odette.
Interviewer:	Elle a quel âge?
Delphine:	Dix ans. Elle a dix ans.

2

Delphine:	Voici mon grand-père.
Interviewer:	Il s'appelle comment?
Delphine:	Quasimodo.
Interviewer:	Et il a quel âge?
Delphine:	Soixante-douze ans.

3

Delphine:	Voici mon frère.
Interviewer:	Ah oui. Il s'appelle comment?
Delphine:	Caspar.
Interviewer:	Et il a quel âge?
Delphine:	Il a huit ans.

4

Delphine:	Et voici ma mère. Elle s'appelle Lucille.
Interviewer:	Pardon? Elle s'appelle Lucille?
Delphine:	Oui, et elle a trente-neuf ans.

5

Delphine:	Bon. Voici mes demi-frères, Antoine et Vincent.
Interviewer:	Ils ont quel âge, tes demi-frères?
Delphine:	Alors, Antoine a treize ans et Vincent a dix-sept ans.

6

Interviewer:	Alors, qui est-ce?
Delphine:	C'est mon père.
Interviewer:	Il s'appelle comment?

Delphine:	Vladimir.
Interviewer:	Et il a quel âge?
Delphine:	Quarante-quatre ans.

7

Delphine:	Ah! Voici ma grand-mère!
Interviewer:	Elle s'appelle comment?
Delphine:	Mathilde.
Interviewer:	Mathilde! Oh là, là!
Delphine:	Oui, elle s'appelle Mathilde et elle a soixante et onze ans! Agh! Toujours des questions! J'en ai marre!

Solution

Lettre	Nom	Age
G	Antoine	13
G	Vincent	17
A	Quasimodo	72
F	Odette	10
D	Lucille	39
B	Mathilde	71
C	Vladimir	44
E	Caspar	8

• Draw attention to *mon, ma* and *mes*.

T: *Comment dit-on 'my' en français?* (Prompt students to volunteer all three possessives, write them on the board and point out.) *Alors, en anglais 'my' et en français mon, ma et mes. Comment dit-on 'my grandfather'? ... et 'my father'? ... et 'my brother'? Alors, 'mon', c'est masculin ou féminin?* (Wait for students to reply and then draw a blue box around *mon*.)

• Repeat the process to elicit *ma* for the female relatives and encourage students to deduce that this is feminine, before drawing a red box around the word *ma*.

• Finally, show that *mes* is used for plurals, such as *mes demi-frères, mes frères, mes sœurs* and underline the *-s* in *mes* and the plural *-s* at the end of each noun, explaining, '*mes', c'est pluriel*.

• Point out the *'Attention!'* feature on page 68 which highlights this point.

At this point you may wish to use Copymaster 82. Students complete notes on the use of *mon, ma* and *mes* and keep them for reference.

c A tour de rôle.

AT 2 – 2, AT 3 – 2/3

• Practise pronunciation of *voici* in combination with *mon, ma, mes* and the various relatives, before giving students the opportunity of practising the possessive pronouns in the pairwork activity.

d Encore une fois de mémoire!

• Students should then repeat the task but this time should cover the picture at the top of the page and try to introduce the relatives from memory, in response to their partner's letter cue. To add an edge to the game, they could score a point for each correct relative.

Differentiation – Extension

• Higher attainers could be encouraged to extend their introduction of each member of Delphine's family by giving additional information about each relative's name and/or age, e.g. *Voici mon père. Il s'appelle Vladimir* etc. Again, afterwards they could try to do this from memory.

Presentation of:
mon oncle / ma tante / mes parents

Ma famille et moi (CM 41)

1 Mots croisés

AT 4 – 2

• In the first activity on this copymaster, students complete an acrostic, by looking at visual clues and filling in the vocabulary for the different relatives.

Solution

2 Remplis les blancs avec mon, ma ou mes!

AT 2 – 3, AT 3 – 3, AT 4 – 1

- The second activity practises the use of *mon, ma* and *mes*. Before beginning, draw attention to the new items of vocabulary: *parents, oncle* and *tante* which are contained in the rhyme. Encourage deduction of the meaning of these new nouns and demonstrate and practise pronunciation.
- Students can then complete the rap with the appropriate possessive pronouns.

Solution

Voici **ma** sœur
Et **mes** parents?
Mon père et **ma** mère?
Voici **mon** oncle
Et **ma** tante Anne
Enfin **mon** grand-père, Jean-François

3 Enregistre ce rap!

- Finally, students read and record the completed raps individually, in pairs or in small groups.

Voici ma famille! (CM 42)

AT 3 – 1, AT 4 – 3/4

- The possessive pronouns *mon, ma* and *mes* are now linked and practised with the 3rd person forms of *s'appeler* and *avoir*, which were introduced earlier in the module.
- Students use the information contained in the family tree and portraits on the copymaster to write short descriptions about different members of the family shown. They take on the role of Claude, so that all descriptions follow the pattern *Voici mon/ma/mes … Il(s)/Elle(s) s'appelle(nt) … Il/Elle a … ans. Ils/Elles ont … ans.*
- Copymasters 36, 37 and 41 can be used to support this activity if necessary.

Solution

Voici mon grand-père. Il s'appelle Victor. Il a soixante-dix ans.

Voici ma mère. Elle s'appelle Louisa. Elle a quarante-trois ans.

Voici mon frère. Il s'appelle Max. Il a quatorze ans.

Voici ma grand-mère. Elle s'appelle Florence. Elle a soixante-huit ans.

Voici mes sœurs. Elles s'appellent Alice et Lise. Elles ont douze ans.

Un problème électronique! (SB p.69)

a Ecoute et lis.

AT 1 – 4, AT 3 – 4

- Having completed the activities on Copymaster 41 and/or Copymaster 42, students should now turn to page 69 where they have the opportunity to consolidate the language of the first objective of the module.
- Direct the class to the electronic letter and support their reading by playing the class cassette. Students will probably need to hear the tape twice and then have an opportunity for quiet reading to familiarise themselves with the text.

Salut! Je m'appelle David et j'ai douze ans. J'habite à Rouen, en Normandie. J'ai un frère. Il s'appelle Stéphane et il a neuf ans. J'ai aussi une demi-sœur. Elle s'appelle Mélanie et elle a quinze ans. Tu as des frères et des sœurs?

Voici une photo de ma famille. Mon père s'appelle Sébastien et ma mère s'appelle Christelle.

Ecris-moi bientôt et parle-moi un peu de ta famille!

b Corrige les erreurs et recopie les phrases.

AT 3 – 2/4, AT 4 – 2

- Students demonstrate understanding of the language in the electronic letter, by correcting the mistakes in the sentences on the computer print-out.

Solution

J'ai un frère et une demi-sœur.

Mon frère s'appelle Stéphane./Mon père s'appelle Sébastien.

J'ai douze ans.

Ma mère s'appelle Christelle./Ma demi-sœur s'appelle Mélanie.

Ma demi-sœur a quinze ans.

Je m'appelle David./Ma demi-sœur s'appelle Mélanie.

c C'est à toi.

AT 1 – 4, AT 2 – 3/4, AT 3 – 4, AT 4 – 3/4

- Using the material on page 69 and the accompanying cassette as support, students consolidate the language of the first objective by writing and/or recording an electronic letter about their own family.

- This activity lends itself to the use of I.T and students should be encouraged to redraft their work. Where multi-media facilities exist, it may be possible to scan in a photograph, add sound and produce a truly multi-media letter. Alternatively, a photograph or drawing could be added to a word-processed letter, mounted within a drawing of a computer screen and could be accompanied by a recording on an audio cassette. If access to word-processors is limited, the letters can be handwritten. Where appropriate, the results can be displayed.

Differentiation – Extension

- Higher attainers could be encouraged to include language from previous modules, to extend the personal details given in their letter, such as school and pastimes.

Objectif 2 Animaux

New language introduced

J'ai un (deux) chien(s)/chat(s)/lapin(s)/cheval (chevaux)/cochon(s) d'Inde/hamster(s)/oiseau(x)/ poisson(s)

une (deux) gerbille(s)/souris/chienne(s)/chatte(s)

Tu as un animal à la maison?

Oui, j'ai …

Non, je n'ai pas d'animal

(En classe)

Pardon, monsieur/madame.

Pardon?

Je peux fermer/ouvrir la porte/la fenêtre?

aller aux toilettes?

Presentation of pets vocabulary

Les animaux (FC 54 – 63)

AT 1 – 1

- Remind the class of the second section of the goals visual on page 64, before using the flashcards to teach the following core pets vocabulary:

  54 *un chien*
  55 *un chat*
  56 *un lapin*
  57 *un cheval*
  58 *un cochon d'Inde*
  59 *un hamster*
  60 *un oiseau*
  61 *un poisson*
  62 *une gerbille*
  63 *une souris*

- A variety of games can be played to consolidate understanding and to maximise opportunities for hearing these pets. (See Teacher's Notes Introduction, page iv.) Students can then move on to Copymaster 43 for oral and further comprehension practice, before copywriting.

Mes animaux (CM 43)

1 Ecoute et regarde les images. Répète.

AT 1 – 1, AT 2 – 1, AT 3 – 1

- The class cassette and self-study cassette accompanying this copymaster contain identical material, so that students can either use this copymaster as a class or individually/at home.

- Students listen to the cassette item whilst looking at the pictures. They then listen again and repeat.

1	un chien
2	un chat
3	un lapin
4	un cheval
5	un cochon d'Inde
6	un hamster
7	un oiseau
8	un poisson
9	une gerbille
10	une souris

You will need Copymaster 43, activity 1. Look at the pictures and listen to the French for each pet.

1 un chien

2 un chat

3 un lapin

4 un cheval

5 un cochon d'Inde

6 un hamster

7 un oiseau

8 un poisson

9 une gerbille

10 une souris

Now rewind the cassette to the beginning of '*Mes animaux*' and listen again. This time pause the cassette after each pet and repeat it.

2 Ecoute. C'est quel numéro?

AT 1 – 1, AT 3 – 1

● Students listen to the cassette and match the pets they hear to the appropriate visuals, or in a few cases to the appropriate words, on Copymaster 43. They should at this stage be familiar with this type of activity, but, if necessary, demonstrate the task.

T: Un chat, c'est quel numéro? (Wait for the correct number and then write number 2 in a replica grid on the board.) Bravo! Alors, écoutez la cassette. Mettez le bon numéro dans la case.

un chat
un poisson
un cheval
une souris
un chien
un oiseau
un lapin

Look at the section '*C'est quel numéro?*' As you hear each pet, write the number of the picture which goes with it in the box.

un chat
un poisson
un cheval
une souris
un chien
un oiseau
un lapin

Solution

2, 8, 4, 10, 1, 7, 3

3 Copie ou mets le bon animal.

AT 3 – 1, AT 4 – 1

● Students then copy/select and write the appropriate pets below each image, choosing from a menu at the bottom of the copymaster.

Solution

2 un chat **3** un lapin **4** un cheval **5** un cochon d'Inde **8** un poisson **10** une souris

● Afterwards, the copymaster could be used for playing class or small group Bingo. Remind them of games language, e.g. *J'ai gagné!*

AT 4 – 2

● The completed copymaster can also be used to support students in their learning of the pet vocabulary. They can test themselves by covering the names of the animals and trying to write them from memory. Remind them of the strategies for learning vocabulary in '*Le vocabulaire? Pas de problème!*' on Students' Book page 13.

Presentation of:
Tu as un animal à la maison? Oui, j'ai ...

Tu as un animal à la maison?

(SB p.70)

a Ecoute. C'est quel animal?

AT 1 – 2

- Ask rhetorically *Tu as un animal à la maison?* and reply as if you have at least two pets.

T: Tu as un animal à la maison? Moi, j'ai un chien … et j'ai un chat. Alors, tu as un animal à la maison? Tu as un chien? Tu as un chat? (Encourage a few replies, prompting) J'ai … . 'Tu as un animal à la maison?', c'est quoi en anglais? (Confirm the meaning and repeat the question, before asking students to open their books at page 70).

- Direct students to the cartoon illustrations. Students listen to the class cassette and find the appropriate image for each dialogue.

T: Regardez la section 'Tu as un animal à la maison?' Vous allez écouter huit français parler de leurs animaux. (Write the numbers 1 – 8 on the board.) Ouvrez les cahiers et écrivez les numéros 1 à 8. (Students write the numbers down.) Ecoutez la cassette. C'est quel animal? Regardez les images et écrivez la bonne lettre!

1
– Tu as un animal à la maison?
– Oui, j'ai un chat.
– Pardon?
– J'ai un chat.

2
– Et toi? Tu as un animal à la maison?
– Oui, j'ai une souris.
– Une souris?
– Oui, j'ai une souris.

3
– Tu as un animal à la maison?
– Oui, j'ai un poisson!

4
– Tu as un animal à la maison?
– Oui, j'ai un chien.

5
– Et toi? Tu as un animal?
– Oui, j'ai un cheval.
– Ah, un cheval.
– Oui.

6
– Bonjour. Tu as un animal à la maison?
– Oui, j'ai un oiseau.

7
– Et toi? Tu as un animal?
– Bien sûr! J'ai un lapin!

8
– Salut! Tu as un animal à la maison?
– Oui, j'ai un cochon d'Inde.

Solution

1 C **2** H **3** D **4** A **5** E **6** G **7** B **8** F

- Having completed the listening comprehension exercise, focus on the statement *J'ai … (+ pet)*, asking the question *Tu as un animal à la maison?* and cueing responses with flashcards. At this stage before the plurals have been taught, oral practice is more straightforward if visual cues are used and personal responses to the question are avoided.

- Move on to teach and practise the question, before setting up pairwork based on the pictures on page 70.

> **Presentation of:**
> *Je n'ai pas d'animal*

b Ecoute et lis.

AT 1 – 3, AT 3 – 3

- This rhyme can be used to consolidate the statements and question covered so far and to introduce the phrase *Je n'ai pas d'animal*. Play the cassette through twice, encouraging students to follow the rhyme in their books.

J'ai un chat et j'ai un chien,
J'ai une souris, j'ai un lapin,
J'ai une gerbille et j'ai un poisson.
Et toi? Tu as un animal à la maison?
A la maison je n'ai pas d'animal,
Mais chez mon oncle j'ai un cheval!

- Check that the meaning of the last two lines is understood, before focusing on and practising the phrase *Je n'ai pas d'animal*. Students can then practise reading the rhyme aloud in pairs and can learn it by heart for homework, using the self study cassette for support.

You will need Students' Book page 70, activity B. Look at the rhyme *J'ai un chat et j'ai un chien'*. Listen to it on the cassette and practise reading it aloud.

J'ai un chat et j'ai un chien,
J'ai une souris, j'ai un lapin,
J'ai une gerbille et j'ai un poisson.
Et toi? Tu as un animal à la maison?
A la maison je n'ai pas d'animal,
Mais chez mon oncle j'ai un cheval!

Moi, j'ai des animaux! (SB p.71)

a Ecoute et lis.

AT 1 – 2, AT 3 – 2

- Introduce the plural forms of the pets, by playing the class cassette. Students listen and follow the text in their books.

J'ai cinq chats, trois chiens, deux poissons, trois lapins, deux hamsters et quatre gerbilles ... et j'ai six souris, quatre cochons d'Inde, deux chevaux et quatre oiseaux!

- Tell students to listen and read the text again and this time pause the cassette and encourage them to repeat the groups of pets.
- Write the singular nouns *chat, chien, poisson, lapin, hamster* and *gerbille* on the board and demonstrate, by contrasting *un chat* and *deux chats* etc., that although an -*s* is added when there is more that one pet, there is no change to the sound. Then contrast the singular and plural versions of *souris, cochon d'Inde, cheval* and *oiseau*, which don't add an -*s* in the way that the

previous pets do. Highlight the fact that the spellings must be learned, although most of the pets, with the exception of *chevaux*, still sound the same.

- To reinforce *J'ai* + singular and plural pets, use combinations of numbers and the pet flashcards to play '*Jeu de morpion*' on the board.

b C'est à toi!

AT 2 – 2

- Students could then play a 'Granny went shopping'-style game orally in groups of three to five. (Student 1: *J'ai deux poissons*. Student 2: *J'ai deux poissons et ... cinq souris*. Student 3: *J'ai deux poissons, cinq souris et ... trois chats*, etc.)
- Alternatively/additionally, they could make up their own cartoon and caption, along the lines of '*Moi, j'ai des animaux!*' and read it out aloud.

Sondage (SB p.71)

a Ecoute et dessine!

AT 1 – 2

- Explain that the class is now going to listen to a survey. Students listen to the dialogues on cassette and draw simple pictures to show understanding of the responses given each time.

T: Maintenant nous allons écouter un sondage. C'est un sondage d'animaux. Alors, écoutez les quatre conversations et dessinez les animaux. (Demonstrate on the board.) Par exemple, Numéro un. 'Tu as un animal à la maison?' 'Oui, j'ai deux lapins.' (Write 1A and draw two rabbits.) 'Et toi, tu as un animal à la maison?' 'Oui, j'ai un chien.' (Write B alongside and draw a dog. Explain also how to record Je n'ai pas d'animal, by drawing a dash.)

1
– Tu as un animal à la maison?
– Oui, j'ai deux lapins. Tu as un animal à la maison?
– Oui, j'ai un chien.

2
– Tu as un animal à la maison?

– Oui, j'ai trois souris. Tu as un animal à la maison?

– Oui, j'ai un chien et deux chats.

3

– Tu as un animal à la maison?

– Non, je n'ai pas d'animal. Tu as un animal à la maison?

– Oui, j'ai quatre oiseaux.

4

– Tu as un animal à la maison?

– Oui, j'ai deux chevaux et un chat. Tu as un animal à la maison?

– Non, je n'ai pas d'animal.

Solution

Students should have drawn the following:

1 A 2 rabbits   B 1 dog

2 A 3 mice   B 1 dog + 2 cats

3 A –   B 4 birds

4 A 2 horses + 1 cat   B –

b Fais un sondage.

AT 1 – 2, AT 2 – 2, AT 3 – 1/2, AT 4 – 1/2/3

- Remind students of the question *Tu as un animal à la maison?* and elicit individual responses. At this stage try to avoid spending a lot of time giving the French for other pets, although if the class is desperate to find out, you could jump ahead to page 72, '*Le glossaire anglais-français*' and work through this before undertaking the survey. Otherwise, tell students that they will find out the French for some more pets very soon, but that meanwhile they should try to stick to the pets which they know.

- Direct them to the model conversation at the bottom of the page. Students can follow this as you read it aloud. Remind them of the negative *Non, je n'ai pas d'animal* and then ask for two volunteers to take over the two roles. Ask for further volunteers, to establish the pattern.

- Decide how wide-ranging the survey is to be – students can either interview all the other members of the class or could interview a minimum number of, say, 10.

T: Faites un sondage dans la classe/dans un groupe de ... personnes. Notez les réponses, par exemple ... (Demonstrate ways in which students can note the responses which they receive – either drawing a simple grid on the board or showing how to record tally marks next to drawings or abbreviations, etc.) *Après, présentez vos résultats, par exemple ...* (Point out the bar chart on page 71. You may also want to suggest that they write up some of their friends' statements, e.g. *Michael: J'ai un chien et un chat*.) *Bon. Commencez!*

- Some students may be able to present their results using I.T.

Le glossaire anglais-français

(SB p.72)

AT 3 – 3, AT 4 – 1

- The activities on this page are designed to encourage simple dictionary skills and to promote the use of the English-French glossary. Before students begin, remind them of the concept of alphabetical ordering by playing some preliminary games as a class or in groups, for example:

- Write each letter of the alphabet on a separate piece of card/paper. Shuffle them and ask students to arrange them in alphabetical order whilst they say the letters in French.

- Write the names of some familiar pets on A4-size pieces of paper/card for students to arrange alphabetically on the board. (Cf. Teacher's Notes page 52, accompanying Students' Book Module 2 page 35, '*Le glossaire, c'est clair!*')

- Show students how to find out the French for other pets. Work through page 72 with the class, reading the instructions aloud and demonstrating and clarifying each stage of the process. Remind students that there are two glossaries at the back of their books, and that to find out the French for a word in English they should first look in the '*Vocabulaire anglais-français*'. Stress, however, that they should always make sure that they have found the correct word, by cross-checking the French in the '*Vocabulaire français-anglais*'.

- When students understand the process, they should use their glossaries to find out the French for the ten pets listed.

Solution

1 une perruche   **2** un canard   **3** un rat   **4** une chèvre   **5** un canari   **6** un chaton   **7** un chiot   **8** un serpent   **9** une oie   **10** un phasme

- Before starting the activities on page 73, collect as many magazine photos of pets as possible. In addition, ask students to bring a photo of one or more pets to the next lesson. (These will be needed in the *'Concours de photos'* activity.) Students can either bring in a photo of their actual pet(s) or can bring a photo or cartoon from a magazine or comic. Those who are unable to find a suitable picture can provide a drawing.

Grand concours d'animaux! (SB p.73)

AT 1 -3, AT 4 – 2

- Questions and statements about names and ages, using the language covered in objective 1 of this module, are now linked with pets.
- Direct students to the cartoon at the top of page 10 and read the speech bubbles of the characters at the pet show to establish the context, asking students to deduce the meaning of *'Concours d'animaux'*.

T: (Ask rhetorically) *Tu as un animal? Il s'appelle comment? Il a quel âge?* (Volunteer information about your own or imaginary pets, e.g.) *Alors, moi, j'ai un chien. Il s'appelle George. Il a deux ans.*

- Point out the *'Attention!'* feature and explain that *chien* and *chat* also have feminine equivalents.

T: **Attention!** *'Un chien', ça c'est masculin: J'ai un chien. Il s'appelle George. 'Une chienne', ça c'est féminin. J'ai une chienne. Elle s'appelle Georgina.* **(Repeat the process, contrasting *un chat* and *une chatte*.)**

- Having established the two new feminine forms and reminded students of questions and responses about names and ages, explain that they are now going to listen to a cassette.

T: **Regardez la page 73. Vous allez écouter six copains au concours d'animaux. Faites une grille comme ça ...** (Point out the grid in the example and, to clarify, draw a larger version numbered 1 – 6 on the board.) ... *et notez les détails des animaux, par exemple ...*

(Fill in the first example on the grid on the board.)

- Students now listen to the class cassette, featuring six longer conversations about pets and their names and ages. Initially, they should focus solely on these three aspects of each conversation. In addition, however, the conversations include familiar language from Module 3 in an unfamiliar context.
- On the second or third hearing, students could be encouraged to listen and note/say what other details they have understood. At this point they could be reminded of the method of listening examined on Students' Book page 60 of Module 3, *'J'écoute – pas de panique!',* ie: *thème, détails, encore des détails.*

1

– Bonjour! Je m'appelle Sébastien. J'ai un chien.
– Il s'appelle comment?
– Simba.
– Et il a quel âge?
– Cinq ans.
– Bon, merci. Voici ton billet. Tu as le numéro dix. Bonne chance!

2

– Bonjour! Je m'appelle Sandrine. J'ai trois lapins.
– Bon. Ils s'appellent comment?
– Tic, Tac et Toc.
– Tic, ça s'écrit T – I – C?
– Oui, et Tac, ça s'écrit T – A – C, et Toc, ça s'écrit T – O – C.
– Merci. Ils ont quel âge?
– Tic a deux ans et Tac et Toc ont quatre ans.
– Un moment ... Tic ... deux ans ... Tac et Toc ... quatre ans. Oh! Regarde comme ils mangent les carottes!

3

– Bonjour! Je m'appelle Marc. J'ai une chatte.
– Elle s'appelle comment?
– Maxi.
– Et elle a quel âge?
– Dix-huit mois.

– Dix-huit mois ... Merci ...
– Oh! Pardon! Elle joue avec votre stylo!

4

– Bonjour! Tu t'appelles comment?
– Olivier. J'ai un oiseau.
– Et il s'appelle comment?
– Bleuet.
– Ah! Bleuet, le perroquet?
– Oui, il chante en anglais et parle français! Il adore la musique!
– Et il a quel âge?
– Quarante-cinq ans.

5

– Salut! C'est Sophie, n'est-ce pas?
– Oui, salut! Alors, j'ai deux souris.
– Deux souris ... Bon. Elles s'appellent comment?
– Winnie et Minnie.
– Elles ont quel âge, alors?
– Dix mois. Ah, Winnie! Arrête!
– Qu'est-ce qu'elle fait?
– Elle fait une promenade dans mon sac!

6

– Bonjour! Je m'appelle Nicole. J'ai un cheval.
– Un cheval! Alors, il s'appelle comment?
– Orage. O – R – A – G – E.
– Et il a quel âge?
– Quinze ans. Euh ... Pardon, monsieur, quelle heure est-il, s'il vous plaît?
– Euh ... Il est une heure et quart.
– Bon. Ça va, Orage. C'est l'heure du déjeuner!

Solution

	animal/animaux	nom(s)	âge
1	1 chien	Simba	5 ans (+ Sébastien is given ticket number 10)
2	3 lapins	Tic	2 ans
		Tac et Toc	4 ans (+ they are eating carrots)
3	1 chatte	Maxi	18 mois (+ she is playing with the man's pen)
4	1 oiseau	Bleuet	45 ans (+ it's the parrot which sings in English and speaks French! He loves music!)
5	2 souris	Winnie et Minnie	10 mois (+ Winnie is going for a walk in Sophie's bag!)
6	1 cheval	Orage	15 ans (+ it's a quarter past 1 and time for the horse's lunch!)

- Before directing students to Copymaster 44, ask them to try to remember as many questions as possible from the cassette. Prompt them if necessary, by asking *Comment dit-on* 'What is he called?' etc. List the questions on the board.

- Remind the class of the use of the different forms of the questions by revising *Tu as des frères et des sœurs?* and showing how to select the appropriate follow-up question in response to information received, depending on the gender and number of siblings. Then show how this same principle applies to pets, by referring to the cartoon again at the top of the page and showing/asking students to deduce how the questions would change if the girl in the cartoon were to say *J'ai une gerbille/J'ai deux lapins* etc.

- Finally, point out that in this context *il* and *elle* can also mean 'it'.

Encore des animaux (CM 44)

1 Relie.

AT 3 – 2, AT 4 – 2/3

- This copymaster practises linking questions and statements about names and ages to pets. In the first activity, students simply link the correct pair of questions to each statement.

Solution

1 E **2** C **3** B or D **4** A **5** B or D

2 Complète les réponses.

AT 3 – 2, AT 4 – 2/3

- Students use their completed first activity to support them in the second task in which they

4 En famille

complete sentences about the names and ages of various pets.

- The whole sheet can then be kept and used for reference.

Solution

2 Elle s'appelle Minnie. **Elle a** trois ans.

3 Ils s'appellent Bill et Ben. **Ils ont** quatre ans.

4 Elles s'appellent Bubble et Squeak. **Elles ont** deux mois.

5 Ils s'appellent Tom et Jerry. **Tom a** deux ans et **Jerry a** six mois.

Concours de photos (SB p.73)

AT 1 – 3, AT 2 – 3, AT 3 – 1/3, AT 4 – 2

- Point to the photo of the dog on page 73 and read through the example interview, using a volunteer to take the role of Nick if possible. Then point out the accompanying note showing the details collected from the interview.

- Explain that students are now going to work in groups of five or six and run their own pet show, using the photos collected earlier. (If snaps of pets or photos/cartoons from magazines are not available, drawings could be made instead.)

- Ask a couple of students up to the front of the class to demonstrate the activity. Greet one of the students and ask him/her to show his/her photo. Then show how to adapt the interview on page 73, by substituting the student's name and the details of the animal in his/her photo, and also changing the questions accordingly, if necessary. Demonstrate how the rest of the group should listen and note the details. Then ask the next student to show his/her photo and help the first student to take over the role of the interviewer, showing again how to substitute the details in the model interview on page 10. Again, explain that the rest of the group should listen and note the details. Finally show how the second student should then interview you about the pet in your photo!

- Show the photos from your demonstration again and demonstrate how each member of the group votes by writing the name of his or her favourite pet on a piece of paper. Then count the votes and declare them, e.g. Jenny, trois votes! Dougal ... etc.

- When students understand what they have to do, help them to organise themselves into groups of

five or six and check that they each have a photo or drawing before starting the activity.

A toi! (SB p.73)

AT 4 – 3/4

- Finally, students can write up a description of their own pet(s) or the one(s) which they entered for the Concours de photos.

Entre-temps ... (SB p.74)

AT 3 – 3/4

- Students should read the selection of articles on this page for personal interest and enjoyment. Copymaster 23 'Mes découvertes' can be used in conjunction with this page, to help students develop reading skills and widen their vocabulary.

> **Presentation of:**
> *Pardon, monsieur/madame.*
> *Pardon?*
> *Je peux fermer/ouvrir la porte/le fenêtre?*
> *aller aux toilettes?*

Aïe! (SB p.75)

a Ecoute et lis.

AT 1 – 4, AT 2 – 2, AT 3 – 4

- Students listen to the class cassette, whilst following the text of the 'Classe d'enfer' cartoon strip on page 75, which features *Je peux ...?* and classroom requests.

Prof: Alors, les devoirs de géo, s'il vous plaît .
Girl: Pardon? Les devoirs? Oh, là. là! ...
Pardon Monsieur, je peux aller aux toilettes?
Prof: Un moment. Les devoirs s'il vous plaît.
Boy: Pardon, monsieur!
Girl: Pardon, monsieur, je peux ouvrir la fenêtre?
Prof: Oui, Oui.
Girl: Pas de panique! ... Aïe!
Monsieur, je peux fermer la fenêtre?

- Play the cassette through once continuously. Then play it a second time and pause the cassette after each frame of the cartoon strip. If necessary, demonstrate the linking of the text to the cassette and encourage students to point to the relevant speech bubbles as they hear the language.

- Refer to the visuals in the cartoon strip and, supporting these with mime, encourage students to work out the meaning of the following phrases:
  Pardon?
  Pardon, monsieur ...
  Je peux aller aux toilettes?
  Je peux ouvrir la fenêtre?
  Je peux fermer la fenêtre?

- Extend these phrases to include the following, prompting students to deduce the substitutions, where possible:
  Pardon, madame ...
  Je peux ouvrir la porte?
  Je peux fermer la porte?

- Point out the convention of preceding the requests with *Pardon, monsieur .../Pardon, madame ...* to make them sound more polite.

- Check understanding by saying all these phrases in random order and encouraging students to respond to them with the appropriate action. The class should then repeat the language along with the mime to practise pronunciation. Finally, students produce the language orally in response to the mime, before taking over the activity themselves as a class, in groups or in pairs.

En classe Pas de panique! (CM 45)

AT 1 –2, AT 2 – 2, AT 3 – 2

- When photocopying this copymaster, it may be preferable to use card rather than paper, so that the spinner at the bottom of the sheet works more effectively when cut out and used in the final activity. Alternatively, the segments can be numbered 1 – 6 and used in combination with a die.

1 Relie les phrases et les images.

- Students first demonstate understanding by linking each phrase to the appropriate visual.

Solution

1 D 2 G 3 B 4 F 5 C 6 A 7 E

2 Ecoute, lis et répète.

- Students now practise pronunciation by listening to the classroom language on the cassette, reading the phrases and repeating each one after the cassette. If the students work independently, using the self-study cassette, they can try reading the phrases aloud and then compare their own pronunciation with that of the cassette.

1 Pardon, monsieur ...
2 Pardon, madame ...
3 Pardon?
4 Je peux fermer la fenêtre?
5 Je peux ouvrir la fenêtre?
6 Je peux aller aux toilettes?
7 Je peux fermer la porte?

You will need Copymaster 45, activity 2. Look at the seven phrases. Listen to the cassette as you read each one. Pause the cassette after each phrase and repeat it.

1 Pardon, monsieur ...
2 Pardon, madame ...
3 Pardon?
4 Je peux fermer la fenêtre?
5 Je peux ouvrir la fenêtre?
6 Je peux aller aux toilettes?
7 Je peux fermer la porte?

3 Jeu de mémoire!

- Finally, students can cut out and make the spinner, using it to cue oral work. This memory game can be played individually, or in pairs for points. As an alternative to making the spinner, the segments can be numbered 1 – 6 and used in combination with a die. To make the game more challenging and promote the use of social conventions, encourage the use of *Pardon, monsieur / madame ...* and *..., s'il vous plaît* with the requests.

Aie!

b Comment dit-on ...? (SB p.75)

AT 2 – 2, AT 4 – 2/3

- Students use the pictures as cues for oral and/or written production of the classroom language. This can be done as a class, group or pairwork activity.

Solution

1 Pardon?   **2** Pardon, monsieur ...   **3** Je peux ouvrir la fenêtre?   **4** Je peux aller aux toilettes?   **5** Je peux fermer la fenêtre?   **6** Je peux fermer la porte?

Differentiation – Extension

AT 1 – 4, AT 2 – 2/4, AT 3 – 4, AT 4 – 2/4

- Working in groups or individually, some students could write and/or act out their own short cartoon strip or playlet based in a classroom, incorporating the new language. Copymaster 45 and the cartoon strip on page 75 can both be used for support.

Objectif 3   Descriptions

New language introduced

Il/Elle est rouge/bleu(e)/jaune/vert(e)/noir(e)/ blanc(he)/gris(e)/brun(e)

Ils/Elles sont rouges/bleu(e)s/jaunes/vert(e)s/ noir(e)s/blanc(he)s/gris(e)s/brun(e)s

Il/Elle est comment?

Ils/Elles sont comment?

... pénible(s)/amusant(s)/adorable(s)/grand (e)s/ petit(e)s/sympa

Revised language

Personal information (name, age, where you live)

Student goals (SB p.64)

- Remind the class of the third section of the goals visual on page 64.

*T: (Point to the third objectif.) **Nous commençons objectif trois – descriptions. Alors, tu as des frères et des sœurs? Ils sont grands ou petits?** (Gesture to indicate tall and short.) **Tu as un chien? Il est grand? Il est petit? Il est noir? Il est blanc?** (Gesture to indicate large and small and point to something black and something white to indicate the colours.)*

Presentation of colours

Les couleurs (FC 64 – 65)

AT 1 – 1, AT 2 – 1

- Use different coloured objects in the classroom and/or flashcards 64 and 65 to teach the following colours:

  rouge
  bleu
  jaune
  vert
  noir
  blanc
  gris
  brun

- Check comprehension, by sticking the flashcards on the board and linking each colour to a number written on the board.

*T: **Rouge, c'est quel numéro? etc.***

- Move on to practise pronunciation and cue oral production of the colours. Play a variety of oral and aural games, after which students should be ready to tackle Copymaster 46.

Les couleurs (CM 46)

- This copymaster practises aural and reading comprehension of colours. Since students need access to colouring equipment and time to colour in, the tasks are more suitable for homework.

1 Ecoute et colorie.

AT 1 – 1

- In the first activity, students listen to the self-study cassette and colour the birds according to the instruction given on the tape.

You will need Copymaster 46, activity 1 and some colouring pencils or felt-tip pens. Look at the picture of eight birds. Listen to the cassette to find out the colour of each one. Pause the cassette after you hear each colour and colour in the bird, following the instruction.

1 bleu
2 jaune
3 brun
4 vert
5 blanc
6 noir
7 rouge
8 gris

2 Lis et colorie.

AT 3 – 1

- In the second activity students colour the balls according to the label on each one. Remind them not to colour over the label itself, so that the sheet can be used for future reference.

Solution

jaune – yellow   noir – black   rouge – red   blanc – white
bleu – blue   brun – brown   vert – green   gris – grey

Presentation of: *Il/Elle est (+* colour*)*

F

Les animaux et les couleurs

(FC 54 – 65)

- Begin linking colours to the masculine pets. Hold up the flashcard of the dog and then point to the splodge of black on the colour flashcard.

T: ***J'ai un chien. Il est noir.***

- Repeat the process with other combinations of masculine pets and colours, encouraging students to join in building up the descriptions.

- Then use combinations of the pet and colour flashcards to contrast the way in which the masculine fish and the feminine mouse, gerbil and a female cat are described. Slightly stress the indefinite article, pronoun and any contrast in the sound of the colour as you do so.

T: ***J'ai un chien. Il est brun. J'ai une souris. Elle est brune. etc.***

- Focus initially on the colours which have a sounded feminine agreement, so that the contrast is more obvious.

- Summarise by asking *Alors, comment dit-on 'green'/'brown'/'grey'/'white' en français?* and encourage students to volunteer the alternative masculine and feminine versions of the adjectives. As they do so, write the masculine forms on the board underneath the flashcards of several masculine pets and write the feminine forms on the other side of the board underneath the flashcards of the feminine pets.

T: **Quelle est la différence? (If no answer is forthcoming, ask.) Les animaux ici sont masculins ou féminins? Et les animaux ici? 'Vert', ça s'écrit comment? Et 'verte', ça s'écrit comment? (Remind them again that il and elle can also mean 'it'.)**

- Having established the principle, leave the subtleties of silent -*e* endings and *rouge* and *jaune* until later and move on to Students' Book page 76.

De quelle couleur?   (SB p.76)

AT 1 – 2, AT 2 – 2, AT 3 – 2

- The class now practises comprehension of pets and colours. At the same time the activity reinforces the contrast between masculine and feminine forms. Students listen to the class cassette, whilst following the short descriptions in their books and then match the appropriate photo to each description.

1 J'ai un lapin. Il est gris.
2 J'ai une chatte. Elle est noire et blanche.
3 J'ai une souris. Elle est grise.
4 J'ai un lapin. Il est brun.
5 J'ai un cheval. Il est noir et blanc.

Solution

1 B   **2** A   **3** D   **4** E   **5** C

En couleurs!   (SB p.76)

AT 1 – 1, AT 3 – 1

- Work through the two rows of colours, contrasting masculine and feminine forms alternately, whilst students follow in their books.

In a *pause anglaise* ask students to recap what they have noticed about the colours. Emphasise the fact that you can nearly always see the difference in spelling, but that you cannot always hear it. Ask them to suggest why *jaune* and *rouge* do not change in the feminine form.

Il est ... Elle est ... (CM 47)

1 Ecoute, lis et répète.

AT 1 – 2, AT 2 – 2, AT 3 – 2, AT 4 – 1/2

- This copymaster builds on Students' Book page 77 and gives students the opportunity to practise adjectives of colour in the masculine and feminine singular forms. The class cassette and self-study cassette accompanying the copymaster contain identical material, so that students can either work through the first activity as a class or individually/at home.

- Initially, students listen to the cassette in which masculine and feminine forms of the colours are given alternately. At the same time they follow the written version of the descriptions in the two dustbins on the copymaster and then they repeat after the cassette.

Il est brun.
Elle est brune.
Il est gris.
Elle est grise.
Il est vert.
Elle est verte.
Il est blanc.
Elle est blanche.
Il est noir.
Elle est noire.
Il est bleu.
Elle est bleue.
Il est jaune.
Elle est jaune.
Il est rouge.
Elle est rouge.

You will need Copymaster 47, activity 1. Look at the words in the two dustbins at the top of the page. Listen to the cassette as you read the words in the left- and right-hand bins alternately. Pause the cassette after each sentence and repeat it.

Il est brun.
Elle est brune.
Il est gris.
Elle est grise.
Il est vert.
Elle est verte.
Il est blanc.
Elle est blanche.
Il est noir.
Elle est noire.
Il est bleu.
Elle est bleue.
Il est jaune.
Elle est jaune.
Il est rouge.
Elle est rouge.

2 Complète les descriptions et colorie!

AT 3 – 2, AT 4 – 1/2

- In the second activity students look at the pictures, read the descriptions of the pets, choose the correct version of the adjective to complete the descriptions and colour accordingly. In some cases they are also required to fill in other missing vocabulary. The 'reference bins' at the top of the copymaster should provide support in choosing the correct form of the adjectives.

Solution

1 noir (+ black rabbit)
2 brune (+ brown mouse)
3 blanche (+ white cat)
4 oiseau; vert (+ green bird)
5 gerbille; Elle; grise (+ grey gerbil)
6 poisson; Il est bleu (+ blue fish)

A toi! (SB p.76)

AT 3 – 2, AT 4 – 2/3

- Direct students back to page 76 and remind them of the handwritten descriptions of pets. They can now write their own description of one or more real or imaginary pets, supplying a photo or picture to accompany each description if desired. Stress, however, that at this stage students should not describe more than one animal at a time.

Presentation of: *Ils/Elles sont (+ colour)*

Ce n'est pas vrai! (SB p.77)

AT 1 – 3, AT 3 – 3

- Use the cassette and the cartoons at the top of the page to introduce the plural adjective endings. Play the class cassette, whilst students follow the texts in the speech bubbles in their books.

– J'ai deux chiens. Ils sont noirs et blancs. J'ai trois gerbilles. Elles sont grises.

– Et moi, j'ai deux chats. Ils sont bleus et verts. J'ai aussi trois souris. Elles sont vertes, bleues et rouges!

- Check that the class understands the meaning of *ils sont* and *elles sont*.

T: *'Ils sont noirs et blancs', c'est quoi en anglais? … Et 'elles sont grises', c'est quoi en anglais? Alors, comment dit-on 'they are …' en français?*

- Use combinations of numbers and pet flashcards with the colour flashcards to illustrate the different masculine and feminine plural forms, building descriptions such as *J'ai trois chiens. Ils sont noirs* and contrasting this with sentences such as *J'ai trois souris. Elles sont grises.* Encourage the class to help you build up similar descriptions, based on number and flashcard cues and to deduce the difference in the use of *ils sont* and *elles sont*.

- Now focus on the plural adjective endings. Direct students back to the descriptions on page 77.

T: *Regardez les descriptions: 'J'ai deux chiens. Ils sont noirs et blancs. J'ai trois gerbilles. Elles sont grises.' Regardez les mots 'noirs', 'blancs' et 'grises' … et regardez les mots pour les couleurs à la page 76 …* (Point out the *'En couleurs'* feature.) *Quelle est la différence?* (If no answer is forthcoming, prompt students.) *Regardez la page 76: Il est noir … 'noir', ça s'écrit comment? Et à la page 77: Ils sont noirs … 'noirs', ça s'écrit comment?*

- Contrast a few more examples, writing the different masculine and feminine singular and plural forms on the board. Then summarise all this as you guide students through the *'Attention!'* feature on page 77.

At this point you may wish to use Copymaster 81. Students complete notes on the agreement of adjectives and keep them for reference.

Differentiation – Consolidation or Extension

- Depending on the degree of support needed, students can now move on to practise the adjective endings using either Copymaster 48 or 49. The same class cassette accompanies both and can be used simultaneously. The tasks on Copymaster 48 include more support and are more graduated than those on Copymaster 49. Also, they do not involve written production of the different forms of the adjectives.

Radio Jeunes – Nos animaux (CM 48)

AT 1 – 3, AT 3 – 2

1 Ecoute. C'est quel numéro?

- In the first activity students listen to the radio phone-in and number the first set of statements about pets in the order of hearing, using the accompanying pictures for support.

1

– Et maintenant … Un sondage! Aujourd'hui, 'Radio Jeunes – Nos animaux'! Allons – y!

– Bonjour. Je m'appelle Elizabeth.

– Bonjour, Elizabeth. Ça va?

– Oui, ça va bien merci.

– Alors, Elizabeth, tu as un animal à la maison?

– Oui, j'ai deux chiens. Ils sont blancs.

2

– Bonjour!

– Bonjour! Tu t'appelles comment?

– Luc.

– Bon, Luc. Tu as un animal à la maison?

– Oui, j'ai deux gerbilles. Elles sont grises.

3

– Salut! Je m'appelle Madeleine.

– Bonjour, Madeleine. Tu as un animal à la maison?

– Oui, j'ai deux souris. Elles sont noires.

– Bon. Merci!

4

– Bonjour.

– Bonjour. Tu t'appelles comment?

– Karine.

– Alors, tu as un animal à la maison, Karine?

– Oui, j'ai deux lapins. Ils sont noirs.

5

– Salut! Je m'appelle Philippe.

– Salut, Philippe. Ça va?

– Oui, très bien, merci.

– Bon. Tu as un animal à la maison?

– Oui, j'ai une souris. Elle est noire.

6

– Salut!

– Salut! Tu t'appelles comment?

– Isabelle.

– Alors, tu as un animal aussi?

– Oui, j'ai une souris. Elle est blanche.

7

– Bonjour. Je m'appelle Jean-Pierre. J'ai un chat. Il est blanc.

– Merci, Jean-Pierre!

8

– Bonjour. Je m'appelle Laurent et j'ai un chien.

– Il est comment, ton chien? –

– Il est noir.

– Merci!

9

– Salut! Je m'appelle Françoise et j'ai deux souris. Elles sont blanches.

– Merci, Françoise. Au revoir!

Solution

4 J'ai deux lapins.

6 J'ai une souris.

3 J'ai deux souris.

7 J'ai un chat.

1 J'ai deux chiens.

9 J'ai deux souris.

2 J'ai deux gerbilles.

5 J'ai une souris.

8 J'ai un chien.

2 Relie la description!

- Students then link the appropriate description from the right-hand set of statements on their copymaster to the correct statement about pets on the left-hand side. This time, in addition to using the pictures, they can also use the 'Rappel' box at the top of the copymaster for support.

Solution

J'ai deux lapins. Ils sont noirs.

J'ai une souris. Elle est blanche.

J'ai deux souris. Elles sont noires.

J'ai un chat. Il est blanc.

J'ai deux chiens. Ils sont blancs.

J'ai deux souris. Elles sont blanches.

J'ai deux gerbilles. Elles sont grises.

J'ai une souris. Elle est noire.

J'ai un chien. Il est noir.

Radio Jeunes – Nos animaux – Extra!
(CM 49)

AT 1 – 3, AT 3 – 2, AT 4 – 3

1 Ecoute la cassette et regarde les images. C'est quelle lettre?

- Higher attainers listen to the same radio phone-in on the class cassette, but must select the letter of the pet described each time, choosing from the accompanying pictures. Unlike students using Copymaster 48, they do not have a list of written statements for support and must base their choice solely on comprehension of the conversations.

1

– Et maintenant … Un sondage! Aujourd'hui, 'Radio Jeunes – Nos animaux'! Allons – y!
– Bonjour. Je m'appelle Elizabeth.
– Bonjour, Elizabeth. Ça va?
– Oui, ça va bien merci.
– Alors, Elizabeth, tu as un animal à la maison?
– Oui, j'ai deux chiens. Ils sont blancs.

2

– Bonjour!
– Bonjour! Tu t'appelles comment?
– Luc.
– Bon, Luc. Tu as un animal à la maison?
– Oui, j'ai deux gerbilles. Elles sont grises.

3

– Salut! Je m'appelle Madeleine.
– Bonjour, Madeleine. Tu as un animal à la maison?
– Oui, j'ai deux souris. Elles sont noires.
– Bon. Merci!

4

– Bonjour.
– Bonjour. Tu t'appelles comment?
– Karine.
– Alors, tu as un animal à la maison, Karine?
– Oui, j'ai deux lapins. Ils sont noirs.

5

– Salut! Je m'appelle Philippe.
– Salut, Philippe. Ça va?
– Oui, très bien, merci.
– Bon. Tu as un animal à la maison?
– Oui, j'ai une souris. Elle est noire.

6

– Salut!
– Salut! Tu t'appelles comment?

– Isabelle.
– Alors, tu as un animal aussi?
– Oui, j'ai une souris. Elle est blanche.

7

– Bonjour. Je m'appelle Jean-Pierre. J'ai un chat. Il est blanc.
– Merci, Jean-Pierre!

8

– Bonjour. Je m'appelle Laurent et j'ai un chien.
– Il est comment, ton chien?
– Il est noir.
– Merci!

9

– Salut! Je m'appelle Françoise et j'ai deux souris. Elles sont blanches.
– Merci, Françoise. Au revoir!

Solution

E, G, C, A, H, B, D, I, F

2 Complète les descriptions.

- In the second activity, students use pictures as a cue for writing statements about pets, following the pattern *J'ai deux … Ils sont …* etc. The copymaster contains the same '*Rappel*' feature as Copymaster 48 for reference, but students must use this actively to produce their descriptions of the pets.

Solution

A J'ai deux lapins. Ils sont noirs.
B J'ai une souris. Elle est blanche.
C J'ai deux souris. Elles sont noires.
D J'ai un chat. Il est blanc.
E J'ai deux chiens. Ils sont blancs.
F J'ai deux souris. Elles sont blanches.
G J'ai deux gerbilles. Elles sont grises.
H J'ai une souris. Elle est noire.
I J'ai un chien. Il est noir.

Animaux fantastiques au marché!

(SB p.77)

AT 2 – 2/3, AT 4 – 2/3

- The class can now return to page 77 and, referring to the cartoon of the market stall, the '*Attention!*'

feature and the example, produce other statements for the alien. This can be a written and/or oral activity.

Solution

(Answers acceptable in any order)

J'ai deux lapins. Ils sont rouges!

J'ai trois gerbilles. Elles sont bleues!

J'ai deux chiens. Ils sont verts!/J'ai deux chiennes. Elles sont vertes!

J'ai deux chats. Ils sont jaunes!/J'ai deux chattes. Elles sont jaunes!

J'ai quatre souris. Elles sont bleues!

Differentiation – Extension

- Higher attainers can study the *'Extra!'* sign beside the market stall and use their English – French glossary or their notes from page 72 to produce statements about the additional animals.

Solution

J'ai deux tortues. Elles sont vertes!

J'ai trois serpents. Ils sont rouges et bleus!

- All students can be encouraged to produce written and/or oral statements about their own fantastic animals.

Mon frère a un crocodile (SB p.78)

AT1 – 2/3/4, AT 2 – 2/3/4, AT 3 – 2/3/4

- Students now listen to the rap, which provides further consolidation of descriptions of pets. It also reinforces the fact that the plural *-s* is silent, and provides support for the *'Comment ça se prononce?'* feature later on page 78.
- Play the rap through once and encourage the class to follow the accompanying text on page 78 of their books. Then play one verse at a time, stopping briefly after each to check understanding. As this process continues and the rhythm becomes familiar, encourage the class to join in with the separate verses, before students finally rap along to the full version.

1 Mon frère a un crocodile.
   Il est grand. Il s'appelle Cyril.
2 Il est vert et il est gros.
   Je préfère *mes* animaux.
3 Moi, j'ai deux petits lapins.
   Ils sont bleus et ils sont bruns.
4 J'ai une souris et elle est grise.
   Elle a cent ans. Elle s'appelle Louise.
5 J'ai deux rats, Alphonse et Mec.
   Ils vont à la discothèque.
6 J'ai un cheval. Il s'appelle Dédé.
   Il regarde la télé.
7 Mon frère a un crocodile.
   Il est grand. Il s'appelle Cyril.
8 Il est vert. Il est très gros.
   Il mange tous mes animaux!
9 Rats, souris, lapins, cheval …
   Maintenant, je n'ai pas d'animal!

1 Mon frère a un crocodile.
   Il est grand. Il s'appelle Cyril.
2 Il est vert et il est gros.
   Je préfère *mes* animaux.
3 Moi, j'ai deux petits lapins.
   Ils sont bleus et ils sont bruns.
4 J'ai une souris et elle est grise.
   Elle a cent ans. Elle s'appelle Louise.
5 J'ai deux rats, Alphonse et Mec.
   Ils vont à la discothèque.
6 J'ai un cheval. Il s'appelle Dédé.
   Il regarde la télé.
7 Mon frère a un crocodile.
   Il est grand. Il s'appelle Cyril.
8 Il est vert. Il est très gros.
   Il mange tous mes animaux!
9 Rats, souris, lapins, cheval …
   Maintenant, je n'ai pas d'animal!

- Afterwards, where appropriate, challenge the class to chant without the support of the cassette as you turn down the volume.

Alternatively/additionally, students could work in pairs, taking it in turns to use a ruler or pen to cover a line or verse of the rap for their partner to say, chant or write from memory.

AT3 – 2/3/4, AT4 – 2

- Finally, students could demonstrate comprehension and accuracy by copying and illustrating one or more verses of the rap for a wall display. They could also learn their chosen section of the text or one or more of their favourite verses by heart.

Comment ça se prononce? (SB p.78)
a Lis, prononce et écoute.

AT 1 – 1, AT 2 – 1, AT 3 – 1

- Recap briefly and remind students that the plural -*s* is silent. They can then work independently to practise reading and pronouncing the singular and plural words listed. After each word they should use the self-study cassette to check pronunciation.

You will need Students' Book page 78. Look carefully at the ten words in activity A at the bottom of the page and read them out loud. After saying each word listen to the cassette to check your pronunciation. Pause the cassette after each number.

1 chien
2 chiens
3 blanc
4 blancs
5 chat
6 chats
7 noir
8 noirs
9 vert
10 verts

b Extra! Lis, prononce et écoute.

AT 1 – 1, AT 2 – 1, AT 3 – 1

- Higher attainers can go on to tackle and practise the words in this activity.

Now look at the five words in activity B. Read them out loud, then listen to the cassette to check your pronunciation.

1 crayons
2 règle
3 cahier
4 livres
5 stylos

Presentation of: *pénible(s) / amusant(e)s / adorable(s)*

Les chiens sont adorables! (SB p.79)

AT 1 – 3, AT 2 – 2/3/4, AT 3 – 3, AT 4 – 2/3/4

- Use page 79 and the class cassette to consolidate the work on pets and their descriptions. Play the cassette as support for this piece of more extended reading, telling students to listen and follow the story in their books.

Louise: A moi!
Marc: Hé!
Boy: Pardon! C'est mon chien! Il est pénible!

Louise: Oh, non! Il est amusant! Il s'appelle comment?
Boy: Bruno.

Louise: Il a quel âge?
Boy: Trois ans.

Louise: Moi, j'aime bien les chiens. Ils sont adorables!

Boy: Tu as un chien?
Louise: Non, j'ai un chat.

Boy: Euh … Il est noir et blanc?
Louise: Oui … Oh, non! … J'aime les chiens, mais, moi, je préfère les chats!

- Draw attention to the following new language, encouraging students to use the context to deduce the meaning of this new vocabulary: *pénible, amusant, adorable(s)*.
- Recap by playing the cassette again while students listen to and read the text. Students could then work in pairs and practise reading the conversation between Louise and the boy.

Differentiation – Extension

- Students could work in pairs and adapt the story to invent their own cartoon and/or conversation, involving one or more different animals. It may be helpful to suggest a few possibilities, e.g. a cat chasing a bird/mouse, a dog chasing a rabbit etc. Use an example to demonstrate how students can substitute details in the speech bubbles to create a new story.

> **Presentation of:** *grand(e)s / petit(e)s / sympa*

Descriptions

AT 1 – 1/2, AT 2 – 1/2, AT 3 – 1/2

- Before proceding to Copymaster 50, teach the following adjectives, some of which will have been touched upon already:
grand, petit, amusant, pénible, sympa.
- Use the adjectives to describe some of the flashcard pets and mythical members of your family/pin people on the board. Support the meaning through mime and gesture and check that students understand.

T: **'*Pénible*', c'est quoi en anglais? etc. (When they are confident in the meanings of the adjectives, ask.)** *Tu as des frères et des sœurs? Il/Elle est comment? Ils/Elles sont comment?* **(Writing the relevant question on the board. Offer a choice, to help students respond to the follow-up question.)** *Il est grand? Ou il est petit? etc.* **(List the masculine singular, feminine singular, masculine plural and feminine plural forms of the adjectives in four different groups on the board.)**

- Focus on the four questions on the board. Check that students understand the meaning and

encourage them to repeat each question after you. Then give a series of statements such as *J'ai un frère, J'ai deux sœurs* etc. and ask them to choose the correct question to find out more information. Remind them that in response to a statement about a mixed group, they will also ask *Ils sont comment?* When students understand the principle, cue questions randomly from the class by giving a statement *J'ai ...* + one or more siblings, and throwing a softball or beachball to a student, who should then ask the appropriate follow-up question, before throwing the ball back to you.

- Then focus on the adjectives on the board and contrast their masculine and feminine singular and plural forms, encouraging students to repeat them after you. Highlight the adjective endings as you do so, before referring students back to the *'Attention!'* feature on page 77. Show that the pattern of endings operates in the same way, except in the case of *sympa*, which never changes.

- Finally, repeat the softball game, but this time encourage students to follow up your statement with a description when they catch the ball, e.g. *J'ai un frère. > Il est grand* etc. Eventually, the ball could be thrown from one student to another to form a chain of statements, follow-up questions and answers, e.g. *J'ai un frère. > Il est comment? > Il est grand. > J'ai deux sœurs. > Elles sont comment? > Elles sont amusantes* etc.

Descriptions! (CM 50)

AT 3 – 2, AT 4 – 1/2

- Students can now build up a reference sheet of the questions and the five additional adjectives relating to descriptions. They complete statements in response to questions, choosing the appropriate adjectives from a menu and sorting them into masculine singular, feminine singular, masculine plural and feminine plural groups.

Solution

Il est grand, petit, pénible

Elle est grande, petite, pénible

Ils sont grands, petits, pénibles

Elles sont grandes, petites, pénibles

Rue St. Lazare (SB p.80)

AT 1 – 4, AT 3 – 4

- The themes and language of the module are now brought together in a new context. In this longer text, a young actor from a television soap introduces himself and describes the character whom he plays in the series and his fictional family.

- Students follow the text, whilst listening to the class cassette. Check that they understand the context and new vocabulary such as *Je joue le rôle de …* and *série télévisée,* before playing the cassette again. They can then have the opportunity for quiet reading to familiarise themselves with the text, before moving on to the activities on page 80.

Salut! Je m'appelle Samuel Pétri. J'ai douze ans et j'habite à Quinzac. Je joue le rôle de Mathieu dans la série 'Rue St. Lazare'! Vous aimez les séries télévisées? Alors, je vous présente 'ma famille'! Dans la série je m'appelle Mathieu Lauret et j'ai treize ans. J'ai un frère et une sœur. Mes parents sont séparés et j'habite à Bordeaux avec mon père et ma sœur …

Alors, voici mon père. Il s'appelle Stéphane et il a quarante-huit ans. Il est assez grand et très sympa. Et voici ma sœur. Elle s'appelle Emmeline et elle a neuf ans. Elle est petite et amusante!

Mon frère habite à Paris avec ma mère. Il a dix-neuf ans et il s'appelle Philippe. Ma mère s'appelle Michèle et elle est très sympa.

Et enfin mon chien! Il s'appelle Astérix et il a deux ans. Il est très grand, brun et pénible!

Interview avec Mathieu! (SB p.81)

AT 1 – 2, AT 2 – 1/2/3/4, AT 3 – 2, AT 4 – 1/2/3

- Students demonstrate understanding of the language on page 80 and their ability to cope with handwritten texts, by answering ten questions, as if they were Mathieu. This can be done orally or as a written activity. The questions listed on page 81 also form a reference for future interviews.

Solution

1 Je m'appelle Mathieu Lauret.
2 J'ai treize ans.
3 J'ai un frère et une sœur.
4 Ils s'appellent Emmeline et Philippe.
5 Emmeline a neuf ans et Philippe a dix-neuf ans.
6 Emmeline est petite et amusante. (+ possibly info. about Philippe from photo)
7 Oui, j'ai un chien.
8 Il s'appelle Astérix.
9 Il a deux ans.
10 Il est très grand, brun et pénible!

Salut, Dominique! (SB p.81)

AT 1 – 4, AT 4 – 1/2

- The class now has the opportunity to listen to an interview with another young actor and to practise their skills in listening to longer passages. They should try to note as many details as possible about Dominique's family. To check comprehension, it might be more appropriate to do this in English. If notes are to be taken in French, it may be helpful to provide some guidance, perhaps in the form of the following grid:

	frère(s)?	sœur(s)?	parents?	animaux?
nom(s)?				
âge(s)?				
comment?				

Et moi, je m'appelle Catherine Dubois. Je joue le rôle de Dominique dans la série. … Et 'ma famille'? Alors, dans la série je m'appelle Dominique Rocher et je suis dans la classe de Mathieu. J'ai quatorze ans et j'ai deux sœurs. Mes parents s'appellent Jean-Claude et Véronique et nous habitons dans la rue St. Lazare.

Mon père a quarante-six ans et il est très amusant. Ma mère a quarante-trois ans. Elle est petite et sympa. Et mes sœurs? Alors, elles s'appellent Nathalie et Vanessa. Elles ont dix ans et elles sont pénibles!

Oh! J'ai complètement oublié! J'ai aussi un cochon d'Inde et un chat! Mon cochon d'Inde s'appelle Georges. Il est brun et blanc. Et mon chat s'appelle Minuit. Il est noir et petit et il regarde la télé – surtout la série 'Rue St. Lazare'!

Solution

	frère(s)?	sœur(s)?	parents?	animaux?
nom(s)?		2; Nathalie Vanessa	Jean-Claude Véronique	cochon d'Inde + chat Georges + Minuit
âge(s)?		10	père = 46 mère = 43	
comment?		pénibles	père – très amusant mère – petite et sympa	G brun et blanc M petit et noir, regarde la télé

Differentiation – Extension

AT 2 – 4, AT 4 – 4

- As an optional extra, having completed the listening activity, students could reconstruct their notes and write or record a text or monologue as if they were Dominique.

A toi! (SB p.81)

AT 1 – 2, AT 2 – 4

- Remind the class quickly of the ten questions listed at the top of page 81. Demonstrate how to use these to interview a partner. In particular, show how to alter questions 4 – 6 and 8 – 10, depending on the answers received in response to questions 3 and 7. Explain that this is summarised in the 'Rappel' feature at the bottom of the page. Students can then work in pairs and take it in turns to interview one another.

Porte ouverte! (SB p.82)
Sommaire (SB pp.82–83)

AT 1 – 2/3/4, AT 2 – 2/3/4, AT 3 – 2/3/4, AT 4 – 2/3/4

- In this summative activity students describe a real or imaginary soap opera family, as if they were acting the role of a member of the family. Before directing students to page 82, return to the goals section on page 64 to show how all the language is leading to the 'Porte ouverte!' activity. Remind the class of the language which they have learned, by referring to each goal in turn and pointing out the relevant pages in the module.

- Talk through the instructions on page 82, making sure that students understand the task and demonstrating how to use page 80 as a model. Also spend some time talking through the summary of the module's language on pages 82 and 83. Show how to refer to this and key pages of the Students' Book and copymasters for support. Give some guidance about presentation – the end products could be word-processed and/or handwritten and should be illustrated. Afterwards they could be displayed for others to read.

- When students have completed the written activity, encourage them all to prepare a list of questions and to interview some friends (set a minimum number) about their soap opera family. They should note the details which they find out, and decide afterwards which friend has the most interesting family.

- Alternatively/Additionally, some interviews could be acted out in the form of a chat show in front of the class. This could be recorded on video or cassette. The rest of the class can listen and take notes, before voting for their favourite soap opera family!

Differentiation – Consolidation and Extension

- It may be helpful to put a limit on the number of people and pets which the lower attainers have to describe.

- Encourage higher attainers to write fuller descriptions and/or to describe more people and pets. If possible, they should try writing a first draft from memory, in pencil or using a word processor. They should then check their spelling and redraft their work if necessary.

At this point you may wish to assess students by using the Assessment Copymasters for Modules 3 and 4 (Assessment Test 2, Copymasters 100–104). Teacher's notes and solutions can be found on Copymaster 105 onwards in the Copymasters book.

5 VISITE SCOLAIRE

In this module students learn how to:

Talk about what they and others are doing, using 'nous'
Nous jouons au foot/allons à la pêche/faisons du canoë-kayak (etc.)

Say when they do certain things
Le soir/Le samedi nous ...

Ask what they are doing and when they do things, using 'vous' (Polite and plural forms)
Que faites-vous? / Vous jouez au tennis? / Vous mangez à quelle heure?

Talk about how they are feeling
Je suis fatigué(e) / J'ai chaud/soif (etc.)

Ask how much something is
C'est combien, s'il vous plaît? / Ça fait combien?

Understand prices and deal with French currency
(Ça fait) Dix francs cinquante (etc.)

Order snacks, ice creams and drinks
Un sandwich au fromage/Une glace au citron/Un café-crème, s'il vous plaît

Ask others whether they would like an ice cream
Tu veux une glace? / Quel parfum? / Une simple ou une double?

Say 'Yes, please'
Oui, je veux bien

Understand a waiter or waitress' questions
Qu'est-ce que vous prenez? / C'est tout?

Say what they will have
Je prends ...

Ask where the toilets are and understand simple directions
Où sont les toilettes, s'il vous plaît? / A droite / Tout droit (etc.)

Ask for the bill
L'addition, s'il vous plaît

Materials needed
Students' Book pages 84 – 103
Copymasters 51 – 60
Flashcards 66 – 88
Class cassette E
Self-study cassette

Objectif 1   Que faites-vous?

New language introduced
Nous jouons au foot/volley/tennis
Nous allons à la pêche
Nous faisons du vélo/du canoë-kayak/de la voile/de la natation
Nous jouons aux cartes
Nous allons en ville
Nous faisons des excursions
Nous regardons la télé/les vidéos
Nous mangeons
Nous écoutons de la musique
Nous arrivons
Nous lisons

Que faites-vous (ce matin)?
Vous faites du canoë-kayak? / Vous jouez au tennis? (etc.)
Le matin/L'après-midi/Le soir/L'après-midi, nous ...
Nous ... à (+ time)
Je suis fatigué(e)
J'ai chaud/froid/soif/faim
Je me sens malade

Revision of
Leisure activities
The time

Student goals (SB p.84)

- Use the top half of the page to familiarise students with the module's main teaching points and goals. Establish the meaning of *Visite scolaire* and then guide students through the visual representation of the three objectives in the usual way, using flashcards, mime etc. to clarify the theme of each. Point to the '*En classe*' bubbles and make a couple of statements such as *J'ai chaud! J'ai froid!*, supported by mime, before finally reminding students that the module will culminate in a '*Porte ouverte!*' activity.

> **Presentation of:**
>
> *Nous allons … / Nous quittons …*

En route! (SB p.84)

AT 1 – 3, AT 3 – 3

- Use the text on page 84 and the accompanying cassette to introduce the idea that the *copains* are going to an activity centre with their class.
- Play the cassette through once and direct students to follow the text and photos in their books whilst they listen.

>
>
> Sandrine: Un, deux, trois, …
> Yannick: C'est lundi le 19 mai. Il est neuf heures moins le quart. Nous allons en classe au centre de vacances. Nous quittons le collège à neuf heures.
> Au revoir!

- Check that students understand the text and in particular that they have correctly deduced the meaning of *Nous allons* and *Nous quittons*, before playing through the cassette again.

> **Presentation of:**
>
> *Nous jouons au foot/volley/tennis*
> *Nous faisons du vélo/du canoë-kayak/de la voile/de la natation*
> *Nous allons à la pêche*

Notre routine au centre de vacances (SB p.85)

a Ecoute et lis.

AT 1 – 1/2/3, AT 3 – 1

- Direct students to the list of activities on the noticeboard at the top of page 85.

T: Voici les activités sportives au centre de vacances: foot, volley, tennis, etcetera. (Begin reading through the list).

- Then tell them to follow the list as they listen to the cassette, in which the teacher explains the various activities to Sandrine, Yannick and the rest of the class. This provides further introduction to present tense 1st person plural forms, using the familiar verbs *jouer, aller* and *faire*.

Differentiation – Extension

- Higher attainers could listen to the cassette two or three times without prior reference to the noticeboard on page 85 and with their books closed, noting as many activities on offer as possible.

>
>
> Alors, les activités sportives pour notre classe: Ecoutez bien … Ce matin nous jouons au foot, au volley, au tennis … ou … nous allons à la pêche … ou bien nous faisons du vélo, nous faisons du canoë-kayak, de la natation, de la voile. Bon. Vous avez la possibilité d'une ou deux activités ce matin. Dans votre groupe faites votre choix, s'il vous plaît!

- Use the symbols on the plan of the lakeside activity centre on page 85 to check that students understand the activities which they have just heard and read.
- First revise the meaning of the familiar activities *foot, volley, tennis, pêche, vélo,* and *natation,* by pointing to the noticeboard and the plan and asking *Foot, c'est quelle lettre?* etc. Then clarify the new vocabulary *canoë-kayak* and *voile* using flashcards 67 and 68, before asking which symbols on the plan these correspond to.

Presentation of:

Que faites-vous (ce matin)?

---

b Quelles activités?

AT 1 – 3

- Students are now exposed to more examples of the 1st person plural forms of *jouer, aller* and *faire,* as they listen to seven short conversations and identify the activities which groups of children are doing at the lakeside centre.

- Explain the context and the task, pointing out the photo on page 85.

T: Les copains regardent la liste d'activités sportives. Après, le prof parle avec les groupes de copains, par exemple 'Yannick, Marc, Sandrine et Sophie, que faites-vous?' C'est à dire 'Vous faites quelle(s) activité(s)?' Les groupes répondent, par exemple 'Nous faisons du canoë-kayak'. Alors, regardez le plan ... Nous faisons du canoë-kayak, c'est quelle lettre? (Wait for the correct response.) Bravo! C'est 'A'. C'est activité 'A'. Bon. Ecoutez maintenant les sept conversations, regardez le plan et écrivez la ou les bonne(s) lettre(s).

1

Prof:	Groupe numéro un: Yannick, Marc, Sandrine et Sophie ... Que faites-vous ce matin?
Yannick:	Nous faisons du canoë-kayak.
Prof:	Du canoë-kayak ... Merci.

2

Prof:	Groupe numéro deux: Louise, Olivier Frédéric et Nicole ... Que faites-vous?
Louise:	Nous jouons au volley et nous faisons du vélo.
Prof:	Pardon?
Louise:	Nous jouons au volley et nous faisons du vélo.
Prof:	Bon.

3

Prof:	Groupe numéro trois ... Que faites-vous?
Boy:	Nous faisons de la voile.
Prof:	De la voile ... Merci.

4

Prof:	Groupe numéro quatre ... Que faites-vous?
Boy:	Nous jouons au foot et nous faisons de la natation.
Prof:	Bon. Merci.

5

Prof:	Groupe numéro cinq ... Véronique, Sébastien, Françoise et Martin. Que faites-vous ce matin?
Girl:	Nous faisons du vélo et nous jouons au tennis.
Prof:	Bon.

6

Prof:	Groupe numéro six, s'il vous plaît ... Que faites-vous?
Girl:	Nous faisons du canoë-kayak et nous allons à la pêche.
Prof:	Merci.

7

Prof:	Et finalement, groupe numéro sept. Que faites-vous?
Boy:	Nous faisons de la voile ... et ... nous faisons de la natation!
Prof:	Bon. Merci.

Solution

1 A **2** F et D **3** C **4** H et G **5** D et B **6** A et E **7** C et G

Nous ...-ons

(FC 33, 34, 37, 42, 44, 51, 66-69)

AT 1 – 2, AT 2 – 1/2

- Using a reference from Students' Book page 84 or the last cassette item if necessary, encourage the class to remind you of the pronoun *nous.*

5 Visite scolaire

T: *Comment dit-on 'we' en français?*

- Move on to focus on the verb forms recently encountered, using flashcard 66 of the group of friends from Albi in combination with the various activity cards to present the following:

  Nous jouons au foot.

  Nous jouons au volley.

  Nous jouons au tennis.

  Nous allons à la pêche.

  Nous faisons du vélo.

  Nous faisons du canoë-kayak.

  Nous faisons de la natation.

  Nous faisons de la voile.

- Check that students understand the meaning of the verbs and play a variety of comprehension games. Then encourage them to repeat the phrases and practise pronunciation, paying particular attention to *Nous faisons du canoë-kayak* and *Nous faisons de la voile* which are new.

- When the class is familiar with the verb forms, write a series of three-part sentences on the board/OHP, using the following pattern:

  Nous jouons   au foot.

- Stick the corresponding flashcard next to each phrase and then gradually rub out different parts of the sentences, until students can produce the complete phrases from memory, using the visual cue provided by the flashcard. They can then be encouraged to use one of these phrases as their password or *passe-partout du jour/passe-partout de la semaine* in order to be able to leave the classroom at the end of the lesson!

Differentiation – Support and Consolidation

Nos activités sportives   (CM 51)

1 a Ecoute, lis et répète.
b Lis, prononce et écoute.

AT 1 – 2, AT 2 – 2, AT 3 – 2

- This copymaster is suitable for independent work at home or in the classroom. Students requiring further oral practice of the 1st person plural forms of *jouer, aller* and *faire* should be directed to the first task in which they practise repetition and pronunciation.

You will need Copymaster 51, activity 1. Look at the phrases on the left-hand side of the page. Listen to the cassette as you read each sentence. Pause the cassette after each one and repeat the sentence.

1 Nous jouons au foot.
2 Nous jouons au volley.
3 Nous jouons au tennis.
4 Nous allons à la pêche.
5 Nous faisons du vélo.
6 Nous faisons du canoë-kayak.
7 Nous faisons de la natation.
8 Nous faisons de la voile.

In a moment, rewind the cassette to the beginning of '*Nos activités sportives*'. Look at the sentences again. This time, read the sentences out loud. After each one listen to the cassette to check your pronunciation. Pause the cassette after each sentence.

2 Mets la bonne activité.

AT 3 – 2, AT 4 – 2

- Afterwards/alternatively, students can practise reading and writing the activities, demonstrating comprehension of the phrases by copying them next to the correct symbol on the plan.

Differentiation – Extension

- To create a more challenging task for higher attainers, cut off the menu of phrases provided in activity 1 and encourage students to label the activity symbols from memory.

Solution

A Nous faisons du canoë-kayak.
B Nous jouons au tennis.
C Nous faisons de la voile.
D Nous faisons du vélo.
E Nous allons à la pêche.
F Nous jouons au volley.
G Nous faisons de la natation.
H Nous jouons au foot.

Notre routine au centre de vacances
(SB p.85)

c Regarde le plan. Qu'est-ce qu'on dit?

AT 2 – 2, AT 3 – 1/2, (AT 4 – 2/3)

- Draw attention to the speech bubbles at the bottom of page 85. Then encourage the class to work in pairs and to use the plan of the lakeside activity centre to produce oral responses for the letter cues in activity C.

Solution

1 Nous jouons au foot.
2 Nous jouons au tennis et nous faisons du vélo.
3 Nous faisons du canoë-kayak.
4 Nous jouons au volley et nous allons à la pêche.
5 Nous faisons de la voile et nous faisons de la natation.
6 Nous allons à la pêche et nous faisons du vélo.

- Students should then repeat the task but this time should cover the plan and try to produce the correct utterances in response to their partner's letter cue. To add an edge to the game, they could score a point for each correct activity.
- Some members of the class could also produce a written record of their answers to the *'Qu'est-ce qu'on dit?'* task, either with or without using Copymaster 51 as support.

> **Presentation of:**
>
> *Le matin / L'après-midi / Le soir / Après nous …*
> *Nous faisons des excursions / Nous regardons la télé / Nous mangeons / Nous jouons aux cartes / Nous écoutons de la musique / Nous allons en ville*

Ici, c'est super! (SB p.86)

a Ecoute la cassette et mets dans le bon ordre.

AT 1 – 4

- Direct students to the photo at the top of page 86.

T: Louise décrit maintenant les activités sportives, les excursions et les passe-temps au centre de vacances.

- Illustrate the meaning of the new vocabulary *excursions*, using flashcard 69. Explain that the class should then listen to Louise's description on the cassette and that they should look at the activity pictures on page 86 and write the letters in the order in which they hear them.
- Demonstrate the task before starting the cassette and stress the fact that although 10 symbols are shown in the book, only nine activities are described on the tape.

Louise:	Ici, c'est super. Le matin nous faisons des activités sportives … Par exemple, nous allons à la pêche, nous faisons de la voile, ou bien nous jouons au volley. Et l'après-midi …
Olivier:	Nous faisons des excursions!
Louise:	Et l'après-midi nous faisons des excursions. Aujourd'hui, par exemple, nous allons en ville. Nous mangeons le repas du soir à sept heures et demie – euh, pardon! Nous mangeons le repas du soir à six heures et demie et après nous regardons la télé, nous écoutons de la musique ou …
Olivier:	ou nous jouons aux cartes!
Louise:	… Pardon! … ou nous jouons aux cartes. C'est vraiment chouette!

Solution

C, G, J, E, I, D, B, H, F

Nous …-ons
(FC 29, 41, 46, 48, 53, 66-69)

AT 1 – 2, AT 2 – 2

- Use flashcard 66 in combination with the various activity flashcards to draw attention to, practise and exploit the following 'new' 1st person plural forms of present tense verbs:

Nous regardons la télé.
Nous mangeons.
Nous faisons des excursions.
Nous jouons aux cartes.
Nous écoutons de la musique.
Nous allons en ville.

5 Visite scolaire

- Play a variey of games, moving from comprehension to repetition and pronunciation practice and paying particular attention to *Nous faisons des excursions* which is new.
- Finally, students could work in groups of three and play a 'Granny went shopping'-style cumulative game for further oral practice. (Cf. Teacher's Notes page 96 – '*Moi, j'ai des animaux*'.)

> At this point you may wish to use Copymaster 83. Students complete notes on the 1st person plural forms of present tense verbs and keep them for reference.

Ici, c'est super! (SB p.86)

b Regarde les phrases et les images. C'est quelle lettre?

AT 3 – 2

- Highlight the '*Attention!*' feature on page 86. Write a selection of the 1st person plural verb forms encoutered so far on the board and underline the *nous* pronoun and the *-ons* verb ending. Encourage students to remind you again of the meaning of these verb forms.

Differentiation – Extension

- If appropriate, point out the link between these and the first person singular forms encountered in Modules 2 and 3 and draw attention to the retention of the letter *e* in *Nous mangeons*.
- The class can then practise comprehension and copywriting in the '*C'est quelle lettre?*' task.

Solution

1B **2**I **3**D **4**F **5**H **6**E

c Et les autres quatre phrases?

AT 3 – 2

- Afterwards, students can write down the additional four phrases 'missing' from the list. This should be done from memory if possible, but if support is needed students can use Copymaster 51.

Solution

Nous faisons du vélo. Nous allons à la pêche. Nous faisons de la voile. Nous jouons au volley.

> **Revision of time**
> **Presentation of:**
> *Nous ... à* (+ time)
> (Time of day) *nous ...*

Notre agenda (CM 52)

AT 3 – 1/4, AT 4 – 2/3/4

- Students now consolidate the work on the 1st person plural forms of familar present tense verbs by completing the gaps in a diary itinerary. They can then use this as a model for writing their own ideal itinerary for two days at an activity centre.

Solution

lundi:

Nous **quittons** le collège à 9 h. A 11h 30 nous **arrivons** au centre de vacances. Nous **mangeons** le déjeuner à la cantine à midi. L'après-midi nous **faisons** du canoë-kayak. Le soir nous **jouons** aux cartes.

mardi:

Le matin nous **faisons** de la voile. L'après-midi nous **allons** en ville. Le soir nous **regardons** la télé ou les vidéos et nous **écoutons** de la musique.

Differentiation – Extension

- To make the first task more challenging, the menu of verbs for the cloze exercise could be removed before giving the copymaster to higher attainers.

Differentiation – Consolidation and Support

- The number of sentences to be produced in the second activity could be limited in advance for lower attainers. Alternatively, they could be instructed to re-read the left-hand diary entry when they have completed it and to then *copy* a set number of sentences *which they would most like to do* on a residential visit onto the right-hand page.

> **Presentation of:**
> *Vous jouez ... ? / Vous allez ... ?*

Vous jouez au tennis? (SB p.87)

AT 1 – 4, AT 3 – 4

- Use page 87 and the class cassette to develop the work on 1st person plural forms of present tense verbs and to introduce 2nd person plural question forms. Play the cassette as support for this piece of more extended reading, telling students to listen and follow the story in their books.

Nicole:	Vous faites du canoë-kayak ce matin?
Marc:	Non, nous faisons du vélo.
Frédéric:	Vous jouez au tennis?
Yannick and Sophie:	Oui, d'accord!
Girl:	Vous jouez au tennis? Oh là, là. C'est ennuyeux! Nous faisons de la voile!
Prof:	Que faites-vous, alors?
Boy:	Nous allons à la pêche.
Prof:	Et vous?
Girl:	Nous faisons de la voile.
Prof:	Je regrette, mais ce n'est pas possible aujourd'hui.
Girl:	Zut!
Girl:	Alors, nous faisons du canoë-kayak ou du vélo?
Yannick:	Mais ce n'est pas possible!
Yannick:	Vous jouez au tennis avec nous?

- Tell the class to find and say as many examples of questions in the text as possible. As they volunteer the questions, list them on the board/OHP. Underline the *vous* pronouns and ask *Comment dit-on 'vous' en anglais?* Encourage students to deduce the meanings of the questions themselves before playing the cassette again while they listen to and read the text.

F Vous ...? (FC 34, 37, 39, 50, 51, 53, 67-69)

AT 1 – 2, AT 2 – 2, AT 3 – 2

- Return to the list of questions on the board/OHP and draw a box around *Que faites-vous?* Ask this question rhetorically, before showing the relevant flashcards.

T: Vous jouez au foot? Vous allez à la pêche? Vous faites du canoë-kayak?

- Encourage the class to repeat all four questions, stressing the intonation. Then take each of the questions *Vous jouez ...?, Vous allez ... ?* and *Vous faites ...?* in turn and encourage students to build other questions containing these verbs, using the flashcards to cue the possibilities.
- Finally, pairs of students could come to the front of the class and mime an activity which the rest of the class can try to guess, asking *Vous ...?* as they do so.

Que faites-vous? (CM 53)

1 Relie.

AT 3 – 2

- Students link French and English equivalents to demonstrate comprehension of a selection of 1st and 2nd person plural forms of familiar present tense verbs. Explain that the French also corresponds to the English 'Do you play?', 'Do you go?', 'we play' and 'we go' etc.

Solution

1 Que faites-vous? What are you doing?
2 Vous jouez au tennis? Are you playing tennis?
3 Vous allez à la pêche? Are you going fishing?
4 Vous faites du canoë-kayak? Are you going canoeing?
5 Nous jouons au tennis. We're playing tennis.
6 Nous allons à la pêche. We're going fishing.
7 Nous faisons du canoë-kayak. We're going canoeing.

2a Ecoute, lis et répète.

b Lis, prononce et écoute.

AT 1 – 2, AT 2 – 2

- After completing the matching activity, students practise pronunciation by repeating each question or statement after the cassette.

5 Visite scolaire

1 Que faites-vous?
2 Vous jouez au tennis?
3 Vous allez à la pêche?
4 Vous faites du canoë-kayak?
5 Nous jouons au tennis.
6 Nous allons à la pêche.
7 Nous faisons du canoë-kayak.

- If they work independently, using the self-study cassette, students can try reading aloud and then compare their own pronunciation with that of the cassette.

You will need Copymaster 53, activity 2. Look at the phrases on the top left-hand side of the page. Listen to the cassette as you read each sentence. Pause the cassette after each one and repeat the sentence.

1 Que faites-vous?
2 Vous jouez au tennis?
3 Vous allez à la pêche?
4 Vous faites du canoë-kayak?
5 Nous jouons au tennis.
6 Nous allons à la pêche.
7 Nous faisons du canoë-kayak.

In a moment, rewind the cassette to the beginning of 'Que faites-vous?' Look at the sentences again. This time, read the sentences out loud. After each one listen to the cassette to check your pronunciation. Pause the cassette after each sentence.

3 Encore des questions!

AT 2 – 2, AT 3 – 2

- In the final task on the copymaster, students work in groups of four and play a guessing game. Invite three students to the front of the class and demonstrate the game, using an OHT version of Copymaster 53 or drawing a replica of the game on the board.
- Point to one of the students and yourself and explain *Nous sommes partenaires* and then point

to the other two students and explain to them *Vous êtes partenaires.*

> **T:** *Bon. A deux regardez la fiche et choisissez une activité.* (Mime.) *Maintenant cochez l'activité … mais attention! C'est un grand secret!* (Mime ticking the chosen activity in a secretive way.) *Et moi et mon/ma partenaire, nous regardons notre fiche et nous choisissons aussi une activité.* (Mime.) *Et nous cochons l'activité* (Mime.) *Maintenant nous devinons l'activité de nos partenaires, par exemple … Vous jouez au foot? Mais attention! Nous avons seulement cinq chances!*

- Take it in turns with your partner to try to guess the opposing pair's activity, encouraging them to say *oui* or *non*, recording the number of guesses as you do. If you do not guess the activity within the five chances, ask *Que faites-vous?* and encourage the opposing pair to say their activity. With the help of the class the other pair should then be encouraged to guess the activity which you and your partner have chosen. When the class understands the principle of the game, they can play in groups of four.

Differentiation – Extension

AT 1 – 4, AT 2 – 2/3/4, AT 3 – 4, AT 4 – 2/3/4

- At this point some students could return to 'Nous les copains' on page 87 and work in groups, adapting the story and inventing their own conversation. Afterwards/alternatively, some members of the class may like to invent their own cartoon strip using the verb forms practised in the module so far.

> **Presentation of:**
> *Vous regardez / Vous lisez / Vous écoutez … ?*

Temps libre (SB p.88)

AT 1 – 2/3, AT 2 – 2, AT 3 – 2/3

- Use page 88 to introduce the 2nd person plural forms of other verbs in the present tense and to remind students of the formal use of *vous.* Tell the class to listen to the cassette whilst following the text in their books.

Marc:	Que faites-vous ce soir, Monsieur Duval?
Louise:	Vous regardez la télé?
Sandrine:	Vous lisez un livre?
Sébastien:	Vous écoutez de la musique classique?
Teacher:	Non! Je fais du patin à roulettes!

- Go on to highlight the '*Attention!*' feature and demonstrate the different uses of *vous*, reminding the class of the plural and formal use of *Vous avez ...?* which they met when asking for classroom equipment in Module 1. (Cf. pages 16 – 17.) Then point out the *-ez* verb ending, together with the contrasting form *vous faites*.

- Students could then practise the formal use of *vous* by trying to guess which of the activities covered in the module you are doing this evening. This could be set up by showing the class a selection of flashcards and then shuffling them all into a pile, concealing the one on top and asking the class *Qu'est-ce que je fais ce soir?* The number of guesses could be limited in advance and the practice carried out in the form of a class v. teacher guessing game, with the class scoring a point if they guess the activity and you scoring a point if they do not!

> At this point you may wish to use Copymaster 84. Students complete notes on the 2nd person plural forms of present tense verbs and keep them for reference.

Que faites-vous ce soir? (CM 54)

1 Ecoute et coche.

AT 1 – 2/3

- Students now have an opportunity for further practice of the 2nd person plural forms of verbs in the present tense. Initially, they listen to the cassette and after each conversation tick the appropriate column(s) of the grid at the top of the copymaster, to show understanding of the verbs. They should then use the information on the completed grid to decide which pairs of children are in the same group.

- Introduce the task briefly and demonstrate what the class has to do, before playing the cassette as many times as is necessary, pausing briefly after each conversation.

1

Boy:	Marc! Yannick! Que faites-vous ce soir? Vous jouez au foot?
Marc:	Oui, nous jouons au foot et après nous jouons au tennis de table. Vous jouez avec nous?
Boy:	Oui! Allons-y!

2

Girl:	Louise! Sandrine! Que faites-vous ce soir?
Louise:	Nous faisons du patin.
Girl:	Et que faites-vous après?
Louise:	Nous écoutons de la musique.

3

Boy:	Ah! Voici Sophie et Véronique! Bonsoir! Vous jouez au tennis avec nous?
Sophie:	Non, nous faisons du vélo. Mais après nous jouons aux cartes. Vous jouez aussi?
Boy:	Oui! A bientôt!

4

Prof:	Bonsoir, Frédéric. Bonsoir, Olivier. Que faites vous ce soir?
Frédéric:	Nous jouons au basket. C'est chouette!
Prof:	Bon. Amusez-vous bien!

5

Sébastien and Martin:	Bonsoir, monsieur!
Prof:	Bonsoir, Sébastien. Bonsoir, Martin. Vous jouez aussi au basket?
Sébastien:	Non, nous regardons la télé. Il y a un match de foot à sept heures et demie.
Prof:	A sept heures et demie? Ah, bon!

6

Girl:	Nicole! Françoise! Que faites-vous ce soir?
Nicole:	Après le repas du soir nous jouons au tennis.
Girl:	Vous faites aussi du patin?
Nicole:	Non, nous jouons au foot.

7

Prof:	Bonsoir, Paul. Bonsoir, Simon. Vous jouez au foot, ce soir?
Paul:	Non, nous faisons du vélo.
Prof:	Et après, vous regardez la télé?
Paul:	Non, nous jouons aux cartes.

8

Michèle and Anne-Marie:	Bonsoir, madame!
Prof:	Bonsoir, Michèle. Bonsoir, Anne-Marie. Que faites-vous ce soir?
Michèle:	Nous lisons et nous écoutons de la musique.
Prof:	Vous ne regardez pas la télé?
Michèle:	Non, les gars regardent le match de foot!

Solution

Les jeunes dans le même groupe sont: Sophie, Véronique, Paul et Simon

2 Complète les questions et la question mystère.

AT 3 – 2, AT 4 – 2

- Afterwards, students should complete the verbs in the gapped sentences and transfer the numbered letters in their answers into the final question, to complete the mystery question. If necessary, they can use Copymaster 53 and Students' Book pages 87 – 88 for support.

Solution

Vous **jouez** au tennis?

Vous **regardez** la télé?

Vous **mangez** le déjeuner?

Vous **lisez** un livre?

Que **faites**-vous?

Vous **parlez** avec des copains?

Vous **écoutez** de la musique?

1 = c 2 = e 3 = n 4 = t 5 = r 6 = e 7 = s 8 = p
9 = o 10 = r 11 = t 12 = i 13 = f

Vous allez au **centre sportif?**

Vous faites quelle activité? (SB p.88)

AT 2 – 2, AT 4 – 2/3

- Students now return to page 88 and ask or write the question corresponding to each odd-angle photograph. If possible, they should be encouraged to do this from memory.

Solution

A Vous faites du vélo?

B Vous regardez les vidéos?

C Vous écoutez de la musique?

D Vous jouez au tennis?

E Vous allez à la pêche?

F Vous lisez un livre?

Differentiation – Extension

AT 4 – 3/4

- Some members of the class could invent and write their own conversation between a group of students and a teacher, adapting the conversation at the top of page 88.

Comment ça se prononce? (SB p.89)
a Ecoute et lis.

AT 1 – 2/3, AT 2 – 2/3, AT 3 – 2/3

- Students listen to the rhyme 'Dépêchez-vous!' on the class cassette, whilst following the written version in their books.

Dépêchez-vous!

Que faites-vous, Sophie et Lucille?

Vous faites de la voile? Vous allez en ville?

Que faites-vous, Jérôme et Yannick?

Vous regardez les vidéos? Vous écoutez de la musique?

Dépêchez-vous, Claire et Marc!

Nous jouons au foot. Nous allons au parc!

- Recap briefly afterwards, making a point of the intonation in the questions and highlighting the elision in *vous allez, vous écoutez* and *nous allons*. Then encourage the class to join in saying the rhyme. This can be done in a variety of ways, e.g.
  - Split the class into three groups and ask each group to chant or rap two lines.
  - Students read the rhyme aloud as a class or in groups, in the same rhythm as the original version.
  - Students jog on the spot whilst chanting the rhyme.
  - Divide the class into groups and conduct them in chanting a round.
  - Students read the rhyme aloud, simultaneously with the cassette. See if the class can maintain the rhythm and speed of the cassette, while you suddenly turn the volume right down. Then turn up the volume again to find out whether or not students have kept pace with the cassette!
- The rhyme is also on the self-study cassette for independent practice.

You will need Students' Book, page 89, activity A. First listen to the rhyme '*Dépêchez-vous*' while you read it in your book. Try to join in. Then try closing your book and join in. Finally, see if you can say it without using your book or the cassette.

Dépêchez-vous!
Que faites-vous, Sophie et Lucille?
Vous faites de la voile? Vous allez en ville?
Que faites-vous, Jérôme et Yannick?
Vous regardez les vidéos? Vous écoutez de la musique?
Dépêchez-vous, Claire et Marc!
Nous jouons au foot. Nous allons au parc!

b Ecoute et lis. Ecoute, lis et répète.

AT 1 – 2, AT 2 – 2, AT 3 – 2

- Students listen to the class cassette whilst reading the parallel questions and statements in the second activity. They then practise pronunciation, intonation and elision by listening, reading and repeating the phrases on cassette.

Que faites-vous?
Vous jouez au foot?
Nous jouons au foot.
Vous regardez les vidéos?
Nous regardons les vidéos.
Vous écoutez de la musique?
Nous écoutons de la musique.
Vous allez au parc?
Nous allons au parc.

c Lis, prononce et écoute.

AT 1 – 2, AT 2 – 2, AT 3 – 2

- Students read and pronounce a selection of questions and statements, before operating the pause button on the self-study cassette and checking their pronunciation, intonation and elision.

You will need Students' Book, page 89, activity C. Look carefully at the six phrases in the pictures at the bottom of the page and read them out loud. After each phrase listen to the cassette to check your pronunciation. Pause the cassette after each phrase.

1 Vous regardez la télé?
2 Vous jouez au volley?
3 Vous arrivez à quelle heure?
4 Nous faisons du canoë-kayak.
5 Nous lisons.
6 Nous allons au cinéma.

Differentiation – Extension

AT 2 – 2/3, AT 3 – 3, AT 4 – 2/3/4

- As possible further exploitation, students can produce their own '*Dépêchez-vous!*' rhyme and illustration by substituting *Vous faites de la voile?*,

Vous regardez les vidéos? and *Nous jouons au foot* with other activites in lines 2, 4 and 6. They could also insert other names instead of Sophie, Jérôme and Claire in lines 1, 3 and 5. Afterwards they could then learn their own or the original version of the rhyme by heart.

Visite d'une journaliste   (SB p.90)

a Ecoute la cassette et note les activités.

AT 1 – 4, AT 4 – 1/2

- The language of the first objective of the module is now drawn together and present tense *nous* and *vous* forms of verbs are combined in longer pieces of listening and reading.
- Direct the class to the title and photo at the top of the page to explain the context of the visiting journalist and that they are now going to listen to an interview.

T: *Regardez activité A à la page 90. Vous allez écouter une interview entre une journaliste et un groupe de copains au centre de vacances. Faites une grille comme ça …* (Point out the grid in the example and, to clarify, draw a larger version on the board.) ***Notez les détails des activités du matin et du soir, par exemple …*** (Fill in the first example on the grid on the board. Show students how to use abbreviations for note-taking.)

- Students listen to the class cassette and complete their grids in their exercise books/on paper.

– Bonjour tout le monde. Je peux poser des questions, s'il vous plaît?
– Oui, d'accord.
– Oui, bien sûr.
– Alors, que faites-vous le matin?
– Nous faisons des activités sportives.
– Vous faites du canoë-kayak?
– Oui, nous faisons du canoë-kayak …
– Et nous, nous faisons de la voile.
– Sébastien et moi, nous allons à la pêche.
– Vous jouez au tennis?

– Oui, nous jouons au tennis, au volley, au foot …
– C'est très bien ça. Et le soir? Que faites-vous le soir?
– Nous regardons la télé et les vidéos.
– Vous jouez aux cartes et au tennis de table?
– Oui, et nous parlons beaucoup. Ici, c'est super!

Solution

le matin	le soir
canoë-kayak	télé
voile	vidéos
pêche	cartes
tennis	tennis de table
volley	nous parlons
foot	

Differentiation – Consolidation and Support

AT 1 – 2/3, AT 4 – 1/2

- To simplify the listening task, students could initially focus solely on the morning activities and listen as many times as necessary to the first section of the interview. They could then go on to listen to the evening activities.

b Lis la carte postale et regarde tes notes. Quelles sont les différences?

AT 3 – 1/3, AT 4 – 2/3

- Students now read the postcard, compare it with their notes from the cassette and note the differences in the activities of the two groups of children. Provide the format below in which to note the differences and encourage as many students as possible to write full sentences.

Différences:

Carte postale	Cassette

Solution

Carte postale:

Nous faisons du canoë-kayak et du vélo.
Nous allons en ville.
Nous jouons au tennis de table, au volley et au foot.
Nous regardons la télé.
Nous jouons avec l'ordinateur.

Cassette:

Nous faisons du canoë-kayak et de la voile.

Nous allons à la pêche.

Nous jouons au tennis, au volley et au foot.

Nous regardons la télé et les vidéos.

Nous jouons aux cartes et au tennis de table.

Differentiation – Consolidation and Support

AT 3 – 1/3, AT 4 – 1/2

- Students who find writing difficult could simply jot down the differences in note form, e.g.

Carte postale	Cassette
canoë-kayak et vélo	canoë-kayak et *voile*

Differentiation – Extension

AT 3 – 3, AT 4 – 3/4

- Higher attainers could write a full postcard as if from the group of children interviewed by the journalist, using their notes from the cassette activity and adapting the existing postcard on page 90. Alternatively, they could imagine that they are staying with a group of friends at an activity centre and invent their own postcard.

c Travail à trois ou à quatre.

AT 1 – 2/3, AT 2 – 2/3/4

- For oral consolidation of present tense verbs in the 1st and 2nd person plural forms, students work in groups and invent their own interview between a journalist and a group of children at an activity centre.
- Direct students needing support to Copymasters 53 and 54 and Students' Book page 88.
- The rehearsed interviews could be acted out in front of the class and/or recorded on video or cassette.

> **Presentation of:**
> *Je suis fatigué(e)*
> *J'ai chaud/froid/soif/faim*
> *Je me sens malade*

J'en ai marre! (SB p.91)

a Ecoute et lis.

AT 1 – 4, AT 2 – 2/3, AT 3 – 4, AT 4 – 2/3/4

- Students listen to the class cassette, whilst following the text of the cartoon strip on page 91 which introduces language used to express feelings and states (e.g. hungry, tired, thirsty).

Prof:	Bon! Nous allons maintenant au château …
Prof:	Dépêchez-vous, s'il vous plaît!
Boy:	Oh, monsieur. Je suis fatigué!
Prof:	Ça suffit. Allez-y! Vite!
Boy:	Monsieur, j'ai chaud!
Girl:	Oh, monsieur, j'ai soif!
Girl 2:	Monsieur, je suis fatiguée!
Boy 2:	Nous mangeons à quelle heure? J'ai faim!
Prof:	Eh bien, vous avez vingt minutes ici …
All:	Chouette!
Prof:	Bon, alors – en route!
Boy:	Brr … J'ai froid! Allez, vite!
Prof:	Eugh! Je me sens malade! Plus lentement, s'il vous plaît!

- Play the cassette through once continuously. Then refer to the visuals in the cartoon strip and, supporting these with mime, encourage the class to work out the meaning of the new language and in particular of the following phrases:

Je suis fatigué.
J'ai chaud.
J'ai soif.
Je suis fatiguée.
J'ai faim.
J'ai froid.
Je me sens malade.

- Check that students understand the difference in the use of *Je suis fatigué* and *Je suis fatiguée* and highlight the difference by drawing a pin-man and a pin-woman on the board and writing the appropriate speech bubble for each.

- Then play the cassette a second time and pause it after each frame of the cartoon strip. If appropriate, demonstrate the linking of the text to the cassette and encourage students to point to the relevant speech bubbles as they hear the language.

- Move on to say and mime the seven new phrases, encouraging the class to repeat both the phrase and the mime. Afterwards, use mimes and drawings to cue them to say the correct phrase. When they are confident, hand over the activity for them to continue in the form of a class, group or pair guessing game.

En classe: Allez-y! (CM55)

1 Relie les phrases et les images.

AT 3 – 2

- Students use the top half of the copymaster to show understanding of the written and spoken form of the phrases indicating feelings and states, by linking each to its appropriate visual.

Solution

1 Je suis fatigué = D
2 Je suis fatiguée = G
3 Je me sens malade = A
4 J'ai chaud = E
5 J'ai froid = B
6 J'ai faim = F
7 J'ai soif = C

2 Ecoute, lis et répète.

AT 1 – 2, AT 2 – 2

- Students then listen to the phrases on the cassette, before reading and repeating the corresponding sentences.

1 Je suis fatigué.
2 Je suis fatiguée.
3 Je me sens malade.

4 J'ai chaud.
5 J'ai froid.
6 J'ai faim.
7 J'ai soif.

- If the students work independently, using the self-study cassette, they can try reading the phrases aloud and then compare their own pronunciation with that of the cassette.

You will need Copymaster 55, activity 2. Look at the seven sentences at the top of the page. Listen to the cassette as you read each sentence. Pause the cassette after each sentence and repeat it.

1 Je suis fatigué.
2 Je suis fatiguée.
3 Je me sens malade.
4 J'ai chaud.
5 J'ai froid.
6 J'ai faim.
7 J'ai soif.

3 Oh, monsieur ... Oh, madame ...

AT 1 – 2, AT 2 – 2

- Finally, students can play a Beetle-style game, to practise the phrases orally. For this each pair will need a die and each individual will need a piece of paper numbered 1 – 6. Students then take it in turns to give statements, cued by the number on the die and the *légende* on Copymaster 55. They can then tick off the corresponding number written on their piece of paper. In each case their partner must answer impatiently, *Ça suffit. Vite!* The winner is the person who manages to go to the café by ticking off all six numbers and saying all six phrases first.

- Before setting up the game, ask a student to come to the front of the class to help demonstrate how to play. (Cf. page 56 of the Teacher's Notes for Module 2, in which a similar game is explained.) Then divide the class into pairs and hand out dice so that they can play.

J'en ai marre! (SB p.91)

b Comment dit-on?

AT 2 – 2, AT 4 – 2/3

- Students use the pictures as cues for oral and / or written production of the phrases expressing feelings and states. This can be done as a class, group or pairwork activity.

Solution

1 Je me sens malade. **2** J'ai chaud . **3** J'ai faim.
4 J'ai soif. **5** Je suis fatigué. **6** J'ai froid.

Objectif 2   Nous avons faim

New language introduced

C'est combien / Ça fait combien (s'il vous plaît)?
(Ça fait) vingt-huit francs/dix francs cinquante.
(etc.)

un hot-dog/hamburger/sandwich au fromage/
sandwich au jambon/croque-monsieur
une crêpe/gaufre/portion de frites/portion de pizza
Une glace simple/double
Une glace au chocolat/café/citron
à la vanille/fraise/menthe.
Tu veux une glace? / Une simple ou une double?
Quel parfum?
Oui, je veux bien

Revision of

Numbers 1 –100
Voilà
Merci
S'il vous plaît/S'il te plaît

Student goals (SB p.84)

- Remind the class of the second section of the goals visual on page 84.

T: **(Point to the second picture.)** *Nous commençons objectif deux – nous avons faim. Alors, regardez les snacks et les glaces. Un hamburger, c'est combien? Dix francs? Onze francs? Douze francs? Et une glace, c'est combien? Huit francs? Neuf francs? Dix francs?* **(Shake some coins to indicate that you are talking about prices.)**

- Then direct students to the introduction to French money on page 92.

T: **C'est combien? Tournez à la page 92 et regardez l'argent français.**

Revision of numbers 1–100
Presentation of:
C'est combien?
Sums of money (e.g. *Dix francs cinquante*)

C'est combien? (SB p.92)

- Read out the introduction to French coins and notes on page 92, guiding students through the labels and visuals and supporting the content with real French money if possible.
- Spend some time in a *pause anglaise,* talking about exchange rates, working out the approximate value of the different coins and notes and comparing the currency with the system in the students' own country.
- Play a variety of aural and oral games and use the song '*Nombres toréadors*' to revise numbers 1 – 100. (Cf. 'Games', Teacher's Notes page iv, and the Teacher's Notes accompanying Modules 1 and 3.)
- Remind the class of the values of the coins and notes on page 92 and check that they understand the title phrase *C'est combien?* Then direct them to the listening comprehension activity at the bottom of the page.

a Ecoute la cassette et écris la bonne lettre.

AT 1 – 2, AT 3 – 1

- Explain that you are going to play eight short conversations featuring prices and that students should look at the selection of prices and write down the letter of the price which they hear. Play the class cassette as many times as necessary, pausing after each price.

1 – C'est combien?
 – Cinq francs.
2 – C'est combien, s'il vous plaît?
 – Vingt-huit francs.

3 – C'est combien?
  – Sept francs cinquante.

4 – C'est combien?
  – Trente-quatre francs.

5 – C'est combien, s'il vous plaît?
  – Dix francs.

6 – C'est combien, s'il vous plaît?
  – Seize francs vingt.

7 – C'est combien?
  – Dix francs cinquante.

8 – C'est combien, s'il vous plaît?
  – Quinze francs.

Solution

1 H **2** F **3** D **4** B **5** G **6** E **7** A **8** C

Les numéros et les prix   (CM 56)

1 Ecoute, lis et répète.

AT 1 – 1, AT 2 – 1

- This copymaster provides oral and aural practice of prices, focusing in particular on the contrasting pronunciation of certain numbers when they are combined with *francs* rather than standing alone.
- In the first activity, students listen to the self-study cassette, whilst reading the contrasting numbers and prices, before repeating them.

You will need Copymaster 56, activity 1. Look at the pairs of numbers and prices at the top of the page. Listen to the cassette as you read each pair. Pause the cassette after each pair and repeat the number and price.

cinq   cinq francs

six   six francs

huit   huit francs

dix   dix francs

dix-huit   dix-huit francs

vingt-cinq   vingt-cinq francs

vingt-six   vingt-six francs

vingt-huit   vingt-huit francs

2 C'est combien? Lis, prononce et écoute.

AT 1 – 1, AT 2 – 1

- Students move on to practise reading prices aloud, before checking their pronunciation on the self-study cassette.

You will need Copymaster 56, activity 2. Look carefully at the prices on the eight items shown in the pictures. Read each price out loud. After each one listen to the cassette to check your pronunciation. Pause the cassette after each price.

1 cinq francs
2 six francs
3 dix francs
4 dix-huit francs
5 vingt-huit francs
6 trente-six francs
7 quarante-cinq francs
8 soixante-cinq francs

3 Ecoute. C'est quelle lettre?

AT 1 – 1

- The third task provides additional listening comprehension practice of prices. Again, students use the self-study cassette and can undertake this individually in the lesson or at home.

You will need Copymaster 56, activity 3. Look carefully at the eight price tags at the bottom of the page. Then listen to the short conversations on the cassette. Pause the cassette after each price and write down the letter of the price you have heard. Then start the cassette again, listen to the next price, pause the cassette and choose the correct letter. Keep going until you have heard all the prices. Then rewind the cassette, listen again and check your answers.

1 – C'est combien, s'il vous plaît?
  – Vingt-cinq francs.

2 – C'est combien, s'il vous plaît?
  – Huit francs cinquante.

3 – Cinquante-six francs, s'il vous plaît.
  – Voilà.
  – Merci. Au revoir.
4 – C'est combien?
  – Soixante-dix francs.
5 – Pardon, monsieur. C'est combien?
  – Dix-huit francs cinquante.
6 – C'est combien, s'il vous plaît?
  – Cinquante-huit francs.
7 – Pardon, madame. C'est combien, s'il vous plaît?
  – Trente-cinq francs.
8 – C'est combien, s'il vous plaît?
  – Soixante-six francs.

Solution

1 D **2** A **3** G **4** E **5** H **6** C **7** F **8** B

C'est combien? (SB p.92)

b A deux! C'est combien?

AT 1 – 2

- Teach the question *C'est combien?*, checking that students remember its meaning, before encouraging them to repeat the question after you.

- When they are confident, write a series of lettered prices on the board and then divide the class in two and play a team game. A member of the first team starts by asking, *'F', c'est combien?* etc. and a member of the second team must answer with the correct price. A different member of the second team then asks the first team, *'D', c'est combien?* and so on. Alternatively, this can be played as a class game, in which a softball is thrown around the class to determine who asks and answers each question.

- Finally students can work in pairs and use page 92 for further practice of asking and giving prices.

Presentation of snacks (see list below)

Les snacks (FC 70 – 78)

AT 1 – 1, AT 2 – 1

- Use the flashcards to teach the following snacks, grouping them according to their gender:

70 *un hot-dog*
71 *un hamburger*
72 *un sandwich au fromage*
73 *un sandwich au jambon*
74 *un croque-monsieur*
75 *une crêpe*
76 *une gaufre*
77 *une portion de frites*
78 *une portion de pizza*

- A variety of games can be played to consolidate understanding and to maximise opportunities for hearing the new vocabulary, before practising it orally. (See 'Games', Teacher's Notes introduction, page iv.)

- Using Copymaster 57, the written word can then be introduced as an aid to comprehension, before students move on to individual oral practice and copywriting.

Les snacks (CM 57)

1a Relie.

AT 3 – 1

- Students begin by reading a list of snacks and linking each one with its corresponding picture on the menu.

Solution

un hot-dog = G   un hamburger = B   un sandwich au fromage = F   un sandwich au jambon = A   un croque-monsieur = H   une crêpe = E   une gaufre = C   une portion de frites = D   une portion de pizza = I

b Ecoute, lis et répète.

AT 1 – 1, AT 2 – 1, AT 3 – 1

- Students listen to, read and repeat each snack. This can be done as a class activity, or individually in the lesson or at home.

un hot-dog
un hamburger
un sandwich au fromage
un sandwich au jambon
un croque-monsieur

5 Visite scolaire

une crêpe
une gaufre
une portion de frites
une portion de pizza

You will need Copymaster 57, activity 1. Look at the list of snacks at the top of the page. Listen to the cassette as you read each snack. Pause the cassette after each one and repeat the snack.

un hot-dog
un hamburger
un sandwich au fromage
un sandwich au jambon
un croque-monsieur
une crêpe
une gaufre
une portion de frites
une portion de pizza

2 Ecris dans l'ordre de préférence.

AT 4 – 1

- The next activity requires the students to copy out the snacks in their own personal order of preference.

3 C'est combien?

a Ecoute. Vrai ou faux?

AT 1 – 1, AT 3 – 1, AT 4 – 1/2

- In the third task, students listen to a series of short conversations linking comprehension of snacks and prices. During each conversation they should compare the information that they hear with the menu on the copymaster and then decide whether the prices on cassette are true or false.

You will need Copymaster 57, activity 3, 'C'est combien?' Look at the price list, 'Tarif', for the snacks at the top of the page. Listen to the conversations. Are the prices that you hear true or false?

1 – Une crêpe, s'il vous plaît. C'est combien?
– Vingt francs.

2 – Un sandwich au jambon, s'il vous plaît. C'est combien?
– Huit francs.

3 – Un hot-dog, s'il vous plaît. C'est combien?
– Vingt-quatre francs cinquante.

4 – Une portion de pizza, s'il vous plaît. C'est combien?
– Trente-deux francs.

5 – Un croque-monsieur, s'il vous plaît. C'est combien?
– Vingt-cinq francs cinquante.

6 – Une gaufre, s'il vous plaît. C'est combien?
– Vingt francs.

Solution

1 vrai **2** faux **3** vrai **4** faux **5** faux **6** vrai

b A deux.

AT 2 – 1

- Finally, students work in pairs, asking and giving information about the prices of the different snacks. At this point remind them if necessary of the use of the formal *s'il vous plaît* when questioning snack bar attendants, waiters, waitresses and other adults.

Differentiation – Consolidation

AT 1 – 1, AT 2 – 1, AT 3 – 1

- Afterwards, groups of students could use the copymaster for playing snack bingo. (Prior to playing, revise the phrase *J'ai gagné!*) Students tick their copymaster or use small objects to cover any agreed number of snacks. Play the game with the whole class first to remind students of the procedure; after one or two games, the activity can be handed over to students to play in groups. They can use their copymaster as a mastersheet for calling the snacks.

Presentation of:
Ça fait combien?
Ça fait (+ sum of money)

Au snack-bar (SB p.93)

a Ecoute et écris les bonnes lettres.

AT 1 – 3, AT 4 – 2

- Explain that the class is now going to listen to a series of short conversations at a snack bar.

T: Maintenant nous allons écouter huit conversations au snack-bar. Ecoutez les conversations, regardez les photos à la page 93 et après chaque conversation écrivez la ou les bonne(s) lettres.

- Demonstrate the first example if necessary. Play the cassette through at least twice and on the second or third hearing instruct the class to listen for the price of each order and to write it down.

1
– Bonjour, monsieur.
– Bonjour.
– Un hamburger et une portion de frites, s'il vous plaît.
– Un hamburger et une portion de frites ... Voilà. Ça fait 30 francs, s'il vous plaît.

2
– Bonjour, madame.
– Bonjour.
– Un sandwich au jambon et une crêpe, s'il vous plaît ... Ça fait combien?
– Trente-huit francs. Merci.

3
– Bonjour, monsieur.
– Bonjour.
– Un sandwich au fromage et un croque-monsieur, s'il vous plaît.
– Un sandwich au fromage et un croque-monsieur ... 41 francs, s'il vous plaît.

4
– Bonjour.
– Bonjour.
– Un hot-dog et une portion de pizza, s'il vous plaît.
– Un moment, s'il vous plaît. Ça fait 43 francs.

5
– Bonjour.
– Bonjour.
– Un hamburger et une gaufre, s'il vous plaît.
– Voilà. Ça fait 46 francs.
– Merci bien.

6
– Bonjour, madame.
– Bonjour.
– Un sandwich au jambon, une portion de frites et un croque-monsieur, s'il vous plaît. Ça fait combien?
– Euh ... Un sandwich au jambon, une portion de frites et un croque-monsieur ... Ça fait 50 francs, s'il te plaît. Merci.

7
– Bonjour.
– Bonjour, monsieur. Un sandwich au fromage, un hot-dog et une crêpe, s'il vous plaît.
– Un sandwich au fromage ..., un hot-dog ... et une crêpe ... Voilà. Soixante-deux francs, s'il vous plaît.
– Merci. Au revoir.

8
– Bonjour.
– Bonjour, madame. Une portion de pizza, un croque-monsieur et une gaufre, s'il vous plaît.
– Une portion de pizza, un croque-monsieur et une gaufre ... Ça fait ... 65 francs 50.
– Merci. Au revoir.

Solution

1 B, H (30 francs)   **2** D, F (38 francs)   **3** C, E (41 francs)   **4** A, I (43 francs)   **5** B, G (46 francs) **6** D, H, E (50 francs)   **7** C, A, F (62 francs)   **8** I, E, G (65 francs 50)

b Ça fait combien?

AT 2 – 2

- Afterwards, students work in pairs and take it in turns to practise being the customer ordering each set of snacks. As an optional activity they could also write out the eight requests.

J'ai faim! (SB p.93)

a Ecoute et lis.

AT 1 – 3, AT 3 – 3

- Direct the class to the cartoon at the bottom of the page and instruct them to listen to the cassette as they read the bubbles.

Boy:	J'ai faim! Bonjour, madame.
Woman:	Bonjour.
Boy:	Un hamburger, une portion de frites, un hot-dog …
Woman:	Voilà.
Boy:	… un sandwich au jambon, un croque-monsieur et une crêpe, s'il vous plaît. Ça fait combien, s'il vous plaît?

- Encourage students to deduce the difference between *Ça fait combien?* which features on this page and *C'est combien?* which they met on page 92 and on Copymaster 57. Give some examples of contrasting usage to help them in their deduction, deliberately contrasting multiple and single snacks.

b A deux. Dialogues au snack-bar.

AT 2 – 3/4

- Practise pronunciation and intonation of *Ça fait combien?*, before organising the class into pairs to invent their own dialogues at a snack bar. Encourage students to use the cartoon on page 93 as support but to substitute their own snacks and to extend the dialogue by using *merci, au revoir*, etc.

c Fais ta bande dessinée au snack-bar!

AT 2 – 3/4, AT 4 – 2/3/4

- Students use their imagination to invent their own cartoon at a snack bar. If preferred they could use cuttings from comics or magazines rather than drawings and add their own handwritten or word-processed speech bubbles. The final versions could be displayed afterwards.

- As a separate homework task students should try to learn as many of the snacks as possible, so that they can say and write them from memory. Remind them of the strategies for learning vocabulary in *'Le vocabulaire? Pas de problème!'* on Students' Book page 13.

Presentation of ice cream flavours (see list below)

Tu veux une glace? (SB p.94)

AT 1 – 1, AT 2 – 1, AT 3 – 1

- Introduce the core vocabulary relating to ice creams, using Students' Book page 94. Begin by presenting the vocabulary and checking that students understand the meaning.

T: Regardez la page 94. Voici des glaces. Voici une glace simple et voici une glace double. (Point to the different sizes of ice cream on the price list at the top of the page.) Une glace simple, c'est combien? Et une glace double, c'est combien? Comment dit-on 'une glace simple' en anglais? etc.

- Go on to present the six different flavours, using the class cassette. Play the cassette through once, whilst students follow in their books. Again check that the meaning is understood, before practising aural comprehension of the new vocabulary.

T: Une glace à la fraise, c'est quel numéro? Numéro cinq, c'est une glace à la fraise. Vrai ou faux? etc.

- Play the cassette again and encourage students to repeat the flavours. Follow this up with further class repetition practice and finally with oral work.

T: Numéro cinq, c'est une glace à la vanille? Qu'est-ce que c'est numéro cinq? etc.

---

1 une glace au chocolat
2 une glace au café
3 une glace au citron
4 une glace à la vanille

5 une glace à la fraise
6 une glace à la menthe

Presentation of:
Tu veux une glace?

Sondage!

AT 1 – 2, AT 2 – 2, AT 4 – 2

- Teach the question *Tu veux une glace?*, asking students around the class if they would like an ice cream. Check that they understand the question and encourage them to respond by choosing the flavour which they would like. Initially offer a choice until they understand the principle and can choose their own flavour in response to the follow-up question *Quel parfum?*

- Practise repetition of *Tu veux une glace?* and encourage students to practise simple dialogues in pairs, along the lines of *Tu veux une glace? Oui, une glace au chocolat, s'il te plaît.*

- When they are confident, explain that the class is going to carry out a survey into the most popular flavour of ice cream.

T: Maintenant nous allons faire un sondage. Quelle est la glace préférée? Une glace au chocolat? Une glace à la vanille?

- Decide whether this is to be a whole class survey or a group survey and then instruct the students accordingly to interview all the other members of the class or a minimum number of students.

T: Vous avez __ minutes pour interviewer __ personnes ... Vous posez la question 'Tu veux une glace?' Vous écoutez la réponse, par exemple 'Oui, une glace au chocolat' et vous notez la réponse. Bon. Levez-vous ... (mime that students should stand up) et circulez. (Mime that students should move around the classroom.) Allez-y!

- Afterwards, students can practise writing the flavours by displaying the results as part of a tally chart or bar chart.

Presentation of:
Oui, je veux bien.
Quel parfum?
Une simple ou une double?

Qui parle? (SB p.94)

AT 1 – 3

- More extended dialogues are now introduced, initially in the form of a listening comprehension activity. Explain that students should listen to the eight conversations, look at the spaghetti diagram on page 94 and decide who is talking each time.

1

Friend:	Tu veux une glace?
Sophie:	Oui, je veux bien.
Friend:	Quel parfum?
Sophie:	Une glace à la fraise, s'il te plaît.
Friend:	Une simple ou une double?
Sophie:	Une simple, s'il te plaît.

2

Friend:	Tu veux une glace?
Olivier:	Oui, je veux bien.
Friend:	Quel parfum?
Olivier:	Une glace à la vanille, s'il te plaît.
Friend:	Une simple ou une double?
Olivier:	Une double, s'il te plaît.

3

Friend:	Tu veux une glace?
Martin:	Oui, je veux bien.
Friend:	Quel parfum?
Martin:	Une glace à la menthe, s'il te plaît.
Friend:	Une simple ou une double?
Martin:	Une simple, s'il te plaît.

4

Friend:	Tu veux une glace?
Marc:	Oui, je veux bien.
Friend:	Quel parfum?
Marc:	Une glace au café, s'il te plaît.
Friend:	Une simple ou une double?
Marc:	Une simple, s'il te plaît.

5

Friend:	Tu veux une glace?
Véronique:	Oui, je veux bien – une glace au chocolat, s'il te plaît.

Friend:	Une simple ou une double?
Véronique:	Une double, s'il te plaît.

6

Friend:	Tu veux une glace?
Yannick:	Oui, je veux bien.
Friend:	Quel parfum?
Yannick:	Une glace au citron, s'il te plaît – une glace simple.

7

Friend:	Tu veux une glace?
Sandrine:	Oui, je veux bien.
Friend:	Quel parfum?
Sandrine:	Une glace au chocolat, s'il te plaît.
Friend:	Une simple ou une double?
Sandrine:	Une simple, s'il te plaît.

8

Friend:	Tu veux une glace?
Nicole:	Oui, je veux bien – une glace à la fraise, s'il te plaît.
Friend:	Une simple ou une double?
Nicole:	Une glace double, s'il te plaît.

Quel parfum? (SB p.94)

a Ecoute et lis.

AT 1 – 3, AT 3 – 3

- Having exposed the class to a series of longer dialogues, begin to look at the content of this type of conversation in detail.
- Playing the dialogue on the class cassette item and encourage students to follow the text in their books.

> – Tu veux une glace?
> – Oui, je veux bien.
> – Quel parfum?
> – Une glace au chocolat, s'il te plaît.
> – Une simple ou une double?
> – Une simple, s'il te plaît.
> – Voilà.
> – Merci.

- Focus on the phrases *Oui, je veux bien, Quel parfum?* and *Une simple ou une double?* and check that their meaning is understood, before giving the class repetition practice of these phrases. Then begin practising the full dialogue, initially dividing the two roles between yourself and the class and then between two halves of the class, before setting up pairwork.

b C'est à vous!

AT 2 – 3/4, AT 4 – 1/2/3

- Having practised the dialogue on page 94, students can be encouraged to invent and act out their own. Optionally, this could be written up afterwards.

Aide-mémoire (SB p.95)

AT 1 – 2, AT 2 – 2, AT 3 – 2/3, AT 4 – 1/2/3

- Summarise the two main categories of vocabulary contained within the second objective of this module – i.e. *les snacks* and *les glaces* – and remind the class of the importance of learning this vocabulary.
- Explain that there are lots of possible ways of learning and that these can be combined with the method outlined in *'Le vocabulaire? Pas de problème!'* on Students' Book page 13.
- Then show that some of these possible methods are listed on page 95. Read out each method, demonstrating it if possible and checking that students understand the technique. Remind them that these are all ways of <u>helping</u> them to learn their vocabulary, often in a way which is fun. Stress, however, that when they are learning the detail (e.g. spelling), they will still probably need to use the learning method illustrated in *'Le vocabulaire? Pas de problème!'* on page 13, i.e. look and say, cover and say, try to remember and write and then check and rewrite if necessary.

Les snacks et les glaces (SB p.95)

- Finally, set students the task of making their own *aide-mémoire* for snacks and ice creams. They should then revise the snack vocabulary and/or learn the ice cream vocabulary by heart for a short spelling and comprehension test.

- Some students may like to make an *aide-mémoire* in the form of a menu or a mobile for display, using desk-top publishing and/or word-processing facilities if desired/available.

Objectif 3   Nous avons soif

New language introduced:

Un coca/café/café-crème/jus d'orange/jus de pomme/chocolat/thé au lait/thé citron/orangina
Une limonade
Qu'est-ce que tu prends?/Vous prenez?
Je prends …
C'est tout?
A gauche/droite
Tout droit
L'addition s'il vous plaît
Où sont les toilettes?

Revision of:

Board games language: *C'est à moi! / Avance / Passe un tour (etc.)*

Student goals   (SB p.84)

- Remind the class of the third section of the goals visual on page 84 in the usual way, before using flashcards to introduce the drinks.

| **Presentation of drinks** (see list below) |

Les boissons   (FC 79-88)

AT 1 – 1, AT 2 – 1

- Use the flashcards to teach the following drinks, grouping them according to their gender:

  79 *un coca*
  80 *un café*
  81 *un café-crème*
  82 *un jus d'orange*
  83 *un jus de pomme*
  84 *un orangina*
  85 *un thé au lait*
  86 *un thé citron*
  87 *un chocolat*
  88 *une limonade*

- A variety of games can be played to consolidate understanding and to maximise opportunities for hearing the new vocabulary, before practising it orally. (See 'Games', Teacher's Notes introduction, page iv.)

Les boissons   (CM 58)

1 Ecoute la cassette et regarde les images. Mets le bon numéro.

AT 1 – 1, AT 4 – 1

- Students begin by listening to a series of numbered drinks and writing the number of each in the corresponding picture on the copymaster. This can be done in the lesson or using the self-study cassette at home.

1 une limonade
2 un café-crème
3 un coca
4 un orangina
5 un thé au lait
6 un chocolat
7 un jus d'orange
8 un thé citron
9 un café
10 un jus de pomme

You will need Copymaster 58, activity 1. Listen to the cassette and look at the pictures of the drinks. Pause the cassette after you hear each drink and write the number in the correct picture.

1   une limonade
2   un café-crème
3   un coca
4   un orangina
5   un thé au lait
6   un chocolat

7 un jus d'orange
8 un thé citron
9 un café
10 un jus de pomme

Solution

A 3 **B** 9 **C** 2 **D** 7 **E** 10 **F** 6 **G** 5 **H** 8 **I** 4 **J** 1

2 Mets le bon mot.

AT 3 – 1, AT 4 – 1

- In the second activity, students use the support list of drinks at the bottom of the page and copy each label underneath the correct picture.

Solution

A 3   un coca
B 9   un café
C 2   un café-crème
D 7   un jus d'orange
E 10   un jus de pomme
F 6   un chocolat
G 5   un thé au lait
H 8   un thé citron
I 4   un orangina
J 1   une limonade

3 Vérifie tes réponses! Ecoute, lis et répète.

AT 1 – 1, AT 2 – 1

- Students then use the self-study cassette to check their answers, before listening to, reading and repeating the drinks.

You will need Copymaster 58, activity 3, 'Vérifie tes réponses!' Listen to the cassette again, to see if you carried out tasks 1 and 2 correctly. Listen to each drink, pause the cassette and check your answer. Correct it in a different colour if you need to, then start the cassette again, listen to the drink and repeat it. Afterwards, go on to the next drink.

A 3   un coca
B 9   un café
C 2   un café-crème
D 7   un jus d'orange
E 10 un jus de pomme

F 6   un chocolat
G 5   un thé au lait
H 8   un thé citron
I 4   un orangina
J 1   une limonade

Differentiation – Consolidation

AT 1 – 1, AT 2 – 1, AT 3 – 1

- Afterwards, groups of students could use the copymaster for playing Bingo.

Presentation of:

Qu'est-ce que tu prends?/vous prenez?
Je prends …

Au café   (SB p.96)

a Ecoute et lis.

AT 1 – 3, AT 3 – 3

- Introduce the café scenario, using the cartoon on page 96 and the accompanying class cassette.

Differentiation – Extension

- Some students could listen first with their books closed and try to deduce what is happening and/or note which drinks are mentioned.

Au centre de vacances
Girl: Oof! J'ai chaud!
Boy: Et moi, j'ai soif. J'ai une idée …

Au café
Boy: Qu'est-ce que tu prends?
Girl: Je prends une limonade, s'il te plaît.

Waiter: Bonjour. Qu'est-ce que vous prenez?
Boy: Bonjour. Un coca et une limonade, s'il vous plaît.

Prof: Que faites-vous, alors?

- Encourage the class to deduce the meaning of the new phrases *Qu'est-ce que tu prends?*, *Je prends …* and *Qu'est-ce que vous prenez?* There will then be the opportunity to hear these phrases in six more conversations.

Presentation of:

C'est tout?

---

b Ecoute la cassette et regarde les photos. Vrai ou faux?

AT 1 – 3, AT 4 – 1

- Explain that students should listen carefully to the six conversations set in a café, look at the photos on page 96 and decide whether the photos match the drinks ordered on cassette.

1

– Qu'est-ce que tu prends?
– Un coca, s'il te plaît, Papa.
– Bonjour. Qu'est-ce que vous prenez?
– Un coca, s'il vous plaît … Et moi, … je prends un jus d'orange, s'il vous plaît.
– Bon. Un coca et un jus d'orange.

2

– Qu'est-ce que tu prends?
– Un thé citron, s'il te plaît.
– Bonjour. Qu'est-ce que vous prenez?
– Un thé citron, s'il vous plaît … Et moi, … je prends un chocolat, s'il vous plaît.
– Bon. Un thé citron et un chocolat.

3

– Qu'est-ce que tu prends?
– Une limonade, s'il te plaît.
– Et moi, je prends un café.
– Bonjour. Qu'est-ce que vous prenez?
– Bonjour. Une limonade et un café, s'il vous plaît.

4

– Qu'est-ce que tu prends?
– Un thé au lait, s'il te plaît.
– Et moi, je prends un jus de pomme.
– Bonjour. Qu'est-ce que vous prenez?
– Bonjour. Un thé au lait et un jus de pomme, s'il vous plaît.

5

– Qu'est-ce que tu prends?
– Un café, s'il te plaît.
– Et moi je prends un chocolat – non, pardon! Je prends un café aussi.
– Bonjour. Qu'est-ce que vous prenez?
– Bonjour. Deux cafés, s'il vous plaît.

6

– Tu prends un jus d'orange?
– Non, je prends un jus de pomme, s'il te plaît.
– Bonjour. Qu'est-ce que vous prenez?
– Bonjour. Un jus de pomme et un thé citron, s'il vous plaît.
– C'est tout?
– Oui, merci.

Solution

1 faux **2** vrai **3** faux **4** faux **5** vrai **6** vrai

c A deux.

AT 1 – 2, AT 2 – 2/3, AT 3 – 2, AT 4 – 2/3

- Revise the phrases *Qu'est-ce que tu prends?*, *Je prends …* and *Qu'est-ce que vous prenez?* again, this time eliciting them from students by asking *Comment dit-on …. en anglais?*

- Give the class the opportunity to practise repetition of the key phrases and then direct students to the pairwork activity at the bottom of page 96. Demonstrate how to use the photos on the page to cue short conversations. Some or all of these could be written up afterwards if desired/appropriate.

J'ai chaud! J'ai soif!   (CM 59)

AT 2 – 2/3, AT 3 – 2, AT 4 – 2/3

- Students now have the opportunity to bring together vocabulary connected with ice creams, drinks and states and feelings and to use it within a slightly more wide-ranging café context.

- Explain that they can fill in each speech bubble with any phrase which is appropriate. Before students begin, demonstrate that there may be several possibilities for any one speech bubble, by pointing to one or two bubbles and asking for suggestions from the class.

5 Visite scolaire

- The completed copymaster can provide support later, when planning role-plays and playlets.

Differentiation – Extension

- Some members of the class could be encouraged to fill in the bubbles from memory.

Presentation of:

A gauche/droite

Tout droit

Directions

AT 1 – 1, AT 2 – 1, AT 3 – 1, AT 4 – 1

- Before moving on to Students' Book page 97, use arrows and written captions on the board/OHP to teach the following directions:

  à gauche

  à droite

  tout droit

- Check aural comprehension of the directions, e.g. by asking the class to draw arrows, following your directions. Then move on to practise the phrases orally.

- When the new vocabulary has been established, set up pairwork. Students could either take it in turns to guide one another around the classroom or could draw arrows following one another's directions. In the drawing activity, if all the arrows are kept approximately one centimetre long, students could draw a shape made up of arrows and dictate it for their partner to draw, for example:

- As a written activity, the class could work together to produce a series of large captioned arrows or signs to guide French-speaking visitors to the classroom from the nearest entrance or from another part of the school.

Presentation of:

L'addition, s'il vous plaît

Où sont les toilettes?

L'addition, s'il vous plaît!   (SB p.97)

a Ecoute la cassette, lis la conversation et note les détails.

AT 1 – 3, AT 3 – 3, AT 4 – 2

- Direct students to page 97 and explain that they are now going to hear another conversation in a café and that they should listen to the cassette and follow the gapped conversation in their books. Encourage them to deduce the meaning of *Monsieur, l'addition, s'il vous plaît* and *... où sont les toilettes?*

- Play the cassette again and ask students to listen and note the missing details, using abbreviations in their exercise books or on paper. Replay the cassette as many times as necessary.

- Point out the *'Attention!'* feature which will help with the spelling of directions.

Sandrine:	Monsieur, l'addition, s'il vous plaît.
Waiter:	Un jus de pomme, un café-crème, une limonade et un orangina, ça fait 60 francs 50.
Sandrine:	Merci, monsieur. Et où sont les toilettes, s'il vous plaît?
Waiter:	A droite.
Sandrine:	Merci. Au revoir.

Solution

1 Un jus de pomme **2** un café-crème **3** une limonade **4** un orangina **5** 60 francs 50 **6** A droite

---

OHT

Ça fait combien?   (CM 60)

AT 1 – 2, AT 2 – 3, AT 3 – 3, AT 4 – 2

- Cut up the copymaster in advance, allowing for one copy between two students. If an OHP is available, also prepare an acetate copy for demonstration. Divide the class into pairs and give out the example conversation from the top section of the copymaster to each pair. Tell the students to follow the conversation as you read it aloud.

- Then, using a larger version of the conversation on the board or OHP for support, focus in particular on the phrases *Monsieur/madame. L'addition, s'il vous plaît* and *Et où sont les toilettes, s'il vous plaît?* Provide a variety of repetition practice for these phrases.

- Go on to rehearse the full dialogue, dividing the roles between the class and yourself and then between the two halves of the class, until students are confident.

- Explain that the students are now going to imagine that they are in a café and work in pairs, interviewing their partner to find out information about the bill and the location of the toilets. Quickly draw a blank grid with the headings *Boissons, Prix* and *Toilettes* on the board and any similar but completed grid below.

T: Vous faites des conversations au café. Vous commencez, 'Monsieur/Madame. L'addition, s'il vous plaît.' (Point to the first line of the example dialogue.) *Votre partenaire regarde cette grille et répond, par exemple ...* (Point to the completed grid and give a statement about the drinks and the price, also showing how this relates to the format used in the second line of the example dialogue.) *Bon. Vous écoutez et vous notez dans votre grille, par exemple ...* (Show how to fill in the *Boissons* and *Prix* columns of the blank grid.) *Alors, vous continuez, 'Merci. Et où sont les toilettes, s'il vous plaît?'* (Point to the third line of the example dialogue.) *Votre partenaire regarde cette grille et répond, et vous notez ici ...* (Show how the partner gives information from the completed grid and how to add an arrow representing his/her response in the *Toilettes* column of the blank grid.) *Vous complétez la conversation, 'Merci. Au revoir.'*

- Continue the demonstration and show how to swap roles and then use the fully complete printed grid on the copymaster to answer the partner's questions. Involve a student in the demonstration to clarify how the information is being exchanged.

- Distribute the remaining two sections of Copymaster 60 amongst the pairs of students, giving part A of the copymaster to one member of each pair and part B to the other member. Then tell the class to start their interviews.

L'addition, s'il vous plaît! (SB p.97)

b A deux.

AT 1 – 2, AT 2 – 3, AT 3 – 3, AT 4 – 3/4

- Students use their imagination to continue the conversation in the cartoon on page 96 (before the arrival of the teacher in the last frame), by asking for the bill and the location of the toilets. After working out and practising a conversation orally, some students may wish to produce a cartoon version of the sequel to the story.

- Alternatively/additionally, students can work in groups of four or five and act out a complete café scenario. Where appropriate, the whole classroom could be converted into a café, accompanying menus could be designed and real drinks served.

Lundi au Café Cool (SB p. 97, CM 72)

AT 1 – 2/3/4, AT 2 – 2/3/4, AT 3 – 2/3/4

- Students now listen to the song, which provides further consolidation of ordering drinks in a café.

- Play the song through once and encourage the class to follow the accompanying text on page 97 of their books. Then play one verse at a time, stopping briefly after each to check understanding. An OHT version of Copymaster 72 may be helpful in focusing students' attention on particular sections of text, whilst masking the rest of the song. As this process continues and the tune becomes familiar, encourage the class to join in singing the separate verses, before students finally sing along to the full version.

1   Bonjour, ma chérie!
    Bonjour. C'est lundi.
    Allons au café.
    Je veux te parler.

2   Bonjour, Pierre. Ça va?
    Il y a une place pour moi?
    Garçon! Je voudrais
    Un coca, s'il vous plaît.

(Refrain) Lundi au Café Cool, Cool, Cool.
    Au Café Cool.
    Seuls au Café Cool il dit:
    Je t'aime, ma chérie ...

3 Bonjour, ma chérie!
Bonjour. C'est mercredi.
Allons au café.
Je veux te parler.

4 Marie. Me voici!
Voilà mes amis.
Garçon! Deux thés
Et dix-huit cafés!

Refrain

5 Bonjour, ma chérie!
Bonjour. C'est vendredi.
Allons au musée.
Je veux te parler.

6 Pierre et Marie!
Vous êtes ici?
Au Café Cool - venez!
Un citron pressé?

Refrain
... je t'aime ma chérie.
... je t'aime ma chérie.

1 Bonjour, ma chérie!
Bonjour. C'est lundi.
Allons au café.
Je veux te parler.

2 Bonjour, Pierre.Ça va?
Il y a une place pour moi?
Garçon! Je voudrais
Un coca, s'il vous plaît.

(Refrain) Lundi au Café Cool, Cool, Cool.
Au Café Cool.
Seuls au Café Cool il dit:
Je t'aime, ma chérie ...

3 Bonjour, ma chérie!
Bonjour. C'est mercredi.

Allons au café.
Je veux te parler.

4 Marie. Me voici!
Voilà mes amis.
Garçon! Deux thés
Et dix-huit cafés!

Refrain

5 Bonjour, ma chérie!
Bonjour. C'est vendredi.
Allons au musée.
Je veux te parler.

6 Pierre et Marie!
Vous êtes ici?
Au Café Cool - venez!
Un citron pressé?

Refrain
... je t'aime ma chérie.
... je t'aime ma chérie.

- Afterwards, where appropriate, lay a ruler or pen across the OHT version of Copymaster 72 and challenge the class to say, sing or write the missing words from memory. Alternatively/additionally students could play this game in pairs, taking it in turns to cover and to reconstruct the song in their textbooks.
- Finally, you may wish to use the music provided on Copymaster 72 to enable students to perform and/or record their own version of the song.

AT 3– 2/3/4, AT 4 – 2)

- Students could demonstrate comprehension and accuracy by copying and illustrating one or more verses of the song for a wall display. They could also learn their chosen section of the text or one or more of their favourite verses by heart.

Revision of board games language (see list below)

Restauration-rapide! (SB p.98)

AT 1 – 2, AT 2 – 2, AT 3 – 1/2

- Before pairs start this board game, which is based on the principle of Snakes and ladders, revise and practise the actual game language which they will need and demonstrate how to play.
- Begin by revising the following language, reminding the class of the meanings if necessary, with actions or symbols on the board:

  C'est à moi!
  C'est à toi!
  Vrai
  Faux
  Avance
  N'avance pas
  Recule
  Passe un tour
  J'ai gagné!

- Check comprehension, write the phrases on the board/OHP, say them through again and practise repetition. Finally, use the actions or symbols in random order to cue students to produce the language orally.
- Clarify the title of the game. Then draw a representative sample of some of the squares from the game on the board and use these to show what to do when landing on each type of square, i.e.
  - A drawing of a snack, drink, ice cream, the toilets or the bill = ask for the item shown
  - A price = say the price
  - The bottom of a drinking straw = move up to the top of the straw
  - An upset tumbler = move down to the end of the trail of the spilt drink
- Ask a student to the front of the class and demonstrate how to play the game. Use the counting rhyme *'Am stram gram'* from Students' Book page 18 to see who starts, and use *C'est à moi!* or *C'est à toi!* as appropriate. Each person then takes it in turn to roll the die and say the number in French, counting forward the number of squares whilst moving their counter, e.g. *Trois: un, deux, trois*. (Prompt the student to do this if he/she starts.)
- Show a representation of the square on the board and ask *Comment dit-on ... au café-restaurant?*, encouraging the class to work out how the player would respond. Point out that all requests should be as full and as polite as possible.

- Demonstrate how to monitor the answers, by prompting the class to say whether the answer is *vrai* or *faux* and show how to keep a tally of correct and incorrect answers for use in scoring at the end of the game. The person who finishes first only wins if he or she has the most correct answers!
- Explain that students should now play in pairs. Circulate while they are playing and encourage them to maintain the use of the target language.

Differentiation – Extension

AT 1 – 2/3, AT 2 – 2/3, AT 3 – 1/2, AT 4 – 2

- As an alternative, students could play the game in groups of four, each with a counter but working as a pair against another pair. Whenever a player lands on a square requiring an oral response, he/she should act out a dialogue with his/her partner, incorporating the key phrase within the role play. To win, both players in a pair must cross the finishing line and must have completed their dialogues successfully.
- When students have played the game a couple of times, they could try making up their own board game, using as much of the language in Module 5 as possible. As a quick alternative, requiring no writing, they could simply write out different snacks, drinks, ice creams and prices on pieces of paper and place these over the existing squares to make an 'instant' new version of the game.

Entre-temps ... (SB p.99)

AT 3 – 3/4

- Students should read the selection of articles on this page for personal interest and enjoyment. Copymaster 23, *'Mes découvertes'* can be used in conjunction with this page, to help students develop reading skills and widen their vocabulary.

Le désert, c'est super! (SB p.100)
a Ecoute et lis.

AT 1 – 4, AT 3 – 4

- The themes and language of the module are now brought together in a new context. Encourage students to practise their listening skills and aural comprehension, by initially listening to the class cassette without the support of the text in their books. Remind them of the techniques outlined

5 Visite scolaire

on Students' Book page 60 in *J'écoute – pas de panique!*', and tell them to listen first for the general theme or gist of the cassette item and then for a gradually increasing amount of detail.

Beau Geste:	Salut! Bienvenue au Fort Sableux. Je m'appelle Beau Geste et voici mes copains.
	Notre routine ici est vraiment chouette. Nous mangeons le petit déjeuner à six heures moins le quart et après nous faisons du sport.
	Nous jouons au volley et au foot. Nous faisons aussi du cheval.
	L'après-midi nous faisons des promenades.
Soldier:	J'ai chaud!
Beau Geste:	Nous mangeons le repas du soir à onze heures et demie. Après nous jouons aux cartes et nous écoutons de la musique.
	Aujourd'hui, c'est dimanche. Nous faisons une excursion! Nous quittons le fort à huit heures moins le quart et nous allons à l'oasis.
Soldier:	Je suis fatigué!
Narrator:	Deux heures plus tard ...
Soldier:	Vous faites de la voile?
Beau Geste:	Non, nous faisons de la natation et après nous allons au café-restaurant.
Soldier:	Tu veux une glace?
Soldier:	Oui, s'il te plaît. Une glace à la vanille.
Waitress:	Bonjour, messieurs. Qu'est-ce que vous prenez?
Soldier:	Un coca, s'il vous plaît.
Beau Geste:	Et pour moi, un hamburger et une portion de frites, s'il vous plaît!

- Afterwards, give the class the opportunity to read the accompanying text on page 17 and clarify any vocabulary necessary, before moving on to the activities on page 101.

b Lis 'Le désert, c'est super!' Vrai ou faux?

AT 3 – 2/4, AT 4 – 1/2

- Students demonstrate understanding of the text on page 100, by deciding whether the eight statements at the top of page 101 are true or false. These statements also provide a simple model text which can be adapted later in the *'Porte ouverte!'* activity. Where appropriate, the class can be encouraged to correct the sentences which are false.

Solution

1 faux – Nous mangeons le petit déjeuner à six heures moins le quart.
2 faux – L'après-midi nous faisons des promenades.
3 vrai
4 faux – Nous mangeons le repas du soir à onze heures et demie.
5 vrai
6 vrai
7 faux – A l'oasis nous faisons de la natation et après nous allons au café-restaurant.
8 vrai

c Copie et complète les questions.

AT 3 – 2, AT 4 – 2

- Using the references elsewhere in the module if necessary, students practise the 2nd person plural forms of verbs in the present tense. In this activity they should manipulate verbs in the original text on page 100 to complete the cloze sentences.

Solution

1 Vous **mangez** le petit déjeuner à quelle heure?
2 Le matin vous **jouez** au foot?
3 Que **faites**-vous l'après-midi?
4 Vous **écoutez** de la musique le soir?
5 Que **faites**-vous le dimanche?
6 Vous **quittez** le fort à quelle heure?

d Réponds aux questions.

AT 3 – 2, AT 4 – 2/3

- Students move on to practise the 1st person plural forms of the verbs, by answering the questions, with the help of page 100 if necessary.

Solution

1 Nous mangeons le petit déjeuner à six heures moins le quart.

2 Le matin nous jouons au volley et au foot et nous faisons aussi du cheval.

3 L'après-midi nous faisons des promenades.

4 Le soir nous écoutons de la musique et nous jouons aux cartes.

5 Le dimanche nous faisons une excursion/des excursions.

6 Nous quittons le fort à huit heures moins le quart.

e A deux. Enregistrez l'interview!

AT 1 – 2, AT 2 – 3/4, AT 3 – 3

● Finally the class should work in pairs and record an interview based on their answers to the previous activities. Where appropriate, they should be encouraged to produce as much of the interview as possible from memory.

Porte ouverte! (SB p.102)

Sommaire (SB pp.102 – 103)

AT 1 – 3/4, AT 2 – 3/4, AT 3 – 3/4, AT 4 – 3/4

● Before directing students to page 102, return to the goals section on page 84 to show how all the language is leading to the 'Porte ouverte!' activity. Remind the class of the language which they have learned, by referring to each goal in turn and pointing out the relevant pages in the module.

● Explain the instructions on page 102, making sure that students understand the tasks and demonstrating how to use page 100 as a model.

Spend some time talking through the summary of the module's language on pages 102 – 103. Show how to refer to this and key pages of the Students' Book and copymasters for support.

a Prépare ta description de la routine au fort.

● In the first of the two summative activities students write an account of their own routine at the fort, as if they were staying there with a group of friends. Encourage redrafting and explain that the account can be word-processed or handwritten and could be illustrated. The final versions could be displayed for others to read.

b En scène!

● In the second activity the class should work in groups of four to six and act out a scene at the oasis restaurant. Students should be encouraged to extend the dialogues to cover all aspects of snacks, ice creams and drinks, including asking for the bill. Props could be brought to the lesson and the playlets could be acted out and recorded on cassette or video. The rest of the class can listen and take notes, before voting for their favourite playlet.

Differentiation – Consolidation and Extension

● It may be helpful to direct lower attainers to the 'Vrai ou faux?' activity on page 101 and encourage them to use this as a model for their written account of their routine.

● Encourage higher attainers to write fuller descriptions and to use their imagination to extend the account of their routine. Also, in the oral activity, they should be encouraged to learn their lines and to perform from memory.

6 TOUR DE FRANCE

In this module students learn how to:

Talk about the weather
Il pleut / Il fait beau (etc.)

Describe where they are and what the weather is like
Aujourd'hui/Ce matin je suis au bord de la mer/à la montagne (etc.)

Ask about the weather
Quel temps fait-il (à/en …)?

Ask permission to do things
Je peux travailler avec …? / Je peux aller voir …? (etc.)

Talk about other people
Il habite à … / Elle aime le sport /
Ils regardent la télé / Elles quittent la ville (etc.)

Ask what someone is doing
Que fait il/elle?

Ask what is happening
Qu'est-ce qui se passe?

New language introduced
Il pleut/neige

Il fait beau/mauvais/chaud/froid
Il fait du soleil/vent/brouillard
Au bord de la mer
A la montagne/campagne
En ville
A (+ name of town)
Aujourd'hui
Ce matin/Cet après-midi/Ce soir
Lundi matin/Samedi soir (etc.)
Je peux travailler avec (+ name)/aller voir (+ name)/aller a mon cours de musique (match de foot)/aller chercher un livre (une chaise)?
Il/Elle/Le premier coureur/Ils/Elles/Les spectateurs monte(nt)/arrive(nt)/quitte(nt)/mange(nt)/ tombe(nt)/ passe(nt)/regarde(nt)/crie(nt)/va (vont)

Materials needed
Students' Book pages 104 – 123
Copymasters 61 – 70
Flashcards 89 – 101
Class cassette F
Self-study cassette

Objectif 1 Quel temps fait-il?

New language introduced
Il pleut/il neige
Il fait beau/mauvais/chaud/froid
Il fait du soleil/du vent/du brouillard
Quel temps fait-il?

Productive language
Il pleut / neige
Il fait beau/mauvais/chaud/froid
Il fait du soleil/du vent/du brouillard
Quel temps fait-il?
A (+ town + weather phrase)
Au bord de la mer
A la montagne/campagne
En ville
Aujourd'hui
Ce matin/cet après-midi/ce soir

En classe
Je peux aller à mon cours de musique/à mon match de foot/voir (+ name), s'il vous plaît?
Je peux travailler avec (+ name)?
Je peux aller chercher une chaise/un livre?

Revision of
Opinions
1st person singular of verbs

Student goals (SB p.104)

- Use the top half of the page to familiarise students with the module's main teaching points and goals. Establish the meaning of *Tour de France* and then guide students through the visual representation of the three objectives in the usual way, using flashcards, mime etc. to clarify the theme of each.

- Demonstrate the *'En classe'* bubbles and make a couple of statements such as *Je peux aller à mon cours de musique?, Je peux aller chercher une chaise?,* supported by mime, before finally reminding students that the module will culminate in a *'Porte ouverte!'* activity.

F

Quel temps fait-il? (FC 89 – 97)

AT 1 – 2, AT 2 – 2

- Introduce the question *Quel temps fait-il?* by peering out of the classroom window and asking the question rhetorically. Give one or two statements in response about the actual weather and support these with the relevant flashcards.
- Go on to use the other weather flashcards to present the following statements, strengthening the visual impact if desired with props, such as an umbrella, gloves, a sunhat/knotted handkerchief, sunglasses etc.
  89 *Il pleut.*
  90 *Il neige.*
  91 *Il fait beau.*
  92 *Il fait mauvais.*
  93 *Il fait chaud.*
  94 *Il fait froid.*
  95 *Il fait du soleil.*
  96 *Il fait du vent.*
  97 *Il fait du brouillard.*
- Check that students understand the meaning of the statements and invite them to invent appropriate actions to accompany the flashcards, before playing a variety of aural comprehension games.

Quel temps fait-il, aujourd'hui?

(SB p.104)

AT 1 – 2, AT 2 – 2, AT 3 – 2

- Students listen to the class cassette featuring different statements about the weather, whilst looking at the selection of illustrated sentences on page 104. After each statement on the cassette they should write the letter of the corresponding visual, to show that they have made the connection between the spoken and written forms of the statements.

1 Il fait mauvais.
2 Il fait froid.
3 Il fait du soleil.
4 Il fait chaud.
5 Il neige.
6 Il fait beau.
7 Il pleut.
8 Il fait du brouillard.
9 Il fait du vent.

Solution

1 C 2 E 3 I 4 D 5 G 6 A 7 F 8 H 9 B

- As a final check of comprehension, the class could listen to the cassette again with their books closed and draw an appropriate weather symbol for each statement.
- Next, use the flashcards again and encourage repetition and pronunciation practice, before playing a variety of games to practise oral production of the weather statements. Move on to teach and practise the question *Quel temps fait-il?* and then demonstrate how students should use the visuals on page 104 for pairwork, taking it in turns to ask questions such as *Quel temps fait-il: D?* and to reply with the appropriate weather statement. To make this more challenging, some students close their books and could try giving the correct response about the weather from memory.
- Students can then be encouraged to use one or more statements about the weather as their password or *passe-partout du jour/passe-partout de la semaine* in order to be able to leave the classroom at the end of the lesson.

Differentiation – Consolidation

Il fait beau, il fait chaud! (CM 61)
1 Relie les phrases et les images.

AT 3 – 2

- This copymaster is suitable for independent work at home or in the classroom. In the first task, students demonstrate comprehension of the written statements about the weather by linking each statement to the corresponding picture.

2 a Ecoute, lis et répète.

b Lis, prononce et écoute.

AT 1 – 2, AT 2 – 2, AT 3 – 2

- The second task then gives the opportunity for further oral practice of the statements.

1 Il fait froid.
2 Il fait mauvais.
3 Il fait du vent.
4 Il fait du brouillard.
5 Il pleut.
6 Il neige.
7 Il fait beau.
8 Il fait du soleil.
9 Il fait chaud.

You will need Copymaster 61, activity 2. Look at the sentences about the weather at the top of the page. Listen to the cassette as you read each sentence. Pause the cassette after each one and repeat the sentence.

1 Il fait froid.
2 Il fait mauvais.
3 Il fait du vent.
4 Il fait du brouillard.
5 Il pleut.
6 Il neige.
7 Il fait beau.
8 Il fait du soleil.
9 Il fait chaud.

In a moment, rewind the cassette to the beginning of *'Il fait beau, il fait chaud!'* Read the sentences again. This time, say them out loud. After each one listen to the cassette to check your pronunciation. Pause the cassette after each sentence.

3 Dessine ou écris.

AT 3 – 2, AT 4 – 2

- Students practise reading and writing phrases about the weather, and demonstrate comprehension of the phrases by drawing an appropriate picture above the corresponding sentence. In addition they can write the missing weather description underneath the pictures given.

Differentiation – Extension

AT 3 – 2, AT 4 – 3

- Encourage higher attainers to cover the top half of the copymaster and to undertake the final task without additional support.

Presentation of:
A (+ town) **il pleut** (etc.)

La météo   (SB p.105)

a Regarde la carte et écoute la météo. Vrai ou faux?

AT 1 – 2, AT 2 – 2, AT 3 – 1

- Before directing the class to the weather map and listening task at the top of page 105, refer to the introductory map of France on page 4 to refamiliarise students with the names and locations of Cherbourg, Calais, Rennes, Paris, Limoges, Bordeaux, Perpignan and Nice.

T: *Regardez la carte à la page 4. Où est Paris? Indiquez et levez la main* (demonstrate).

- Once students have been reminded of the map of France, play the class cassette and encourage them to look at the map on page 105 whilst following the weather summary on the cassette. Explain that some of the symbols on the map are wrong, but that the cassette version is correct.

Bonjour! Voici la météo.

1 A Cherbourg il fait froid.
2 A Calais il pleut.
3 A Rennes il fait mauvais.

4 A Paris il fait beau.
5 A Limoges il fait du soleil.
6 A Bordeaux il fait du vent.
7 A Perpignan il pleut.
8 A Nice il fait chaud.

- Play the cassette again and ask students whether the symbols on the map are true or false.

T: Maintenant, regardez la carte à la page 105. Où est Paris? ... Oui. Et quel temps fait-il à Paris? ... Oui, très bien. Mais attention! Il y a des erreurs dans les images. Ecoutez la cassette et trouvez les erreurs. Par exemple ... (Write 1 on board and play first item.) Regardez la carte. C'est vrai ou faux? Oui. C'est faux – il fait froid (Write X next to 1.) Continuez comme ça.

Solution

1 faux 2 faux 3 faux 4 vrai 5 vrai 6 faux 7 vrai 8 vrai

(FC 89 – 97)

- Use a couple of examples from the cassette to draw attention to the construction à + town + weather. Write *A Cherbourg* on the board and stick the flashcard representing cold weather alongside. Ask *Quel temps fait-il à Cherbourg?* and encourage students to produce the sentence *A Cherbourg il fait froid*. Then cue other sentences by changing the name of the town and the weather flashcard, gradually removing the cues and encouraging the class to make up sentences of their own.

b Ecris la météo.

AT 2 – 2, AT 3 – 1/2, AT 4 – 2/3

- Students use the map on page 105 to write and then read out the weather summary shown. Draw attention to the lack of accent on the capital letter, contrasting *A Cherbourg il fait du vent* with *J'habite à Cherbourg* and *Quel temps fait-il à Cherbourg?*
- To add enjoyment to the oral part of the activity, students could take it in turns to act out the part of a television weather person, using a large cardboard box with a television screen cut out of one side and placing this over their head as they give the summary. Alternatively, students could present their weather report orally, using a map and symbols on the OHP. As most weather reports are brief, give them a two-minute 'TV slot' to present their report.

Differentiation – Consolidation and Extension

AT 2 – 2/3, AT 3 – 2

- Some members of the class could literally read out the weather forecast with the support of a television auto-cue, while others could be encouraged to give the summary from memory or to make up and give a completely new forecast.

c A toi! Prépare une météo différente.

AT 1 – 2, AT 2 – 2/3

- Direct the class to the weather notes shown and clarify the abbreviation convention and the note-taking technique shown. Write *Ch. = Cherbourg* and *Ca. = Calais* on the board and then ask *Re., c'est quelle ville? Pa., c'est quelle ville?* etc., before inviting students to offer abbreviations for other towns shown on the map. Go through a similar process with the weather abbreviations and demonstrate how to abbreviate a whole phrase such as *Il fait du soleil* to *sol*. In a *pause anglaise*, explain that students only need to use the last word of each phrase, abbreviated.
- When students understand the principle, explain that they should make up their own abbreviated weather summary. Demonstrate this on the board, referring to the model given. Explain that students should write down their own abbreviated towns and weather.

d A deux.

AT 1 – 2, AT 2 – 2/3

- Students then work in pairs and find out their partner's weather. Practise the question *Quel temps fait-il à ...?* and demonstrate the example, by calling one student out to the front and playing one role yourself, showing how students make notes about their partner's weather. Once they have completed this, they should reverse roles.
- Encourage pairs to check one another's notes at the end of the activity and to correct any errors.

e Fais un aide-mémoire.

(AT 3 – 2), AT 4 – 2/3

- Finally encourage students to make up their own *aide-mémoire* or mobile featuring weather vocabulary. Encourage students who design an *aide-mémoire* to think of alternative formats in which to present the vocabulary e.g. clouds, an umbrella, a thermometer etc. These can be kept for personal use or displayed around the classroom as an aid in learning the new vocabulary. Allocate homework time for learning by heart and remind students of the learning strategies outlined on Students' Book page 13.

Comment ça se prononce? (SB p.106)

AT 1 – 2/3, AT 2 – 2/3, AT 3 – 2/3

a Ecoute la météo.

- Play the weather forecast rhyme on the class cassette twice.

Voici la météo. Aujourd'hui
A Beaune, à Bordeaux et à Beauvais
Il fait chaud, il fait beau, il fait mauvais.

- Check that students understand the meaning of the rhyme and then focus on the *au/eau/o* sound in individual words. Draw attention to the various spellings representing the sound *au* etc. by asking students to come to the board/OHP and to fill in the missing letters in a selection of the words from page 106 as you say them, e.g. Write *ch__d* and say *chaud*. Write *b___* and say *beau* etc. Underline the various alternative spellings at the end of the words, whilst making the phonetic sound.
- Move on to encourage repetition of words, phrases, lines and eventually the whole rhyme. To add variety, this can be done with increasing and decreasing volume and in different tones e.g. happy, sad, angry etc.
- For additional practice, the rhyme is also provided on the self-study cassette.

You will need Students' Book page 106, activity A. Listen and read.

Voici la météo. Aujourd'hui
A Beaune, à Bordeaux et à Beauvais
Il fait chaud, il fait beau, il fait mauvais.

b Ecoute et lis. Ecoute, lis et prononce.

- Students then listen to statements combining towns and weather before using the words and picture-prompts in their books to produce these again and check their pronunciation. This can be done as a class or independent activity.

1 Voici la météo.
2 A Bordeaux il fait chaud.
3 A Beauvais il fait mauvais.
4 A Beaune il fait beau.

You will need Students' Book page 106, activity B. Listen and read.

1 Voici la météo.
2 A Bordeaux il fait chaud.
3 A Beauvais il fait mauvais.
4 A Beaune il fait beau.

Now rewind the cassette and listen again. This time pause the cassette after each sentence and repeat it.

c Lis, prononce et écoute.

- Students then move on to read and pronounce other previously encountered words containing the same sound before listening to the cassette and checking their pronunciation after each word.

1 coca	**2** tableau
3 jaune	**4** gaufre
5 C'est rigolo!	**6** oiseau

You will need Students' Book page 106, activity C. Try to pronounce the words, then listen carefully to see how well you have done.

1 coca	**2** tableau
3 jaune	**4** gaufre
5 C'est rigolo!	**6** oiseau

d Copie et complète.

AT 4 – 1/2

- Students copy and complete the *aide-mémoire* to use for future reference, as part of an ongoing reminder of sounds and spelling.

- Finally, students could learn to say and/or write the rhyme '*Voici la météo*' from memory, if appropriate, using the self-study cassette for support.

> **Presentation of:**
> *Au bord de la mer*
> *A la montagne/campagne*
> *En ville*

F

A la montagne (FC 98 – 101)

AT 1 – 2/3, AT 2 – 2

- Use the flashcards of the landscapes to present and practise the following vocabulary:
  - **98** *à la montagne*
  - **99** *au bord de la mer*
  - **100** *à la campagne*
  - **101** *en ville*
- Check understanding and give students opportunities for oral practice of the new vocabulary before directing them to Students' Book page 107.

Au bord de la mer (SB p.107)

a Regarde les images et les phrases. Fais les paires.

AT 3 – 2, AT 4 – 2/3

- Students demonstrate comprehension by matching the illustrations with the appropriate phrase.

Solution

A au bord de la mer **B** à la montagne
C à la campagne **D** en ville

b Ecoute. C'est quelle image?

AT 1 – 2

- Move on to the second task in which students identify the correct illustration as they listen to longer spoken utterances on the class cassette.

Differentiation – Extension

- The first time that the cassette is played, students should focus solely on the landscape mentioned in each conversation. On the second or third hearing, however, they could be encouraged to listen and note/say the weather and any other details which they have understood. It may be helpful to remind them of the method of listening presented on page 60, '*J'écoute – pas de panique!*', i.e.: *thème, détails, encore des détails.*

1 Il fait mauvais en ville. Je vais au cinéma. Et toi?

2 Il fait du soleil au bord de la mer. C'est fantastique!

3 – A la campagne il fait beau aujourd'hui.
 – Super! Alors, je fais du vélo.

4 Il fait chaud aujourd'hui. Nous allons au bord de la mer. Dépêche-toi!

5 – Quel temps fait-il à la montagne, aujourd'hui?
 – Shh! J'écoute la météo.
 – A la montagne il fait froid et il neige.

6 Bon, nous faisons une promenade à la campagne, aujourd'hui. Il fait du soleil. C'est super!

Solution

1 D **2** A **3** C **4** A **5** B **6** C

c Fais une description des images.

AT 4 – 2/3

- Afterwards, students should describe the illustrations on page 107 orally and/or in writing, following the example given at the bottom of the page.

AT 4 – 2/3/4

- Finally, students could find magazine/holiday brochure pictures or make drawings of different landscapes and write accompanying descriptions about the landscape and the weather. Where possible, encourage them to extend the descriptions, e.g. by imagining what activity they do in each location and by giving an opinion. If necessary remind them of the relevant vocabulary in Modules 2 and 3.

> **Presentation of:**
>
> *Aujourd'hui*
> *Ce matin/cet après-midi/ce soir*

Jeu de météo (CM 62)

AT 1 – 2, AT 2 – 2, AT 3 – 2, AT 4 – 1/2

- Before beginning work on this copymaster, present the new phrases:

  aujourd'hui

  ce matin

  cet après-midi

  ce soir

- Write up on the board yesterday's date, today's date and tomorrow's date. Circle today's date and write *aujourd'hui* next to it. Add times of the day: *9 h – 12 h* and label this *ce matin*, *2 h – 5 h cet après-midi* and *5 h – 10 h ce soir*. Check students' comprehension of the new phrases, then practise pronunciation by pointing to the times on the board.

- Students look at Copymaster 62. Explain that this is a version of Battleships. Introduce the copymaster task – if necessary quickly sketch a grid headed *moi* on the board/OHP and work

through the instructions, filling in the grid with nine weather symbols or words and leaving seven blank, as shown in the example at the top of the copymaster. Say the French equivalent for each as you do so, particularly stressing the seven examples of *C'est blanc*. Point out the time phrases on the vertical axis of the grid and the landscape phrases on the horizontal axis.

- Then refer to the *'Joue avec ton/ta partenaire'* rubric and the accompanying example at the top of the copymaster, asking *Quel temps fait-il ce soir* (point to *ce soir* on the vertical axis) *à la montagne?* (point to *à la montagne* on the horizontal axis). Choose a student likely to give the correct reply and help him or her to produce the phrase *Il fait beau.*

- Show how to fill in the response in the *mon/ma partenaire* section of the grid and ask a few more questions until the principle of the game has been established, making sure that students know to give the response *C'est blanc* and to swap roles if a blank square is chosen. Rehearse students in producing other questions, showing them how to use the grid for support in adapting the example question to compile other questions such as *Quel temps fait-il aujourd'hui au bord de la mer?*

- When the class understands the task and is confident in the production of questions and answers, tell students to work in pairs. Explain that they should first complete the *moi* section of their copymaster, before exchanging information with their partner. The first person to obtain all nine of their partner's weather statements is the winner. Alternatively, a time limit could be imposed and the winner is the person who obtains the greater number of weather statements in the time allowed.

C'est pas vrai! (SB p.108)

a Ecoute et lis.

AT 1 – 3/4, AT 3 – 3/4

- Students listen to the cassette, whilst reading three short postcards which combine time of the day, weather, location and activities. Check understanding, then use the activity flashcards from Modules 3 and 5 for revision of the 1st person singular.

Aujourd'hui c'est lundi. Je suis à la montagne. Ce matin il fait froid et il neige. Je fais du ski. C'est super! Ton ami, Robert

samedi, le 20 juin
Salut! Cet après-midi je suis à la campagne. Il fait beau. Je vais à la pêche avec mon père. Bisoux, Marie

mercredi
Ce soir je suis en ville. Il pleut et il fait mauvais. C'est moche! Je vais au cinéma – c'est un film de James Bond – en anglais! Grosses bises, F

(FC 34 – 53, 89 – 97)

- Put selected activity flashcards up on the board. Gradually build up sentences by first writing a time of the day (e.g. *ce matin*) in front of each one for oral practice. Then add *je suis* + location flashcards and practise. Next, add weather flashcards and finally add smiling or unhappy faces to cue opinions. Students now produce whole sentences orally.

b Décris tes vacances.

AT 2 – 3, AT 4 – 3/4

- Leave the models on the board. Students can now tackle activity B, working with a partner to produce sentences orally and then in writing.

c Ecris ta carte postale!

AT 4 – 3/4

- Students use the postcards at the top of page 108 and/or their classwork to produce their own.

Presentation of:

Je peux aller à mon cours de musique?/à mon match de foot?/voir (+ name), s'il vous plaît?
Je peux travailler avec (+ name)?
Je peux aller chercher une chaise/un livre?

Asseyez-vous, svp! (SB p.109)
a Ecoute et lis.

AT 1 – 4, AT 3 – 4

- Students listen to the class cassette, whilst following the text of the *'Classe d'enfer'* cartoon strip on page 109, which features *Je peux …?* and more classroom requests.

Boy:	Oh non! L'éducation civique!
Prof:	Bonjour la classe. Asseyez-vous s'il vous plaît.
Boy:	Pardon, Madame, je peux aller à mon cours de musique?
Prof:	Oui, oui. Ça va.
Girl:	Zut!
Girl:	Madame, je peux travailler avec Daniel, s'il vous plaît?
Prof:	Oui, mais dépêche-toi!
Prof:	Bon. Tournez à la page trente-deux.
Boy 2:	Aïe! Doucement!
Boy 2:	Je peux aller voir Madame Périgaud, s'il vous plaît?
Prof:	Monique! Assieds-toi!
Girl:	Je peux aller chercher une chaise, s'il vous plaît?
Prof:	Ça suffit! Dépêche-toi!
Prof 2:	Je peux vous aider?!

- Play the cassette through once continuously. Then play it a second time and pause the cassette after each frame of the cartoon strip. If necessary, demonstrate the linking of the text to the cassette and encourage students to point to the relevant speech bubbles as they hear the language.
- Refer to the visuals in the cartoon strip and, supporting these with mime, encourage students to work out the meaning of:
Je peux aller à mon cours de musique?
Je peux travailler avec Daniel?
Je peux aller voir Madame Périgaud?
Je peux aller chercher une chaise?
Je peux vous aider?

- Extend these phrases to include the following, prompting students to deduce the substitutions, where possible:

  Je peux aller à mon match de foot?

  Je peux travailler avec Monique?

  Je peux aller voir Monsieur Moriot?

  Je peux aller chercher un livre?

- It may be appropriate to encourage the class to try to remember the other requests beginning *Je peux ...?* which they met in Module 4.

Pardon, monsieur ... Pardon, madame ... (CM 63)

1 Relie les phrases et les images.

AT 3 – 2

- Students demonstrate understanding by linking each written request to the appropriate visual.

Solution

Je peux ...

travailler avec Daniel? **G**

travailler avec Monique? **D**

aller à mon cours de musique? **A**

aller à mon match de foot? **H**

aller voir M. Moriot? **E**

aller voir Mme. Périgaud? **C**

aller chercher un livre? **B**

aller chercher une chaise? **F**

2 Ecoute, lis et répète.

AT 1 – 2, AT 2 – 2, AT 3 – 2

- Students then listen to the classroom language on the cassette whilst reading the phrases and practise pronunciation by repeating each request.

- If they work independently, using the self-study cassette, students can try reading the phrases aloud before comparing their own pronunciation with that of the cassette.

Je peux travailler avec Daniel?

Je peux travailler avec Monique?

Je peux aller à mon cours de musique?

Je peux aller à mon match de foot?

Je peux aller voir M. Moriot?

Je peux aller voir Mme. Périgaud?

Je peux aller chercher un livre?

Je peux aller chercher une chaise?

You will need Copymaster 63, activity 2. Look at the eight questions in the middle of the page. Listen to the cassette as you read each question. Pause the cassette after each phrase and repeat the question.

Je peux travailler avec Daniel?

Je peux travailler avec Monique?

Je peux aller à mon cours de musique?

Je peux aller à mon match de foot?

Je peux aller voir M. Moriot?

Je peux aller voir Mme. Périgaud?

Je peux aller chercher un livre?

Je peux aller chercher une chaise?

Asseyez-vous, s'il vous plaît! (SB p.109)

b Comment dit-on ...?

AT 2 – 2, AT 4 – 2/3

- Students use the pictures as cues for oral and / or written production of the classroom language. This can be done as a class, group or pairwork activity.

Solution

1 Je peux travailler avec Daniel?

2 Je peux aller chercher une chaise?

3 Je peux aller à mon cours de musique?

4 Je peux aller voir Mme. Périgaud?

5 Je peux aller à mon match de foot?

6 Je peux aller chercher un livre?

Image animée (CM 63)
Image animée: En classe (CM 64)

AT 4 – 2/3

- Look at the cartoon on Copymaster 64 with students and ask some questions to familiarise them with the classroom scene shown.

T: Voici la classe de sixième. Il y a le prof et combien de garçons? ... et il y a combien de filles? Ils posent des questions, n'est-ce pas? Quelles sortes de questions? Ce garçon, (pointing to one of the boys in the cartoon) *dit par exemple ...* (Pause and wait for suggestions, prompting students if necessary, before repeating the process with one or two other characters in the picture. Also encourage students to reuse classroom language from previous modules.)

- Write one or two of the questions suggested by the students on the board/OHP and enclose each in a speech or thought bubble. Then direct the class to the empty bubbles and caption boxes on Copymaster 63. Demonstrate how they can be completed, cut out and stuck onto the cartoon on Copymaster 64, so that students can create their own classroom language picture. Refer to the completed speech or thought bubbles on the board/OHP to help.

T: Regardez l'image ... (Point to the cartoon on Copymaster 64.) *... et regardez aussi les bulles sur cette fiche* (Point to the empty bubbles on Copymaster 63.) *Vous, vous allez compléter ces bulles pour l'image, par exemple ...* (Point to the corresponding bubble on the board.) *Je peux aller à mon cours de musique?' Puis, vous allez couper ces bulles et les coller sur votre image animée.* (Take a pair of scissors and some glue and mime cutting out and pasting the completed bubbles onto Copymaster 64.)

- Indicate how extra language such as *Pas de panique!* from previous *'Classe d'enfer'* cartoons could be used to complete the empty caption boxes on Copymaster 63.

Differentiation – Extension

AT 1 – 4, AT 2 – 2/4, AT 3 – 4, AT 4 – 2/4

- Working in groups or individually, some students could write and/or act out their own short cartoon strip, scene or playlet based in a classroom, incorporating the new language. The cartoon strip on Students' Book page 109 and the completed Copymasters 63 and 64 can be used for stimulus and/or support.

Objectif 2   Interviews

Productive language

Ils/elles/les spectateurs (etc.)
arrivent/montent/crient/tombent/regardent/
continuent/passent/quittent/mangent/regardent/ont/
parlent/lisent/font/vont/ sont
Il/elle
arrive/monte/tombe/regarde/fait/s'appelle/a/
habite à /aime/va/est/joue
Que fait-il/elle?
Qu'est-ce qui se passe?

Revision of

1st and 2nd person plural of verbs
Singular adjective agreement
(Extension: plural adjective agreement)
Personal details (name, age, where you live, family and pets)

Student goals   (SB p.104)

- Remind the class of the second objectif for this module.

T: (Point to the second picture on page 104.) Nous commençons objectif deux, 'Interviews'. Nous allons écouter un reportage de la grande compétition de vélo, le Tour de France et des interviews des cyclistes et des enthousiastes. Et vous, vous allez faire des descriptions aussi. Alors d'abord le Tour de France.

> **Presentation of 3rd person plural**
>
> *Ils/les spectateurs (etc.)*
> *arrivent/montent/crient/tombent/regardent/*
> *continuent/passent/quittent*

Les coureurs arrivent!   (SB p.110)

a Ecoute.

AT 1 – 3

- Students are now introduced to 3rd person plural forms of present tense verbs within the context of the Tour de France. Play the class cassette through once, whilst they follow the photos on Students' Book page 110.

Tour de France: première étape. Ce soir il fait beau et il fait chaud … Les coureurs arrivent! Ils arrivent à la rivière … Ils montent en ville … Les spectateurs crient … C'est fantastique! … Mais … qu'est-ce qui se passe? Oh non, ils tombent … Oh là, là … Les spectateurs regardent l'accident … Les autres coureurs continuent … Ils passent devant les spectateurs … Ils quittent la ville et ils continuent à la campagne. Michel Dubois. Tour de France.

b Relie le texte avec la bonne photo.

AT 1 – 3, AT 3 – 2/3

- Play the cassette through a second time, pausing after each stage of the description, and help the class to use the support of the photos to deduce the meaning of the new vocabulary, e.g. *les coureurs arrivent/montent/passent, les spectateurs crient* etc.
- Then give them time to match the photos and captions before playing the cassette again, pausing after each photo and confirming the answers.

Solution

1 C **2** E **3** D **4** B **5** A

AT 2 – 2/3

- Draw attention to the silent *-ent* verb endings and encourage students to read the captions aloud in the correct order, with as much expression as possible. Initially, this can be done as a class activity, but eventually students could be encouraged to read aloud in pairs or individually and to produce their own broadcasts.

T: *Regardez et écoutez* (Write *ils arrivent* on the board.) *Ils arrivent* (Cover the *-ent* ending and say it again. Do the same for *ils montent*.)

- In a *pause anglaise* ask students to explain what they notice about the pronunciation of the *-ent* ending.

- Afterwards, in a *pause anglaise*, encourage the class to volunteer any information which they know about the Tour de France and give a brief explanation of this annual event. For homework, students could visit the library and/or use reference materials to find out more about the race. If possible, they can be encouraged to follow newspaper and/or television reports in July and to collect information, articles, pictures, drawings etc. for a classroom display about the Tour. Some of their classwork and homework from the rest of the module can also be added to the *coin cyclisme*.

c Regarde le texte 'Les coureurs arrivent' (page 110). Fais les bonnes phrases.

AT 3 – 2/3, AT 4 – 2

- Students return to the text on page 110 and use this for support in sorting out the split sentences at the top of page 111 and writing out the full sentences. These can later be reused as headings for items brought in for the *coin cyclisme*.

Solution

1 Ils arrivent à la rivière.
2 Ils montent en ville.
3 Les spectateurs regardent l'accident.
4 Ils passent devant les spectateurs.
5 Ils quittent la ville.

> **Revision of 1st and 2nd person plural of verbs**
> **Presentation of 3rd person plural**
> *Ils mangent/regardent/ont/parlent/lisent/ font/vont/sont*

La première équipe: Interview
(SB p.111, FC 29, 31, 45, 46, 49, 53)

AT 1 – 4, AT 3 – 2

- Before tackling this activity, revise aurally the nous form using flashcards *manger* (29), *parler* (31), *faire une promenade* (45), *regarder* (46), *lire* (49), and *aller en ville* (53).

a Ecoute.

- The class listens to the interview between a journalist and a group of race competitors. This features familiar questions and answers in the *vous* and *nous* forms, before the range of 3rd person plural verbs is extended in the accompanying interview notes on page 111. Students should listen to the dialogue once, either with or without their books open.

– Bonsoir messieurs.
– Bonsoir.
– Je suis journaliste. Je peux vous poser des questions?
– Oui, bien sûr. Allez-y.
– Que faites-vous le soir pendant le Tour de France?
– Bon alors ... à sept heures nous mangeons le repas du soir à l'hôtel.
– Nous avons faim!
– Et après?
– Nous regardons bien sûr le Tour de France à la télé.
– Nous parlons un peu, nous lisons des magazines de vélo et les reportages du Tour de France.
– Ou bien nous allons en ville et nous faisons une petite promenade.
– Mais en principe nous sommes au lit à dix heures et demie.
– A dix heures et demie?
– Oui, nous sommes très fatigués, vous savez.

b Ecoute et mets les images dans le bon ordre.

• Students listen again whilst looking at the pictures and note down the order in which they occur.

Solution

C, A, D, F, G, B, E, H

c Ecoute et regarde les notes du journaliste. Vrai ou faux?

• They should then look at the journalist's note pad and read through the notes. Check comprehension of the phrases. Finally, they should listen to the cassette as many more times as is necessary and decide whether the notes are true or false.

Solution

1 faux **2** vrai **3** vrai **4** vrai **5** vrai **6** faux **7** faux **8** vrai

d A deux.

• Highlight the regular *-ent* ending shown in the left-hand *'Attention!'* feature at the bottom of page 111. Check comprehension of the *ils* pronoun and stress again that the ending is silent, reminding students of *ils s'appellent* which they met in Module 4.

• Then direct the class to the accompanying pairwork activity, in which they find as many verbs as possible on pages 110–111 with this ending. Afterwards, students can be encouraged to read out their list or to compare it with another pair to see how many sentences they have between them.

• Use the same flashcards as before for oral practice of the 3rd person plural of all the verbs.

• In a *pause anglaise*, move on to contrast the meaning, spelling and pronunciation of the irregular verbs *ils font, ils ont, ils vont* and *ils sont* in the right-hand *'Attention!'* feature at the bottom of the page. Students then carry out a similar pairwork activity and use the verbs to build other phrases, e.g. *ils font du vélo, ils ont chaud* etc.

At this point you may wish to use Copymaster 85. Students complete notes on the 3rd person plural form of the present tense and keep them for reference.

Presentation of:

Elles (+ verbs in present tense)

Interview avec des jeunes (SB p.112)

a Ecoute et regarde les photos. Qui parle?

AT 1–3

• Play the class cassette in which six groups of teenagers are interviewed about cycling and other activities. Initially, students should listen without the support of the photos on page 112 to practise gist understanding and to elicit the general theme. They should then listen again whilst looking at the photos to decide which group of teenagers is speaking each time.

1
– Salut!
– Salut!
– Vous faites du vélo?
– Oui, mais nous préférons le tennis. Nous jouons au centre sportif lundi et mercredi soir.
– Et le week-end?
– Le dimanche nous faisons du canoë-kayak.

2
– Salut! Ça va?
– Salut! Ça va bien, merci.
– Vous faites du vélo?
– Oui, nous faisons du vélo le week-end.
– Vous regardez le Tour de France?
– Oui, nous regardons le Tour de France à la télé tous les soirs.

3
– Et vous? Vous faites du vélo?
– Non. Nous ne sommes pas très sportifs. Le soir nous restons à la maison.
– Nous sommes très fatigués!
– Que faites-vous comme passe-temps?
– Eh bien, nous écoutons de la musique, nous regardons la télé …
– … et nous faisons les devoirs!

4
– Salut!
– Salut!
– Vous faites du vélo?
– Oui, bien sûr. Nous sommes très sportives.
– Que faites-vous comme sport?
– Nous allons au centre sportif et nous jouons au basket et au volley.

5
– Bonjour!
– Bonjour!
– Vous faites du vélo?
– Oui, le week-end. Nous faisons du vélo à la campagne et nous allons chez des copains.

6
– Salut!
– Salut!
– Vous faites du vélo?

– Oui, nous faisons du vélo; du vélo tout terrain. Nous allons à la montagne à vélo. C'est super.
– Oui, c'est très bien ça. Moi, j'adore la montagne.

Solution

1 B **2** A **3** D **4** E **5** C **6** F

b Relie le texte et la bonne photo.

AT 3 – 2/3

- Point out the captions at the bottom of page 112, saying *Voici des descriptions des photos.* Read out a representative mixture of the captions and write the pronouns *ils* and *elles* on the board/OHP. Ask *Comment dit-on 'ils' et 'elles' en anglais?* to elicit the answer 'they'. Remind students that in a mixed group, you use *ils* to mean 'they'.

- Draw three sets of pictures on the board/OHP, showing a group of three pin boys, a group of three pin girls and a mixed group of pin boys and pin girls. Point to each picture in turn and ask the class *ils ou elles?* After each correct response, write the appropriate pronoun underneath the relevant picture.

- Then summarise: *En français 'ils', 'elles', 'ils'. En anglais 'they'.* Encourage students to repeat the pronouns as you point to each picture in turn. Then direct them to the second task on page 112, explaining that they should match each caption at the bottom of the page to the appropriate photo.

Solution

1 A **2** E **3** F **4** D **5** C **6** B

AT 2 – 2/3

- Set up and demonstrate pairwork, as follows.

T: *Travail à deux. Regardez page 112. Personne A choisit une photo, par exemple 'c'. Personne B décrit les images, par exemple 'Ils font du vélo à la campagne. Ils vont chez des copains.' Puis personne B choisit une photo, etc.*

Differentiation – Extension or Consolidation

- Higher attainers could be encouraged to cover the captions at the bottom of page 112 and to describe the pictures from memory.

- Students requiring additional support could undertake an alternative pairwork activity, in which person A simply reads out one of the captions at the bottom of page 112 and person B says the letter of the picture which matches.

Jeu d'activités (CM 65)

AT 1 – 1/2, AT 2 – 1/2, AT 3 – 1/2, AT 4 – 1/2

1 Fais des paires.

- Photocopy Copymaster 65 onto card and cut up the top half of the copymaster. Use the copymaster or an OHT version of it to demonstrate how students should work in pairs and play pelmanism, matching the *ils* and *elles* forms of present tense verbs. Remind them of the contrasting *-ent* and *-ont* sounds and tell them to say each verb aloud as they turn it over. As students find pairs, they should lay them out on the desk, ready for the next activity, as follows:

  ils mangent, elles mangent

  ils arrivent, elles arrivent

  etc.

2 Fais des phrases.

- Hand out the cut up versions of the first 10 cards from the bottom half of Copymaster 65. Demonstrate how students should now work in twos and add an appropriate card to each of their verb pairs, building phrases such as:

  ils mangent ⎫
  elles mangent ⎭ *une crêpe*

- The completed phrases can be practised orally and/or copied into exercise books.

Differentiation – Extension

- Higher attainers can work with all 20 cards from the bottom half of the copymaster and build a phrase for each verb from the top half, e.g.

  ils mangent une crêpe

  elles mangent le repas du soir

> **Revision of masculine and feminine plural adjective agreement**

Differentiation – Extension

Extra! D'accord? (CM 66)

AT 3 – 2, AT 4 – 1/2

- Students who are capable of coping with an extra layer of information and grammar at this stage could extend the work on *ils/elles sont*, using Copymaster 66 to revise and practise adjective agreement.

- Direct them through the *'Rappel'* section at the top of the copymaster. Begin by reminding them of the work covered in Module 4 relating to pets, highlighting *ils sont noirs* and *elles sont noires* at the top of the page. Then extend this into a reminder of descriptions for male, mixed, and female groups of people.

- Students should then follow the written and visual clues to complete the crossword with the correct forms of the adjectives. Encourage students to insert accents above appropriate letters. They can do this with or without the support of the *'Rappel'* section of the copymaster.

Solution

Horizontalement

3 grandes **5** petites **9** pénibles

Verticalement

1 sympa **2** fantastiques **4** amusants **6** grands
7 fatiguées **8** fatigués

> **Presentation of:**
>
> *Il/elle arrive/monte/tombe/regarde/fait*
> *Que fait-il / elle?*
> *Qu'est-ce qui se passe?*

Qu'est-ce qui se passe? (SB p.113)

AT 1 – 3, AT 2 – 2/3, AT 3 – 3

- Use the *'Nous les copains'* cartoon strip on page 113 and the class cassette to introduce 3rd person singular forms of present tense verbs and the questions *Que fait-il?*, *Que fait-elle?* and *Qu'est-ce qui se passe?* Play the cassette as support for this piece of more extended reading, telling students to listen and to follow the story in their books.

Crowd:	Bravo!
Annie:	Qu'est-ce qui se passe, Marc?
Marc:	Je ne sais pas, Annie.
Annie:	Qu'est-ce qui se passe, Yannick?
Yannick:	Le premier coureur arrive!

Crowd:	Bravo, Michel!
Annie:	Que fait-il?
Claire:	Il monte en ville.
Crowd:	Oh, non! Michel! C'est pas vrai!
Annie:	Que fait-il?
Man:	Il tombe.
Annie:	C'est impossible! … Un moment …
Claire:	Annie! Que fait-elle?
Yannick:	Annie?
Man:	Elle regarde l'accident.
Yannick:	Er … Annie, qu'est-ce qui se passe?

- After the first hearing encourage students to work out the meaning of the three questions from the context. Listen to the tape again. Practise the questions. The pronunciation of *Qu'est-ce qui se passe?* can be broken down into three parts e.g. *Qu'est-ce/qui/se passe?* and given to three groups to say in a Mexican wave. Alternate the parts so that each group has the chance to say a different part of the question.

- Use the questions for some simple comprehension work based on *'Nous les copains'*.

T: ***Regardez la deuxième image*** (Point if necessary.) ***Qu'est-ce qui se passe? … Regardez la troisième image, Michel que fait-il?*** (Write the three questions on the board and read aloud. Students repeat.)

- Draw attention to the use of *il* and *elle* and extend the activity to encourage the students to produce the language. In pairs students choose an action within learned language e.g. playing football. Student A performs the mime and student B asks the class the appropriate question, referring to the board for support if necessary.

- Encourage the class to deduce the meanings of the new verb forms and questions, before playing the cassette once more whilst students listen to and read the text. Provide opportunities for repetition practice and oral work, before organising students into groups to read the story aloud and act it out.

> **Presentation of:**
> *Il/elle s'appelle/a* (+ age, brothers and sisters)/ *habite à* (+ location)/*aime* (+ noun)/ *va/est/joue*
> **Revision of masculine and feminine adjective agreement**

Les enthousiastes (SB p.114)

AT 1 – 2, AT 2 – 2, AT 3 – 3

- Allow the class time to read the first description at the top of page 114, which introduces other familiar verbs in the 3rd person masculine singular form of the present tense. Ask simple questions, either in the order of the sentences or in random order.

T: ***Thierry est enthousiaste du foot? Il a quel âge? Il habite à Limoges? etc.***

- Then repeat the process with the second description, which introduces the 3rd person feminine singular forms.

- Afterwards, point out the *'Attention!'* feature. Check that the class remembers the meanings of the pronouns *il* and *elle* and contrast the verbs which end in *-e* in the 3rd person singular forms with the irregular verbs *il/elle a, il/elle est, il/elle fait* and *il/elle va*. Work through each item in the *'Attention!'* panel in turn and invite students to find examples of sentences on pages 113 – 114 which contain the verb endings and/or verbs shown.

> At this point you may wish to use Copymaster 86. Students complete notes on the 3rd person singular form of the present tense and keep them for reference.

Encore des descriptions (CM 67)

AT 1 – 3, AT 2 – 2, AT 3 – 2, AT 4 – 1/2

- Having been introduced to the 3rd person singular forms of the present tense, students now have the opportunity of further familiarisation with these forms on Copymaster 67, before moving on to oral and written practice. If you did not use the *'Extra!'* Copymaster 66, you may wish to revise the masculine and feminine singular of the adjectives from Module 4. The activities on the copymaster can be undertaken independently in lesson time or for homework.

1 Ecoute et remplis les cases.

- Initially, students listen to the two descriptions on the self-study cassette and complete the missing information on the sheet. The completed descriptions form a model which can be used in later written and oral activities.

You will need Copymaster 67, activity 1. Look at the description of the boy at the top of the page, on the left. Listen to the cassette as you read it through. Then rewind the cassette to the beginning of the description and listen again. Pause the cassette as often as necessary and fill in the missing information in the boxes.

Je vous présente un jeune homme.
Il s'appelle Nicolas.
Il a quinze ans.
Il est amusant.
Il habite à Paris.
Il a un frère et une soeur.
Comme passe-temps, il fait du patin à roulettes et il joue avec l'ordinateur.

Now look at the description of the girl at the top of the page, on the right. Listen to the cassette as you read it through. Afterwards, rewind the cassette to the beginning of the description and listen again. Pause the cassette as often as necessary and fill in the missing information in the boxes.

Je vous présente une jeune fille.
Elle s'appelle Marie.
Elle a quatorze ans.
Elle est sympa.
Elle habite à Calais.
Elle a deux soeurs.
Comme passe-temps, elle va en ville avec des copains.
Elle adore le football.

Solution

Il a **15** ans.
Il est **amusant.**
Il habite **à Paris.**
Il a **un frère** et **une soeur.**

Comme passe-temps, il fait **du patin à roulettes** et il joue avec **l'ordinateur.**

Elle a **14** ans.
Elle est **sympa.**
Elle habite à **Calais.**
Elle a **deux soeurs.**
Comme passe-temps elle va **en ville avec des copains.**
Elle adore **le football.**

2 Prononciation. Ecoute, lis et répète.

- The second activity highlights the contrast between the two commonly confused verbs *il est* and *il a*. Students are given the opportunity to practise reading, listening to and pronouncing these verbs, before moving on to more open-ended written and oral work.

You will need Copymaster 67, activity 2. Listen to the cassette as you read the eight phrases on the copymaster. Pause the cassette after each one and repeat the phrase.

Il est ...
Il a ...
Elle est ...
Elle a ...
Il est sympa.
Il a douze ans.
Elle est sympa.
Elle a treize ans.

In a moment, rewind the cassette to the beginning of activity 2. Look at the phrases again. This time, say the phrases out loud. After each one listen to the cassette to check your pronunciation. Pause the cassette after each phrase.

3 Qui est-ce?

4 A deux

- These tasks provide additional mixed-skill practice of 3rd person singular descriptions. Students use the models at the top of the copymaster to prepare a description of one of their classmates, either individually in the lesson or at home, and complete box A on the left. They then work in pairs in the lesson and take it in turns to read out their description. The partner must listen and complete the information in the space provided (box B), before guessing who is being described.

- Use an OHT version or draw the boxes on the board and demonstrate the activity.

T: ***Choisissez une personne dans la classe – (name), par exemple, ou (name) et écrivez dans les cases, mais en secret!*** (Fill in the blanks, pretending to hide the page from the class.) ***Maintenant, travaillez avec un(e) partenaire.*** (Call a student out to demonstrate/ role-play with you.) ***(Name) Lis ta description, s'il te plaît.*** (Fill in part B of the OHT version as the student reads.) ***Hmm. C'est (name)?... Non? C'est ...?*** *etc.*

Décris Jean-Pierre et Marianne
(SB p.114)

a A deux.

AT 1 – 2/3, AT 2 – 2/3, AT 3 – 2/3, AT 4 – 1/2/3

- Students return to page 114 and quickly read through the descriptions of Thierry and Françoise once more. They then use these descriptions and the *'Attention!'* feature to help them copy and complete the descriptions of Jean-Pierre and Marianne, following the visual cues. The activity can be done orally or in writing, in pairs or individually.

Differentiation – Extension

- Afterwards students could play a memory game. Give the class two or three minutes to read through the descriptions of Thierry and/or Françoise and tell them to try to remember as much of the text(s) as possible. While they are doing this, copy the description(s) onto an OHT. At the end of the predetermined time limit, tell the students to close their books. Then lay a ruler diagonally across the description(s), deliberately obscuring parts of the text or, alternatively, obscure words with pieces of paper. Students then work in teams and take it in turns to volunteer a missing part of the text. The game can be repeated as many times as desired and the

position of the ruler or paper can be changed to hide different or larger parts of the text.

- When students understand the principle of the game, they can play it in pairs. Explain and demonstrate how, in a similar way, they can use a ruler, classroom objects or pieces of paper to cover the descriptions on page 114 of their books. They should then work together to try to reconstruct the text from memory.

b Décris une personne différente.

AT 3 – 2/3, AT 4 – 2/3/4

- Finally, for homework, students can find a magazine picture or photo of a celebrity, relative or friend and write a description of the person. Encourage them to redraft their work, using word-processing facilities if available. The final versions could then be mounted as a wall display.

Differentiation – Consolidation and Extension

- Redirect lower attainers to the descriptions at the top of Copymaster 67 for support. Demonstrate how to use the model provided and how to change the details in the boxes to create new descriptions.

- Encourage higher attainers to extend their descriptions and to include details beyond those given in the descriptions on page 114, e.g. likes and dislikes re. school subjects, times/times of the day for the activities, details about pets etc.

Le triathlon: première étape
(SB p.115)

a Ecoute et mets dans le bon ordre.

AT 1 – 3/4

- Third person singular and 3rd person plural forms of present tense verbs covered so far are now combined. Keeping their books closed, students initially practise gist comprehension, as they listen to the class cassette which describes part of a triathlon race.

Il fait chaud aujourd'hui pour le triathlon.
Ce matin c'est la course à vélo, cet après-midi la

natation et ce soir la course à pied. Laurent le Lièvre et Thérèse la Tortue sont prêts.

Un – deux – trois …

Ils commencent! Mais qu'est-ce qui se passe?

Ce n'est pas vrai! Thérèse tombe! Laurent continue.

Il arrive à la rivière. Bravo! Il monte la colline … mais il est fatigué. Que fait-il? Mais c'est impossible!

Il mange une carotte! Il parle avec les spectateurs! Et Thérèse? Elle arrive … Elle passe devant Laurent … Lui, il ne regarde pas! Thérèse arrive à la fin. Elle a gagné! Et Laurent?

- Students then look at the cartoons on Students' Book page 115 whilst listening to the cassette again as many times as necessary and write the letters of the cartoons in the order corresponding to the cassette.

Differentiation – Consolidation

- Alternatively, to simplify the task, the cassette can be paused at appropriate intervals, so that students match the appropriate cartoon to each short piece of taped description.

Solution

C, F, A, E, D, B, G

Jeu du Triathlon (CM 68)

AT 1 – 2, AT 2 – 2, AT 3 – 2

- Students now have the opportunity for further practice of 3rd person masculine and feminine forms of present tense verbs as they play the game on Copymaster 68. Before introducing the copymaster revise (by rerunning the mime activity) the questions *Qu'est-ce qui se passe?*, *Que fait-il?* and *Que fait-elle?* which were first introduced on Students' Book page 113. Write these on the board for reference.

- Then direct the class to the *'Comment jouer'* section of the copymaster and, with the aid of an OHT version of the game or a replica of some of the squares on the board, demonstrate how they should play the game in groups of four.

T: (Invite four students up to the front of the class for the demonstration.) *Vous jouez en groupes de quatre. Chaque personne choisit*

une lettre – A, B, C ou D. (Encourage each student to choose a letter.) *Bon. La personne A commence et jette le dé, par exemple … deux: un … deux.* (Engineer this first example to coincide with the copymaster and encourage student A to move his or her counter accordingly. *La personne B pose une question, par exemple …* (Point to the question *Qu'est-ce qui se passe?* or *Que fait-il?* on the board and encourage student B to ask the question.) *La personne A répond et coche la bonne case, par exemple …* (Point to the artwork for the relevant square and also to the corresponding phrase on the grid in the centre of the game and encourage student A to respond *Il fait du vélo* and to tick his/her corresponding square on the grid.) *Maintenant la personne B jette le dé, la personne C pose la question et la personne B répond, par exemple …* (Help students B and C to demonstrate. Encourage student C to choose a picture of a girl to prompt *Que fait-elle?* etc.) *Puis la personne C jette le dé, la personne D pose la question et la personne C répond, etcetera.* (Continue the demonstration for as long as is necessary to establish the principle of the game. Explain how to win the game, saying, *La première personne qui complète la grille gagne.* Demonstrate by ticking off all the squares in one column of the grid and saying *J'ai gagné!*)

- Organise the class into groups of four to play the game, encouraging them to use as much games language as possible while they are playing, e.g. *C'est à moi, C'est à toi, Vite!* etc.

> **Revision of 1st person singular and plural of verbs**

Le triathlon: première étape

(SB p.115)

b Décris le triathlon.

AT 1 – 3, AT 2 – 2/3/4, (AT 3 – 2), AT 4 – 2/3/4

- Finally, the work in this objectif covering 3rd person singular form of present tense verbs is consolidated as students make up their own description of the race shown in the cartoons on page 115. Direct the class back to the page and play the cassette again to refresh their memories.

Then explain that students should work in pairs to describe the cartoons. This could be done in the form of a written account or an oral broadcast, which could be narrated and mimed in groups of three in front of the class. Remind the class of the *'Attention!'* feature on Students' Book page 114.

Differentiation – Consolidation and Extension

- Students requiring more support for their description could be shown how to adapt some of the sentences on Copymaster 68.
- Higher attainers could be encouraged to write and/or narrate an extended account of the race, giving additional information.

Mais samedi ils dansent toute la nuit
(SB p. 115, CM 73)

AT 1 – 2/3/4, AT 2 – 2/3/4, AT 3 – 2/3/4

- Students now listen to the song, which provides further consolidation of present tense verb forms and the language of previous modules.
- Play the song through once and encourage the class to follow the accompanying text on page 115 of their books. Then play one verse at a time, stopping briefly after each to check understanding. An OHT version of Copymaster 73 may be helpful in focusing students' attention on particular sections of text, whilst masking the rest of the song. As this process continues and the tune becomes familiar, encourage the class to join in singing the separate verses, before students finally sing along to the full version.

1 Voici ma mère. Elle adore la cuisine.
Elle fait des omelettes à la strychnine.
Des gâteaux de rat et du serpent rôti ...
Mais samedi elle danse toute la nuit!

2 Voici mon père. Il s'appelle Vladimir.
Il est prof de sports au Collège Vampires.
Il joue au volley toujours à minuit ...
Mais samedi il danse toute la nuit!

3 Voici ma soeur. Elle s'appelle Odette.
Elle fait du vélo et joue au cricket.
La balle est la tête de ma Tante Bigoudi ...
Mais samedi elle danse toute la nuit!

4 Voici mes frères, Antoine et Vincent.
Ils sont pénibles. Ils sont méchants.
Ils mangent mes gerbilles. Ils détestent les souris ...
Mais samedi ils dansent toute la nuit!

5 Voilà ma famille. Mes parents formidables.
Mes frères grotesques et ma soeur adorable.
Viens chez moi, mon cher ami
Et samedi tu danses toute la nuit!

1 Voici ma mère. Elle adore la cuisine.
Elle fait des omelettes à la strychnine.
Des gâteaux de rat et du serpent rôti ...
Mais samedi elle danse toute la nuit!

2 Voici mon père. Il s'appelle Vladimir.
Il est prof de sports au Collège Vampires.
Il joue au volley toujours à minuit ...
Mais samedi il danse toute la nuit!

3 Voici ma soeur. Elle s'appelle Odette.
Elle fait du vélo et joue au cricket.
La balle est la tête de ma Tante Bigoudi ...
Mais samedi elle danse toute la nuit!

4 Voici mes frères, Antoine et Vincent.
Ils sont pénibles. Ils sont méchants.
Ils mangent mes gerbilles. Ils détestent les souris ...
Mais samedi ils dansent toute la nuit!

5 Voilà ma famille. Mes parents formidables.
Mes frères grotesques et ma soeur adorable.
Viens chez moi, mon cher ami
Et samedi tu danses toute la nuit!

- Afterwards, where appropriate, lay a ruler or pen across the OHT version of Copymaster 73 and challenge the class to say, sing or write the missing words from memory. Alternatively/additionally, students could play this game in pairs, taking it in turns to cover and to reconstruct the song in their textbooks.

AT 3 –2/3/4, AT 4 –2)

- Students could demonstrate comprehension and accuracy by copying and illustrating one or more verses of the song for a wall display. They could also learn their chosen section of the text or one or more of their favourite verses by heart.
- Finally, you may wish to use the music provided on Copymaster 73 to enable students to perform and/or record their own version of the song.

Objectif 3   En route!

> **Revision of:**
> Simple negative (*ne/n'... pas*)

Student goals   (SB p.104)

- Remind the class of the third section of the goals visual on page 104. Point to the third picture and say *Nous commençons objectif trois – 'En route'.* Then turn to the appropriate pages and outline the activities.

T: *D'abord il y a un dessin animé, l'entre-temps, vous allez faire des recherches et finalement vous allez faire un interview et une page d'un magazine.*

Le Rallye de Mauville

                               (SB pp.116 – 117)
AT1 – 4, AT3 – 4

- Students listen to and read a cartoon story of a whacky car race. The language is presented on two levels: the speech bubble version and the corresponding narrative. Students will hear the narrative first then the characters speaking. Direct students to the story which they follow frame by frame, supported by the tape (including sound effects).

Narrator:	Ce matin, c'est le Rallye de Mauville. Il fait chaud.
Starter:	Partez!
Spectator:	Ils commencent!
2nd spectator:	Allez!
Narrator:	Voici Charlotte et Charlot, le copilote.
Charlotte:	Ça va Charlot?
Charlot:	Ça va bien Charlotte.
Narrator:	Simon l'Espion et Simone parlent.
Simone:	Tu es fantastique, Simon.
Simon:	Oui, c'est vrai. Je suis super!
Narrator:	Docteur Dodo n'a pas de copilote. Il est dix heures mais le copilote n'arrive pas.
Docteur:	Quelle heure est-il? Que fait-il?
Narrator:	Et voilà Mémé et Mamie avec le chien, Mimi. Mémé a faim. Elle mange. Mamie n'a pas faim. Elle ne mange pas!
Mamie:	Que fais-tu Mémé?
Mémé:	Je mange une glace. J'ai chaud et j'ai faim.
Narrator:	Voilà ils commencent ... mais il pleut ...
Docteur:	Je suis intelligent!
Narrator:	Ils quittent la route et Docteur Dodo passe devant.
Simon:	Qu'est-ce qui se passe?
Charlotte:	Ce n'est pas vrai!
Mamie:	Zut, alors!
Narrator:	Simon et Simone montent dans l'air. Mais ils ont faim et ils vont au restaurant.
Simone:	Tu as faim?
Simon:	Oui. Nous allons au restaurant.

Narrator:	Mémé et Mamie passent devant Charlotte.
Mémé:	Ils gagnent! Vite, Mamie!
Narrator:	Mimi n'aime pas les chats. Mémé et Mamie vont à gauche.
Charlot:	Mm. J'aime le chiens.
Mimi:	Je n'aime pas les chats!
Mémé:	A gauche! Vite!
Narrator:	Docteur Dodo a un problème.
Docteur:	Zut!
Narrator:	Charlotte et Charlot arrivent. Ils passent devant Docteur Dodo ... Ils gagnent le rallye. Bravo!
Charlotte:	J'ai gagné!

- After the first hearing, encourage students to deduce the meaning of new words e.g. *rallye/copilote/ils gagnent*. Point out the significance of the names of the characters i.e. *Charlot/Charlotte* (play on *chat*), *l'Espion* (spy), *Mémé* and *Mamie* (grannie), *Dodo* (sleep). They will probably need to hear the tape twice straight through but on a next hearing it could be helpful to go frame by frame inviting students to join in class reading. Afterwards give volunteers the opportunity to take on roles (including the cat and dog) and speak, using the speech bubbles. The rest of the class can narrate with teacher support.

Differentiation

- If appropriate, students could now take over a performance of the story of the race with or without actions! The task of producing the sound effects requires careful listening/following the story and can provide a useful extra role. Students could either act it using the speech bubble version or they could present the complete story. Encourage more able students to speak the characters' lines from memory.

> **Revision of:**
> *ne/n' ... pas*

Qu'est-ce qui se passe?   (CM 69)

1 Regarde le texte 'Le Rallye de Mauville'. Fais des phrases.

AT 3 – 2, AT4 – 1

- Students study the Students' Book text *'Le Rallye de Mauville'* again and reconstruct the main points of the story and select appropriate verb forms from a menu to complete a gap-fill activity.

Differentiation – Extension

- Students could complete the sentences without referring to the text/menu.

Solution

(**a**) parlent   (**b**) a   (**c**) a   (**d**) faim   (**e**) quittent   (**f**) montent   (**g**) ont   (**h**) vont   (**i**) aiment   (**j**) arrivent

- Draw attention to the use of the negative in the story. Encourage students to give the meaning of the examples given in the *'Rappel'* section and to search for further examples in the story e.g. *Mémé n'a pas faim*.
- Draw attention to the page reference where they originally met the negative in Module 3, Students' Book page 53. Revise this page and lighten the grammatical emphasis by having another sing of the positive and negative song on Copymaster 31. Then go on to the next activity on Copymaster 69.

2 Mets au négatif.

AT3 – 2, AT4 – 1

- Students put positive statements into the negative continuing the theme of the story by inserting *ne/n' ... pas*. An apostrophe is inserted to support students in putting in the *n'* form. If appropriate encourage students to explain why the *n'* is used i.e. before a vowel sound.

Solution

2 Le copilote n'arrive pas.

3 Mamie n'a pas faim.

4 Elle ne mange pas.

5 Ils ne commencent pas.

- Practise putting key verbs into the negative by drawing pin boys and girls on the board alongside some of the activity flashcards. Add a cross to indicate the negative. Students construct sentences using *il/elle/ils/elles/ne/n' ... pas,* orally.

AT1 – 2/3 /4, AT2 – 2/3/4, AT3 – 2/3/4, AT4 – 2/3/4

- Students can put this to communicative use by describing a member of the class, or a group of people e.g. a pop group and guessing who it is. In class pick up other known verbs e.g. *aimer/être/avoir/jouer/faire/aller* in the 3rd person(s) (plural) putting them into a useful sentence in the negative to give support, e.g. *Il/elle ne joue pas au football; Ils/elles ne jouent pas ...; Il/elle ne fait pas de devoirs; Ils/elles etc; Il/elle n'aime pas le français etc.; Il/elle n'a pas de soeurs etc.; Il/elle n'est pas grand(e).*

- First establish the activity, before asking students to write a description for homework. Familiarise students with the question *Qui est-ce?* and establish its meaning. Students take it in turns to give and listen to their descriptions and ask *Qui est-ce?* A limit of five guesses can control the guessing time and if the person(s) remain unidentified they should be revealed in response to a final *Qui est-ce?*

Jeu de verbes (CM 70)
Encore des familles (CM 71)

AT3 – 1

- Students have now met all persons in the present tense. Copymasters 70 and 71 bring them together in paradigms. Students begin by using the first part of Copymaster 70 to show understanding of the pronouns, by linking the French and English. Students then use the middle section of the copymaster, cut-up, to reassemble the paradigm of *regarder.* The infinitive should be included to complete the picture.

- In a *pause anglaise* draw students' attention to the 'family name' (infinitive) without making a grammatical issue of it. Give the students the term infinitif making sure that they understand that it is the official word for the 'family name'. Next, encourage students to make up their own shapes for the paradigm of any other known regular *-er* verbs (e.g. *quitter, jouer, arriver, écouter, habiter.*) On the board, remind them of the use of

j' with *arriver, écouter, habiter* etc. This could be a homework activity.

- Students then move on the use the final part of Copymaster 70 and all of Copymaster 71 to reassemble the paradigms for *avoir, être, faire* and *aller.*

- Alternatively or additionally the shapes could be assembled as a collage and put on permanent display in the classroom. Different members of a group could work on each paradigm.

- Direct students to the *pages grammaire* at the back of the Students' Book where they will see the paradigms of the verbs that they have assembled and remind them of their value for reference/checking.

Entre-temps ... (SB pp.118 – 119)

AT3 – 2/3/4

- Encourage students to use these pages as independently as possible and to read the selection of texts for interest and enjoyment. Encourage students to think of their reading strategies i.e. cognates, visuals, context, glossary to assist them in understanding the texts that contain some unfamiliar language and unfamiliar contexts: e.g. students will need to use the glossary for some of the items in the quiz,'*Les pièces du vélo*'. Encourage students to give their opinion of the texts using known language e.g. *C'est intéressant! C'est difficile! C'est nul! C'est amusant!*

Solutions

Les pièces du vélo

1 B **2** C **3** E **4** D **5** A **6** F **7** G

L'arc-en-ciel

Le bon ordre= rouge, orange, jaune, **vert, bleu,** indigo, violet

Recherche! (SB p.120)

AT1 – 3, AT3 – 3

- This study skills page assists students in finding references to previously learnt language to support language activities in the '*Porte ouverte!*' activity. Work through the page step by step. First set the objective i.e. an interview on pastimes.

T: ***Vous allez faire un interview sur les passe-temps.*** **(Point to and read the first speech bubble.)** ***Parle de tes passe-temps!*** **(Mime a puzzled expression.)** ***Une interview sur les passe-temps? Oh là, là, les questions?*** **(Write a question mark in a speech bubble on the board with a look of dismay.)** ***Et les réponses?*** **(Draw an empty replying speech bubble on the board. Direct students to the thought bubbles in the book and read through with appropriate mime. Mime a bright idea as if enlightenment has dawned.)** ***J'ai une bonne idée. Regardez la méthode!*** **(Point to this next section.)**

1 Regarde les deux premières pages de PASSE-PARTOUT.

- Read the instruction and repeat the the objective *Une interview sur les passe-temps.* Encourage students to work out what the instruction means, then direct students to the contents page of the book and encourage them to look for the appropriate module.

T: ***Les passe-temps, c'est quel module?***

- When students have identified the module, ask *Alors, c'est quelle page?* The class turns to the appropriate page.

2 Regarde le bon objectif et les pages dans ton cahier.

- Read the next instruction and ask the students what they have to do next. Direct students to the objectives collage within the identified module and encourage them to pick out the most useful objectives and pages. Ask them to read through and to jot down the most most useful page numbers/activities.
- Encourage students to look in their exercise books/files for any more helpful references/activities. They can mark the pages by inserting book markers.

3 Regarde le sommaire du module.

- Read the next instruction and ask students what they can do if they have forgotten the meaning of the French. Direct them to the 'Sommaire' of the identified module as illustrated on the page. You may wish to give a few more examples to establish the use of the 'Sommaire'.

Differentiation – Extension

4 Encore des détails?

- This section may well be largely appropriate only for a number of students for independent use but initially you may wish to direct students to it provided that it does not add an unnecessary level of difficulty: '*A la discrétion du prof*'. It should assist those who wish to pick up those verbs which may have appeared in the book in a different form to the one that they wish to use e.g. *Nous faisons de la voile.*
- This section helps students to adapt the language to meet their individual needs and also to check the correct form of the verb. It directs students to the English/French glossary where they will find the phrase in the form in which it appeared in the book. They then pick the appropriate verb form from the paradigm. Students will already be familiar with this process and with the *pages grammaire* cf Teacher's Notes for Copymaster 70.
- Read out the thought bubble, *Comment dit-on … ?* Read out the instruction. Students explain in English what they have to do and find the page in the book as indicated on page 120. Ask them to note down the glossary entry i.e. *je fais de la voile* and give them the infinitive.
- Then direct students to the *page grammaire.* Point to the verb *faire* and explain that the phrase can be adapted by using a different part of the verb, e.g. *Nous faisons de la voile.* Students may benefit from repeating the process either with different verbs or different parts of the verb if they are to work through the process independently, e.g. Do you go sailing? You go horse riding. We go to the sports centre.
- Above all avoid the danger of introducing levels of difficulty that might create an obstacle to confident language use, when students come to the '*Porte ouverte!*' activity.

- Give students a second language area e.g. *Interview. Parle de ton collège.* Direct students to Students' Book page 120 to use the *Méthode* independently, making notes both from the book and from their exercise books/files. Students should classify useful questions (using both *tu* and *vous* forms and possible answers using *je* and nous) referring to their own or to an assumed identity. It is important to stress keeping within the boundaries of learned language. This activity coupled with the research on passe-temps should set them up for the first part of the 'Porte ouverte!' activity on Students' Book page 121.

Porte ouverte! (SB p.121)

Sommaire (SB pp.122–123)

a Ecoute la cassette. Note quatre questions de 1 et 2.

AT1 – 3/4, AT4 – 3/4

- Students listen to the cassette featuring two interviews. In the first a girl interviews a boy so that the questions and replies are in the *tu* and *je* forms. In the second item, a boy interviews a boy and a girl who are brother and sister.

- Direct students to look at the first photo and listen to the first interview. Play the cassette again and ask students to listen specifically for the questions. Students can compare the questions that they have drawn up from their '*Recherche!*' activities with those used on the cassette. The instruction suggests four questions but the number can vary according to the needs of the class. Encourage students to identify any questions used on the tape that are different to those they have found. Encourage them to pick out the use of *tu* and to explain why it is used.

- Listen to the second interview and repeat the process. Draw out the use of *vous* in the questions and *nous* in the responses.

1

– Salut!
– Salut!
– Tu t'appelles comment?
– Je m'appelle Victor Vampire!
– Tu as quel âge?
– J'ai 13 ans.
– Tu as des frères et des soeurs?
– Oui. J'ai une soeur. Elle s'appelle Mangetout et elle a 15 ans.

– Tu as un animal à la maison?
– Oui. J'ai 66 souris.
– Que fais-tu comme passe-temps?
– Je fais du vélo à minuit. Je vais au château de Dracula.
– C'est intéressant. Merci, Victor. Au revoir.

2

– Salut!
– Salut!
– Salut!
– Tu t'appelles comment?
– Didier Dodo.
– Et toi?
– Je m'appelle Dorothée Dodo.
– Vous aimez le Tour de France?
– Oui nous sommes enthousiastes du Tour.
– Vous avez quel âge?
– Moi, j'ai 12 ans.
– Et moi, j'ai 12 ans aussi.
– Vous habitez où?
– Nous habitons à Calais, au bord de la mer.
– Que faites-vous comme passe-temps?
– Nous faisons de la voile …
– et nous faisons de la natation.
– Finalement. Vous aimez le collège?
– Oui, nous aimons le collège …
– et nous adorons les sciences!

b Prépare un interview avec une personne imaginaire.

AT1 – 3/4, AT2 – 3/4, AT4 – 3/4

- Working in pairs or small groups, students plan their interview. Set a minimum number of exchanges according to the needs of the class. Lower attainers need to feel confident in tackling the task and will find it daunting if the task is not scaled down to their particular needs. The language is familiar so it is reasonable to expect a fair number of exchanges.

- Encourage students to work as far as possible from notes or from memory rather than writing and reading a full script. Remind them of the language provided in the '*Sommaire*' on pages 122 – 123. Draw their attention also to the notes they have already made and to Students' Book page 120 to encourage their independence. This will encourage more natural communication skills and a higher intensity of listening to one another. Allow rehearsal time and the opportunity to perform in front of the teacher/another pair.

c Fais l'interview.

AT 1 – 3/4, AT 2 – 3/4

- Encourage students to give their performance interview either in front of another pair/small group, record their interview or give it in front of the video camera. This will give the sense of purpose and encourage a feeling of achievement.

Differentiation – Extension

- Encourage appropriate students to prepare two interviews – one of an individual and one of a group to use the full range of verb forms i.e. *tu/vous/je/nous*. The students can still work and plan in pairs. Two pairs can then come together for the second interview. As each pair comes fresh to the interview without being part of the preparation, students will need to exercise a higher degree of oral/aural competence to respond appropriately to the questions.

d Lis 'Presse des jeunes'.

AT 1 – 4, AT 3 – 3/4, AT 4 – 3/4

- The magazine items serve as a model for students when they come to make their own magazine page. The written description of the characters featured on the cassette reminds students of the use of the 3rd person singular and plural. The same characters are chosen to reduce unfamiliarity with the subject matter and language – it is not intended as a blue print for students to change their own interviews into the 3rd person. This would add an unnecessary layer of grammatical difficulty.
- Direct students to the section *'Presse des jeunes'*.

T: Regardez 'Presse des jeunes'. C'est une page d'un magazine. Il y a deux articles avec des photos, un quiz et la météo. Regardez le premier article sur Victor Vampire. (Read aloud or encourage a student to do so. Then give students time to read it for themselves.) *Il s'appelle comment?* (Elicit the reply *Victor Vampire.* Write the name on the board, then cross the name out and write up *Victoria.*)

Imaginez que ce n'est pas Victor mais c'est Victoria. Regardez la description. Victoria est féminine. Alors on ne dit pas il mais … (Wait for student response *elle,* and write *elle …* on the board.) *Continue. Il est nécessaire de changer la description, e.g. Elle s'appelle Victoria Vampire.* (Encourage students to reread the description making the substitutions.)

- Move on to the second description and follow the same process, this time changing the character of Didier to e.g. Denise to rework the description using *elles.* Encourage students to make a note of the alternative use in preparation for their own two descriptions. Some students will feel safer following the models on the page but encourage appropriate students to think of using the alternatives.
- Direct students to the quiz which gives the model for a similar quiz for their own magazine page.
- The limited weather forecast links the weather with the last lap of the Tour de France. Students may wish to make a more detailed forecast.

e A trois/quatre.

AT 1 – 2/3/4, AT 2 – 2/3/4, AT 3 – 2/3/4, AT 4 – 2/3/4

- Working in groups of up to four, students make their own magazine page to include as a minimum the elements in *'Presse des jeunes'*. Encourage students to bring in photos or use magazine pictures so that the main focus is on language production. This is not an exclusive list and students may wish to incorporate other ideas e.g. a simple commentary on the Tour de France, a cartoon race, a game. Equally students may wish to work beyond a single page or on a larger display sheet.
- Students should delegate tasks between the members of the group and work to an agreed time schedule e.g. two lessons for writing and final production for display. Display the pages in a prominent area as a celebration of the students' learning or alternatively collate the pages into a 'book' either for future reference for the group or to use as exemplar material for next year's cohort!

At this point you may wish to assess students by using the Assessment Copymasters for Modules 5 and 6 (Assessment Test 3, Copymasters 114–117). Teacher's notes and solutions can be found on Copymaster 118 onwards in the Copymasters book.